Teaching the Big Ideas in Economics

Economics as a subject helps equip young people with the knowledge and skills they need to understand and navigate the complexities of the world around them. This book supports teachers, particularly those that are new to the profession or who may not be economics specialists, in teaching the key topics so they can plan and deliver lessons that maximise students' understanding.

Covering the specifications at GCSE and A-level, each chapter outlines the 'big picture' in each topic and explores common misconceptions students have. This is followed by an example of how to effectively explain the topic to students alongside case studies and assessment for learning questions to check students' understanding. Chapters cover the following:

- Price elasticity of demand and supply
- The law of diminishing marginal returns and short-run cost curves
- Long-run average cost curves and economies of scale
- Oligopoly and game theory
- The long-run aggregate supply curve and macroeconomic equilibrium
- Inflation and price stability
- The Phillips curve and natural rate of unemployment
- Financial institutions and money markets

Highly practical and packed with strategies that teachers can use immediately in the classroom, this is essential reading for all economics teachers, especially nonspecialists.

Antony Pazik is Head of Business and Economics at a school in Northeast London.

Teaching the Big Ideas in Economics

Antony Pazik

LONDON AND NEW YORK

Designed cover image: © Getty Images

First published 2026
by Routledge
4 Park Square, Milton Park, Abingdon, Oxon OX14 4RN

and by Routledge
605 Third Avenue, New York, NY 10158

Routledge is an imprint of the Taylor & Francis Group, an informa business

For Product Safety Concerns and Information please contact our EU representative GPSR@taylorandfrancis.com. Taylor & Francis Verlag GmbH, Kaufingerstraße 24, 80331 München, Germany.

British Library Cataloguing-in-Publication Data
A catalogue record for this book is available from the British Library

ISBN: 978-1-041-20779-5 (hbk)
ISBN: 978-1-041-20309-4 (pbk)
ISBN: 978-1-003-72417-9 (ebk)

DOI: 10.4324/9781003724179

Typeset in Melior
by Apex CoVantage, LLC

Contents

1 Introduction

Introduction

Economics is a wonderful subject to teach. There are so many 'aha' moments for students across the course of a two-year A-level or GCSE. It is a subject that provides students access to powerful knowledge that helps them understand the world around them more insightfully. This makes it a pleasure to teach.

It is also a highly rigorous, technical subject. Many of the concepts studied in the curriculum are not encountered in our everyday lives. It is rare, for example, for most of us to encounter short-run cost curves or the transmission mechanism of quantitative easing on a day-to-day basis. A strong conceptual understanding of such concepts relies on carefully planned, explicit explanations from teachers to students. Effective explanations need to emphasise key elements within a concept and tackle common misconceptions that students have. Teachers then need to systematically check that students have understood these examples with a variety of differentiated questions.

All of this sounds like common sense, and I am sure many readers will be nodding their heads as they read this: 'Tell us something we don't know!' However, despite 'explaining stuff' being such a fundamental aspect of teaching, it is something that we typically receive little training or guidance on. The UK teachers' standards do not currently reference the importance of clear, planned explanations. My PGCE teacher training curriculum focused on behaviour management techniques and formative assessment techniques, but there was no explicit reference to how to craft an effective teacher explanation.[1]

Now, I am not the first person to point this out or try to provide some appropriate guidance. Teachers like Adam Boxer and Pritesh Raichura have been banging this drum in various blog posts or podcasts over recent years. References to their work can be found at the end of this chapter.[2]

Carefully worded explanations are something I have been thinking about a lot in the last couple of academic years. I have been working with teachers who haven't necessarily taught economics before, and I've been supporting them with ideas on

DOI: 10.4324/9781003724179-1

how they could explain some of the trickier concepts in both GCSE and A-level specifications. As part of that process, we have thought carefully about the following:

1. What is the big picture that we are trying to communicate to students here? When concepts are technical, it is easy to get bogged down in that technical content. For example, when teaching the law of comparative advantage, we can get so caught up in explaining opportunity cost ratios that we neglect the fact that what we are really trying to tell is the story of how international has developed over time. Reminding ourselves of the big picture ensures that we always anchor our examples in the big picture.
2. Why do students find this content difficult, and what are the common misconceptions? We know that students find proportionate change difficult when learning elasticity and that the concept of marginal changes can seem nebulous. If we map these difficulties out before we plan our explanations, then our explanations are more likely to tackle these issues effectively.
3. How do we then explain these concepts effectively? What are the examples and analogies to use that are most effective? Similarly, what are the non-examples we should use to show the boundaries of the concept?
4. How do we then effectively check that students have 'got it'? How can we be confident that students have gained an in-depth understanding of the concept, as opposed to a surface-level understanding?

The resources created as a result of this process have formed the basis of this book. Each chapter aims to answer each of the question outlined earlier in relation to a different topic in either micro or macroeconomics.

Purpose and teaching approach

The purpose of this book is to provide practical examples and strategies for teachers to use when teaching each concept. The primary audience is teachers new to the profession or those that are teaching economics as a non-subject specialist. A general shortage of economics teachers has meant that, increasingly, schools are asking teachers from departments such as the humanities or maths to teach economics. The book is primarily written with those teachers in mind. Having said this, I hope all teachers of economics, regardless of experience, may find something useful within the approach.

Each chapter is based on the following principles:

1. *Novice students learn best through precise, carefully-planned, teacher-led instruction*, as opposed to some form of discovery-based learning. The book features many examples step-by-step explanations that can be given when introducing topics to students.

2. Difficult concepts should be taught through the use of examples and help students go from *concrete to abstract*. Non-examples also need to be included as part of the teaching sequence to help define the boundaries of a concept. Non-examples often share the same or similar features to an initial example but have some defining characteristic that make them different.

3. Teacher explanations should be accompanied by *live drawing* to help students focus on the critical elements of a concept. This can be done on a classroom whiteboard or using a visualiser.

4. Teachers should use a *series of questions to check student understanding* after an explanation. These should be generally answered by all students on mini-whiteboards to maximise the participation ratio.

5. Carefully planned follow-up questions and case studies can then be used as a method for both further checking of students' understanding and a *deepening of their understanding*.

The primary aim of this book is to be practical. As such, it is not my intention to provide a literature review of the pedagogical research that provides the foundation for the approach taken in this book. Instead, I provide a reference list of some of the works that have informed my practice over the years at the back of this chapter. These are absolutely excellent resources, written by some brilliant educationalists who have produced insights on pedagogy that are far better than anything I could produce! It is not an exhaustive list, but the reference list at the back of this chapter should provide an excellent starting point for a deeper theoretical understanding of this approach. The value I hope to add is through their practical application to economics.

Many of the explanations contained in this book will simplify economic concepts to make them understandable for A-level students at an 'average comprehensive school' in the UK (if such a thing exists!). This is a necessary part of translating concepts from a complex subject discipline into a school curriculum. However, whenever we make such simplifications, we need to do our best to maintain fidelity to the concepts themselves. When making a simplification, I have tried to ask myself the following questions:

1. Is this simplified so much that it creates a barrier to students' understanding the concept properly? As such, would it limit their ability to answer an exam question on the topic?

2. If students never studied economics again in their lives, would I be comfortable with them entering the world with an understanding of the concept as I have presented it to them?

If I am able to answer no to the first question and yes to the second question, then I have included the example.

Finally, there are always different approaches to teaching topics, and some of you may have effective methods that you have used in the past. This is the nature of teaching, and its important as professionals that we are always seeking opportunities to improve our practice and consider alternatives. I would love to hear from you if you've got something that you think works well. Further, this book can't cover all the 'big ideas' in economics. This would be too large a task! Rather, I hope what this book provides is a methodology for approaching difficult content, and some ideas of how this could be put in place.

A note on AI

I know that many teachers are using AI to help them plan and develop resources.

I don't deny that AI is an extremely helpful resource in teacher planning. In the past, I have tried running some teaching ideas through an AI programme and asked it to check for consistency and clarity of thought. I encourage teachers to use AI as an aide that helps them improve their practice.

However, I also caution:

1. There are limits to the effectiveness of AI. I have experienced several instances where an AI programme has recommended a pedagogical approach that I do not believe is effective. For example, standard, unprompted AI models tend to prefer an approach that moves from abstract to concrete, instead of the other way round. It is only through the process of carefully thinking through examples yourself that you will be able to spot these limitations when you then look to use an AI model for support.

2. We should not encourage the outsourcing of teacher thought across the profession. This is important for two reasons. Firstly, thinking deeply and carefully about an explanation and subsequent comprehension questions means that teachers are well-versed in that problem. As such, we are likely to be able to engage more critically in conversations with students during the lesson that deepens their understanding. Secondly, regular cognitive outsourcing is likely to de-skill teachers. As Peps Mcrrea points out, whoever does the thinking gets the learning. If, as teachers, we regularly do not do the thinking, then we are likely to become de-skilled in these areas over time.[3]

Key takeaways

The key pedagogical principles that each chapter will follow are the following:

1. Novices learn best through precise, carefully planned, teacher-led instruction.

2. Difficult concepts should be taught through examples that move from concrete to abstract.

3. Teacher explanations should be accompanied by live drawing.
4. Teachers need to check students' understanding through the use of formative assessment questions.
5. Teachers need to extend students' thinking with the use of case studies and more challenging formative assessment questions.

Notes

1 I should mention that I was fortunate enough to have an excellent lead instructor, Polly Clegg, as part of my Teach First training at University College London. I still remember Polly modelling the way in which she explains the product life cycle to students and how clear this explanation was. I don't remember this being an explicit part of the training syllabus. I think Polly just recognised it was something that our cohort would find useful.

2 Adam Boxer and Pritesh Raichura have written some excellent blogs on teacher explanations that can be found in the bibliography (Boxer, 2021; Raichura, 2019).

3 The idea of 'cognitive outsourcing' is something that Peps Mccrea discussed in one of his email newsletters. Mccrea referenced a paper by Zhai, C.; Wibowo, S. and Li, L.D. (2024) in his email. The paper is called '*The effects of over-reliance on AI dialogue systems on students' cognitive abilities: a systematic review*'.

References

Books

1. Boxer, A., 2021. Teaching Secondary Science: A Complete Guide. Woodbridge: John Catt Educational.
2. Boxer, A. & Bennett, T. E., 2019. *The Research Ed Guide to Explicit & Direct Instruction: An Evidence-Informed Guide for Teachers.* London: John Catt Educational.
3. Christodoulou, C., 2024. Seven Myths About Education. 1st ed. London: Routledge.
4. Engelmann, S. & Carnine, D., 1982. Theory of Instruction: Principles and Applications. Oregon: NIFDI Press.
5. Lemov, D., 2021. Teach Like a Champion 3.0: 63 Techniques that Put Students on the Path to College. 3rd ed. s.l.: Wiley.

Journal articles

On cognitive science and its implications for classroom practice:

1. Kirschner, P. A., Sweller, J. & Clark, R. E., 2006. Why Minimal Guidance during Instruction Does Not Work: An Analysis of the Failure of Constructivist, Discovery, Problem-Based, Experiential, and Inquiry-Based Teaching. Educational Psychologist, Volume 41, pp. 75–86.
2. Atkinson, R. & Shiffrin, R., 1968. Human Memory: A Proposed System and Its Control Processes. Psychology of Learning and Motivation, Volume 2, pp. 89–195.
3. Sweller, J., van Merrienboer, J. & Paas, F., 1998. Cognitive Architecture and Instructional Design. Educational Psychology Review, Volume 10, pp. 251–296.

4. Reed, S. & Bolstad, C., 1991. Use of Examples and Procedures in Problem Solving. Journal of Experimental Psychology, Volume 17(4), pp. 753–766.
5. Sweller, J. & Chandler, P., 1994. Why Some Material is Difficult to Learn. Cognition and Instruction, Volume 12(3), pp. 185–233.
6. Sweller, J. & Cooper, G., 1985. The Use of Worked Examples as a Substitute for Problem Solving in Learning Algebra. Cognition and Instruction, Volume 2, pp. 59–89.

Blog posts

1. Boxer, A., 2021. Education in Chemistry. [Online] Available at: https://edu.rsc.org/ideas/3-ways-to-improve-your-explanations/4013808.article [Accessed 14 December 2025].
2. Raichura, P., 2019. Bunsen Blue. [Online] Available at: https://bunsenblue.com/2019/10/20/clear-teacher-explanations-i-examples-non-examples/ [Accessed 15 December 2025].

2 Demand, supply and the market mechanism

What's the big picture?

The market mechanism is the method by which goods and services are allocated in a free market. It is a voluntary exchange system that enables millions of people to cooperate with each other to allocate resources in the most efficient manner.

In theory, the market mechanism operates without any form of government intervention, such as taxes and subsidies. In a perfectly efficient market, the interaction of demand and supply will ensure that a price is set which results in demand for a product equaling supply. This forms the very basis of microeconomic analysis at A-level and is a concept that students need to understand clearly. The market mechanism is fundamental to students' understanding of the following:

1. How markets are efficient in allocating resources
2. How markets fail
3. Arguments for and against government intervention in markets and, on a more macro level, arguments regarding the structure of an economy
4. Market structures, such as monopoly and oligopoly
5. Wage setting in competitive labour markets
6. How exchange rates are set in floating exchange models
7. How interest rates are set according to the loanable funds theory

The earlier list is not exhaustive. However, it does demonstrate that an understanding of demand, supply and the market mechanism provide the foundation for so much that is studied in economics.

Why do students find this topic difficult?

On the face of it, this may seem like a topic that students seem to understand quite easily. After a couple of months on the course, *most* students can accurately draw

DOI: 10.4324/9781003724179-2

a supply-and-demand diagram, identify equilibrium and shift either curve to show a change in the factors affecting supply or demand. It, therefore, might seem like a strange topic to start with in a book about teaching some of the trickier concepts in economics.

However, I think performance often masks a lack of deeper conceptual understanding. I find that students conceptually understand why the demand curve slopes downwards, and most understand why the supply curve slopes upwards. After that, many students often struggle with the following:

1. They believe a change in the price of the product will lead to a shift in either of the curves. They believe that a decrease in the price of a product will cause an outward shift of demand or vice versa.
2. They often confuse the impacts of a change in the price of a substitute and complement good.
3. They often have a superficial understanding of the functions of the price mechanism. They have learnt that equilibrium occurs where the 'two lines cross' and X marks the spot! They regularly struggle to understand why the market clears at the equilibrium price and quantity. This limits their understanding of why the market mechanism is argued to be so effective and reduces the depth of arguments when considering resource allocation and economic structures.

In my experience, point 3 is particularly pertinent among GCSE and A-level students in the UK.

Explaining this content

Mistakes to avoid

It's important that students understand *why* demand and supply curves shift. In the past, I would assume that this seemed obvious: of course, if levels of income increase, then consumers are going to purchase more of the product at the same price. However, I failed to emphasise the key part here is that consumers will purchase more *at the same price*. In my haste, I would explain that the outward shift of demand shows a higher quantity being purchased, and I wouldn't emphasise the price part. This is likely to be part of the reason for the confusion demonstrated by point 1 in the '*Why do students find this topic difficult*?' section.

Secondly, don't assume that students understand the firm and production costs! Many students won't have previously considered the various costs that businesses need to pay and how this impacts supply decisions. Again, the explanation provided should provide guidance on how this can be done slowly and deliberately.

Finally, don't rush the functions of the market mechanism. Spend time going through these slowly and precisely.

Explaining this content

This is the longest chapter in the book because it tries to tackle quite a lot! It's recognised that the teaching of demand, supply and the market mechanism will probably take around four to five lessons, and the sequence in this book is not intended to be completed during one double period! The chapter is broken down into the following sections:

1. The law of diminishing marginal utility
2. The demand curve
3. The supply curve
4. The market mechanism

I would envisage that each of these sections would take one to two lessons to complete, but this will be dependent on the timetable at your school.

This content requires lots of independent practice by students to achieve mastery. While this is signaled at some points in the chapter, I do not always provide instruction as to where this independent practice should be. This will be down to you to decide based on your knowledge of the pupils in front of you and appropriate chunking of your lessons.

Explaining this concept – the law of diminishing marginal utility

Start with the law of diminishing marginal utility:

> *Let's imagine you are walking home from school in the summer, and you are quite hot and thirsty. You walk past the shop and go in to buy a drink.*
>
> *You buy the drink and step outside, open the bottle and have some of the drink. How good does that first sip taste? Pretty good right! The first drink when we are thirsty always tastes so good.*
>
> *Let's imagine we had some way of measuring how much satisfaction we get from that first unit of the drink. Economists refer to this satisfaction as 'utility', and the measure of utility is a 'util'. Now this is a little bit arbitrary, and economists have developed ways that we can measure this in a slightly more robust manner, but let's stick with it for now.*
>
> *Let's say that first bottle of drink gave us '10 utils' worth of satisfaction.*
>
> *Now, let's imagine that you have finished your drink and are still a little bit thirsty. You are feeling better, but you can tell there is still a little bit of*

> *dehydration! You go back into the shop, and you buy another bottle. You come out, you have some of the drink. Does it taste* **as good** *as the first bottle? Probably not . . . remember, that first bottle always is the one that tastes the best! However, it* **does still taste pretty good**. *Maybe this second bottle gives us '7 utils' of satisfaction.*[1]

The parts highlighted in bold demonstrate perfect moments for a change of intonation and emphasis. We really want students to hear the message that the second bottle is still good but not *as* good.

Run this example for another couple of iterations until, perhaps on the fourth bottle, you suggest that students are starting to feel a little bit sick from drinking so much. If anything, utility at this point is becoming negative. At the same time, I would be accompanying your explanation with a table on the board that is highlighting the key points you are making. This might look a little bit like Table 1.1.

Then carry on your explanation:

> *This is interesting! The first bottle of drink gave us 10 units of satisfaction. The second gave us 7 – still very positive but not quite as positive as the first. The third bottle still did give us satisfaction – we* ***enjoyed the drink but much less than the 1st and 2nd bottle***. *But look at the fourth bottle – t****hat is actually making us feel less satisfied than we did before!***
>
> *If we tried to find out 'total' utility that we have received from buying and drinking those four drinks, we'd simply need to add together the extra utility we received from each one. So, our total utility might look a bit like this [Table 1.2].*

Table 1.1 Marginal utility example

Bottle of drink	Extra utility from each bottle
1st	10
2nd	7
3rd	2
4th	−1

Table 1.2 *Total utility example*

Bottle of drink	Extra utility from each bottle	Total utility
1st	10	10
2nd	7	17
3rd	2	19
4th	−1	18

Notice that so far, we haven't used the word 'marginal' in our explanation. Marginal analysis is something that students tend to find quite tricky. I find that using the word 'extra' to begin with helps students gain an understanding of the concept before they need to worry about the technical term. This follows the same idea as our principle of concrete to abstract.

Once this is complete, check students' understanding of these concepts with a few simple mini-whiteboard (MWB) checks for understanding. They might look a little bit like the one in Box 1.1.

BOX 1.1 MWB CHECK FOR UNDERSTANDING ON UTILITY

MWB checks for understanding

Alice goes to an all-you-can-eat Chinese buffet. Alice is really hungry and has been waiting all day for this meal. Alice fills up her first plate of food and tucks in. She really enjoys that first plate and, if she could, would give it a ranking of 20 utils.

She's still hungry after her first plate an so fills up again. She enjoys this plate and gives it a ranking of 12 utils.

Alice still feels like she can have another plate, which gives her a util ranking of 4. Alice goes up at the end for one more small plate, but this makes her feel a little bit sick. Alice feels like the last plate gave her a util ranking of −2.

Questions

Plot a table that shows the following:

1. The extra utility that Alice receives from each plate of food
2. The total utility that Alice gains from the whole meal

The question in Box 1.1 is designed to be simple and a quick whiteboard activity – possibly lasting no more than two minutes. The question isn't designed to challenge or deepen students' thinking too much at this stage. Instead, you are using it to check that they are ready to move on.

Once the MWB check for understanding is complete, you can introduce students to the graphs for marginal and total utility (although you may still be referring to marginal utility as 'extra utility' at this point). I'm not a big fan of plotting these curves on exactly to scale using graph paper. I think this means that students spend most of their time thinking about *how* to plot the graph accurately as opposed to think about what the graph is showing them. Instead, I would demonstrate to students on the board how you can plot these two curves to show the shape of each without needing to use the numbers too exactly. When drawing the graph, highlight a few things:

1. Initially label the marginal utility curve as 'extra utility', consistent with how we have described it up to now. However, then tell students that the technical name we use is marginal utility, and I would update the label so that it reads: 'Extra utility = marginal utility'. Make sure that students know this is how they should refer to the curve from now on.

2. The point at which the marginal utility curve crosses the X axis is the point at which the total utility curve is at its maximum point (this bit should be drawn accurately!). Use the table that you have previously drawn to show why this is the case: up until the point where marginal utility becomes negative, total utility is growing.

I have previously spent a lot of time going over the relationship in point 2 with students. I have used it as an opportunity to explain that this relationship between marginal and totals will come up again, and so it is important that students understand it. I now don't do this. Instead, when it comes up again, perhaps with marginal and total cost, I remind students that we saw the same rule when we studied marginal and total utility. This second example confirms the rule that they have seen previously, and the two examples are likely to help them form a more concrete understanding of the rule.

Finally, ask students to draw a marginal and total utility graph for the scenario of Alice at the Chinese buffet. Check that students are labelling their axes and curves correctly and that they accurately demonstrate the rule in point 2.

Explaining this concept – demand

We now need to make the link between the law of diminishing marginal utility and the demand curve. This sequence should be taught in the following order:

1. Link the law of diminishing marginal utility to an individual's demand curve
2. Derive a market demand curve from the individual demand curve
3. Extensions and contractions in demand
4. Shifts of the demand curve

The link between diminishing marginal utility and demand can cause some confusion when thinking about the price that an individual consumer would pay for a good. Start with a non-example of how the price mechanism works:

> *Now in an ideal world, we would pay a different price for every individual unit of a product that we could buy. For example, the first bottle of drink that we purchased gave us the most utility so maybe we would be willing to pay £5 for this. The marginal utility gained from the second bottle was less than*

the first, so maybe we would be willing to pay £3 for this bottle. For the third, where marginal utility fell further, we might be willing to pay £1.50 for the bottle. But we know the real world doesn't work like this – you can't go into a shop and buy two bottles of drink but pay different prices for each based on the marginal utility gained.

Make sure this is displayed on the board with the price that the consumer is willing to pay for each individual unit. It's important that students have a visual aid to tie the next part of the explanation to. This bit needs to be gone through slowly, with emphasis on the parts in bold:

So instead, we need to consider the quantity that you wish to purchase and the ***single price*** *that you would be willing to pay per unit. Now luckily, this is straightforward – the single price that we would be willing to pay per unit is equal to the price we would be willing to pay for the* ***last unit****. So, for example, if you wanted to purchase two bottles of water, you would be willing to pay* ***£3 for each*** *because this is what you are willing to pay for that second bottle of drink based on the utility it gives you. If you wanted to purchase three bottles, you would be willing to pay* ***£1.50 for each*** *because this is the marginal utility you gain from the* ***last unit*** *purchased.*

This can take a moment to sink in for students, as it can feel a little abstract. If students are struggling, explain the following to them:

1. In the real world, you can't pay different prices for each unit of the same product that you purchase.
2. If you purchased three bottles of drink, you wouldn't be willing to pay £5 per bottle when the second and third bottles give you less utility than £5 worth.

From this, we can start to plot an individual's demand curve with price on the Y axis and quantity demanded on the X axis. Explain to students that this shows the quantity an individual would be willing to purchase at various price levels, which has been derived from the law of diminishing marginal utility. Then add in the additional detail that this demand also assumes consumers are *able* to purchase the given quantity at the given price. As such, our definition of demand becomes the quantity that consumers are willing and able to purchase at any given price.

Check students' understanding with some straightforward MCQ questions. For example, you may show them an individual's demand curve and ask students to identify the price a consumer would be willing to pay if they purchase six units of a given good.

Finally, explain to students that you will spend much of the course discussing market demand, as opposed to an individual's demand. This market demand curve is derived from an accumulation of individual demand curves. So, for example, you would take the aggregate number of consumers willing to purchase a bottle of drink for £3, and this would signal the demand for that product at that price. Clearly differentiate this to students by giving an example where market demand is likely to be in the thousands and label your X axis accordingly.

Explaining this concept – movements along the demand curve and shifts of the demand curve

Once the demand curve has been constructed and you are confident that students understand the reason for its shape, introduce students to the ideas of 'extensions' and 'contractions' in demand when the price of product will change. For example:

> *Imagine a local pizza company that currently charges £12 for each pizza that it sells. At this price, there are 4,000 customers in the local town that are willing to purchase pizza at that price. Essentially, there are 4,000 customers that think the utility gained from purchasing that one pizza will give them satisfaction that is worth £12 to them.*

Draw a dashed line from £12 on the Y axis along to the demand curve and show that this would result in a quantity demanded of 4,000 by drawing a dotted line down from the demand curve to the X axis.

> *Now what is going to happen if the pizza company reduces the price of their pizzas to £10? Well, there are going to be more customers in the town who are now willing and able to pay £10 for a pizza because there will be more people who think the utility, they gain from the pizza is worth at least £10.*

Demonstrate to students that this would lead to a higher quantity demanded by showing the decrease in price on the Y axis and increase in quantity demanded on the X. Explain to students that this represents an extension along the demand curve, and label this as so. Then repeat this process for a contraction in demand. Emphasise that a change in the price of the pizza is causing an extension or contraction along the demand curve.

Then introduce shifts of the demand curve and the factors that cause this. The key part to highlight here is that a shift occurs because more (or fewer) customers are willing to purchase a product at the same price level. Start with an increase in incomes:

> *Let's now imagine that in the town, average incomes increase. As a result, on average, people in the town earn £1,000 more each year than they did before. What do you think that is going to do to the number of consumers that are willing and able to pay £12 for a pizza . . . Sasha?*
>
> *Exactly – there are going to be more consumers who are willing and able to pay £12 for a pizza because people have got more money! Their purchasing power has increased. Now what is that going to look like on our demand curve?*

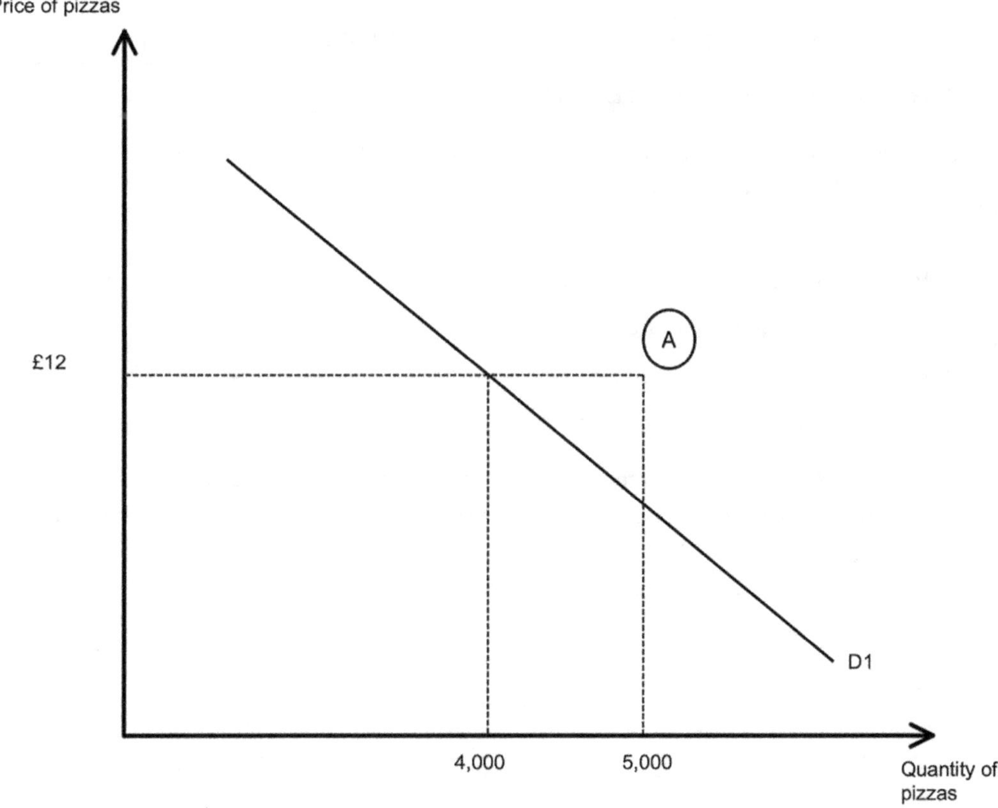

Figure 2.1 Outward shift of demand explanation

Model to students the diagram shown in Figure 2.1. Don't rush to show them a new demand curve straightaway. Instead, show them that more customers are willing and able to purchase pizzas *at the same price* and so the new level of demand doesn't sit on the existing demand curve. This shows us there has been a change in economic conditions, and as a result, the old demand curve no longer accurately shows the willingness and ability of customers to purchase pizzas in the town at various prices. As a result, we must move on to a new demand curve.

At the end point of this explanation, you can then show an outward shift of demand. However, it is important that you have spent time explaining to students the point earlier before they see the shift in demand. This should help to emphasise that a factor that causes a shift means that there is a change in the level of demand at the same price level. This helps to embed the idea that changes in price do not cause a shift in demand, as per point one in the list of student misconceptions.

Finish this sequence by checking students' understanding. Some examples of questions you may ask are shown in Box 1.2.

BOX 1.2 MWB CHECK FOR UNDERSTANDING

MWB checks for understanding

1. Which of the following changes will lead to an outward shift in the demand for a product? There may be more than one correct answer.
   A. An increase in consumer incomes
   B. A decrease in the price of a substitute good
   C. A decrease in the price of a product
   D. A decrease in the price of a complement good
   E. A decrease in spending on advertising

Answers A and D are correct. C is included to check students understand that a change in the price of a product causes an extension or contraction in demand, rather than a shift.

Changes in demand

For each scenario below, show the change in quantity demanded for Apple's products. Identify the factor affecting demand and provide an explanation for the change that you have shown.

Scenario	Graph	Factor affecting and explanation
There is an increase in consumer incomes		
Apple decrease the amount of advertising that they do		
There is an increase in the price of Samsung phones		

Figure 2.2 Example resource

As explained in the earlier pages of this chapter, it is then extremely important that students get lots of practice of shifting demand curves and explain the shift shown. Figure 2.2 shows an example of a resource that can be used for independent practice in lesson or as homework. Figure 2.2 shows three examples, but your resource should have more rows of scenarios that can test students' understanding of inward and outward shifts of demand and their ability to explain the shift occurring.

Explaining this concept – supply

Students find the concept of supply less intuitive than demand. This is likely to be because they can picture themselves as consumers but do not have experience running a firm. They cannot link their learning to their everyday experiences as easily.

Explain to students that you have considered the quantity demanded for various products at different prices and you are now going to consider the other side of a transaction: how many firms will be willing to supply at various prices.

Provide them with a basic example of four pizza restaurants with different cost structures. This is shown in Table 1.3.

Take time to explain why each restaurant has different costs. Perhaps restaurant four is in a busy area and, therefore, has expensive rent to pay or sources their raw materials from a more expensive supplier. Explain to students that we are assuming that 'cost to produce each pizza' encompasses all costs a business needs to pay.

Then model different prices that the restaurants could charge, and question whether firms will be willing to supply at that price. For ease of the example, assume that firms will supply if they are making any sort of profit. For example:

> *Let's imagine that each restaurant is thinking about charging £5 per pizza. At this price, how many of the restaurants would be willing to supply? Probably only one! Restaurants two, three and four are all going to make a loss if they sell their pizzas for £5.*
>
> *What about if they charged £6 per pizza? Well now Restaurant two can make a little bit of profit, so they would start supplying. This would mean supply in the market has increased as the price has increased from £5 to £6.*

Keep going through this example and by increasing the price incrementally and showing new suppliers entering the market. Use this example to derive the upward sloping supply curve and explain extensions/contractions in supply to students in the same way you did for demand.

Table 1.3 Pizza restaurant cost structure

Restaurant	Cost to produce each pizza
Restaurant one	$4.40
Restaurant two	$5.40
Restaurant three	$6.40
Restaurant four	$7.40

Once this is done, move on to factors that cause a shift in the supply curve. These factors will vary between exam board specifications but can always be linked back to the costs of production facing firms. Highlight to students that the factor determining whether each restaurant was willing to supply at each given price was the costs each firm faced. As a result, any factor that will cause a change in those costs will cause the supply curve to shift.

Finish by checking students' understanding of the concept with questions like the ones included in Box 1.3.

BOX 1.3 MWB CHECKS FOR UNDERSTANDING

MWB checks for understanding

1. Which of the following changes will cause an inward shift of supply of a product? There may be more than one correct answer.
   A. A decrease in labour productivity
   B. An increase in the minimum wage rate
   C. A decrease in corporation tax
   D. An increase in income tax rates
   E. An increase in the cost of technology

Answers A, B and E are correct. Students often frame a question positively (e.g. assume outward shift), and misreads are common mistakes made. This question is designed to ensure students read the question carefully.

Explaining this concept – the market mechanism

Finally, introduce students to the concept of equilibrium. Explain to students that over the past few lessons, you have been studying supply and demand and that you are now going to put these concepts together.

Pick a market, such as the market for smartphones, and plot a supply-and-demand diagram for this market. Then set a price above equilibrium (although don't mention this term to students yet!). Your graph should look a little like the one in Figure 2.3.

You need to annotate the graph to show the excess supply on the X axis. However, go through this slowly and step-by-step. Remember, this is the first time students will have put both supply and demand onto the same graph, and each additional line that you add is going to add to the demands on working memory. Instead, emphasise that at £2,000, there are not many customers willing and able to purchase a smartphone, but there will be lots of smartphone produces who can make a profit at this price. As a result, the quantity demanded will be much lower than the quantity supplied. This means we get 'too much' supply in this market. You can then refine your terminology to state that 'too much supply' is referred to as 'excess supply'.

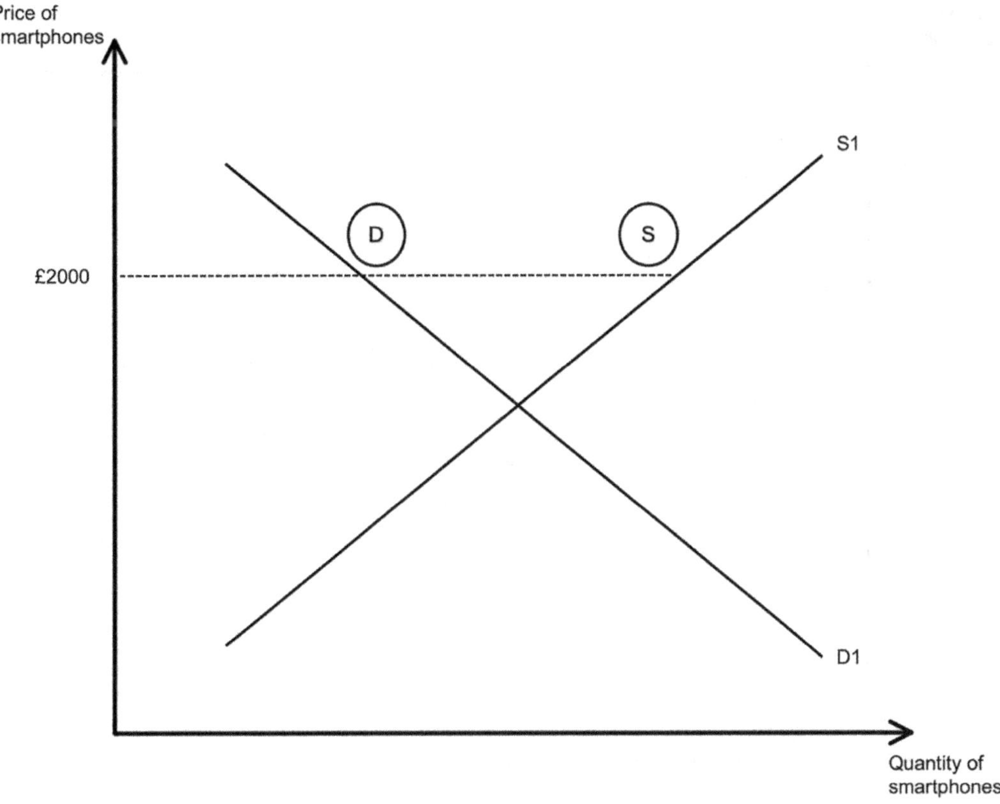

Figure 2.3 Price set above equilibrium

Go through a similar example when price is set below the equilibrium level and excess demand occurs. Then set price to the equilibrium level, and show students that this is the price at which the market 'clears'. the number of consumers willing and able to purchase a product is equal to the number of firms willing and able to supply the product. Tell students that we call this 'market equilibrium', and provide a definition of the term.

Once we have modelled excess supply, demand and equilibrium, we can then consider changes in the equilibrium position. For example:

Now, let's imagine that consumer incomes increase. What is this going to do to the demand for smartphones . . . Richard?

Excellent, we are going to get an outward shift of demand because more customers are willing and able to purchase smartphones at the given price. Let's have a think about what that would look like on our diagram.

The key here is to first model the outward shift of demand *without* a change in price level. Your diagram may look a little like the graph in Figure 2.4.

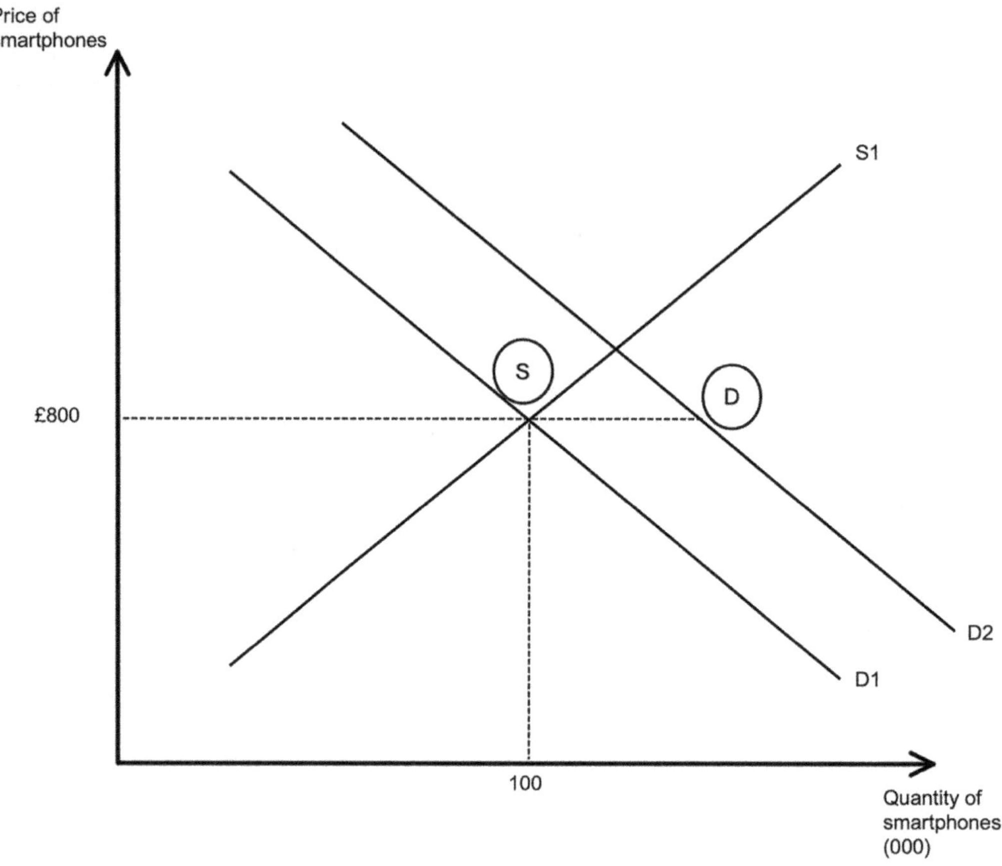

Figure 2.4 The market mechanism

Continue your explanation:

We can see that if price doesn't change, the outward shift of demand is going to mean that there is excess demand in our market. As a result of the increased consumer incomes, there would be too many customers willing and able to purchase smartphones at £800. So, what needs to happen? The price of smartphones needs to rise in response to the change in economic conditions! But how does that happen?

Then label the functions of the price mechanism one by one on the graph that you have drawn. Annotating the diagram directly to explain the price mechanism reduces the split attention effect, as students are not required to look at the diagram and then look elsewhere for the explanation. The diagram you draw may look a little like Figure 2.5. Please note that this diagram looks *very* busy and should not be presented to students as a finished piece. Instead, add on each mechanism sequentially, ideally using a different colour for each.

Then check students' understanding with questions like the one in Box 1.4.

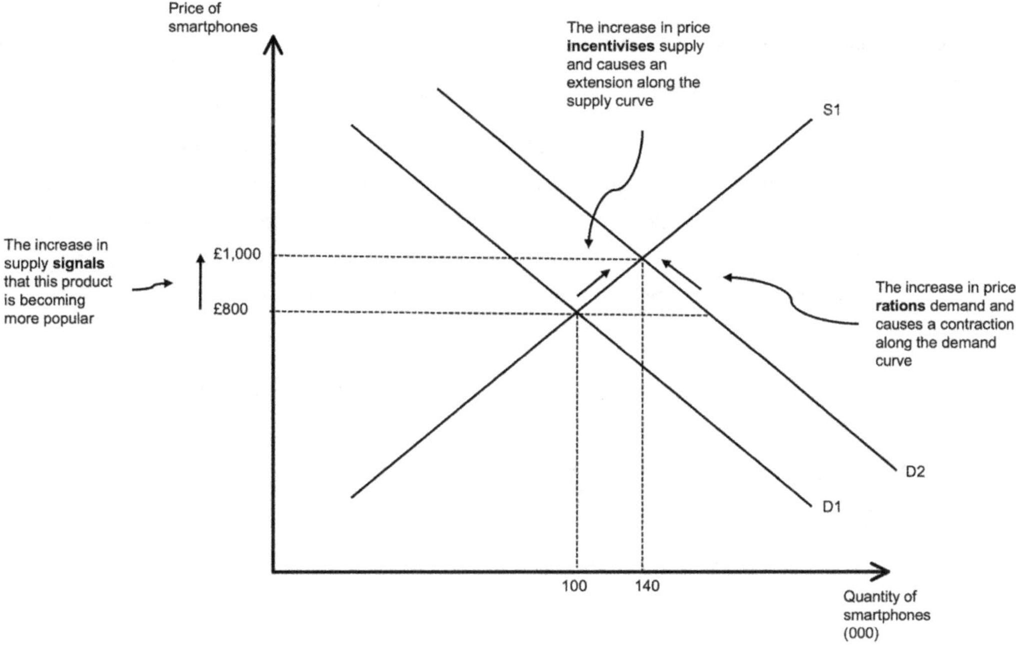

Figure 2.5 Functions of the market mechanism

BOX 1.4 MWB CHECKS FOR UNDERSTANDING

MWB checks for understanding

1. Which of the following is a correct explanation of a function of the price mechanism? There may be more than one correct answer.

   A. A decrease in price will ration the amount of demand for a product.

   B. A decrease in price will signal to firms that a product is less popular.

   C. An increase in price will incentivise firms to produce a certain product.

   D. An increase in price will ration the supply of a product.

   E. An increase in price will signal to firms that a product is becoming more popular.

   B, C and E are correct answers. The only mechanism that is not accurately described earlier is the rationing function. A useful follow-up activity is to ask students to create an additional response that would correctly explain the rationing function. This would test whether students are able to explain in their own words a function of the price mechanism.

2. How could the quantity sold of a product increase and price remain the same?

   A. Demand shifts outwards and supply shifts inwards.

   B. Demand shifts outwards and supply shifts outwards.

C. Demand shifts inwards and supply shifts inwards.

D. Demand shifts inwards and supply shifts outwards.

The correct answer is B. This is a good question to encourage students to use their diagrams to help them answer a question. It also is a good question to generate conversation amongst students by asking if B would always be correct. Students may recognise that this would depend on the relative sizes of the shifts in each curve. For example, a more-than-proportionate outward shift in demand would cause prices to rise despite the increase in supply.

3. Which of the following is likely to cause an extension along the demand curve? There may be more than one correct answer.

   A. An increase in consumer incomes

   B. An increase in the price of a substitute good

   C. A decrease in advertising spending

   D. An increase in labour productivity

   E. A decrease in the quality of technology

The only correct answer is D. This is a question that students find difficult and checks that they understand extensions and contractions. An extension in demand would occur because the supply curve shifts outwards, resulting in a new equilibrium at a lower price. Answer D is the only answer that would cause an outward shift of the supply curve.

Some students may identify A and B as correct answers because they will conflate factors causing an outward shift of demand with an 'increase' in demand and, therefore, extension along the curve. This is a key signal to you that they don't fully understand the difference between movements and shifts!

Finally, finish this sequence by using a case study like the one shown in Box 1.5.

The case study in Box Y is designed to get students shifting supply and demand curves and changing equilibrium in a real-world scenario. It also implicitly exposes students to the idea that the word 'market' can refer to several things: Is this about global demand for chocolate bars, is it the market in China and India, or is it the market in European countries? We can define the market for the same product in different ways based on the supply and demand conditions in certain areas, and it is useful for students to see this early in the course.

BOX 1.5 CASE STUDY

Case study

Chocolate bar producers were hit by a significant supply shock in 2022. Cocoa, which is a key ingredient in chocolate bars, tripled in price over the course of one year. This was caused by severe droughts in West African countries such as Ghana and the Ivory Coast, where nearly 60% of the world supply of cocoa comes from. Cocoa is a key ingredient for chocolate bar producers, along with dairy and sugar. Chocolate bar producers will also have to pay for packaging, transport and marketing costs.

At the same time, there has been changing levels of global demand for chocolate products over the past ten years. This is because of increasing income levels in countries like India and China, where large sections of the population are becoming middle-income earners. This has led to increasing levels of demand in the Asian market. However, in Western markets, demand for chocolate has fallen in many European countries. This is partially due to increasing concerns about children's diets and government campaigns to reduce obesity levels in young people.

Questions

1. Use a demand-and-supply diagram to show how supply shocks in the cocoa market are likely to impact equilibrium price and quantity of chocolate bars.
2. Use a demand-and-supply diagram to show how changing income levels in India and China are likely to impact the equilibrium price and quantity of chocolate bars in those markets.
3. With reference to question 2, explain the three functions of the price mechanism.
4. Use a demand-and-supply diagram to show how changing trends in some European countries are likely to impact the equilibrium price and quantity of chocolate bars in those markets.
5. Do you think chocolate bars are likely to have risen in price in India and China? Explain your answer.
6. Do you think chocolate bars are likely to have risen in price in European countries? Explain your answer.

To finish this sequence, I think it is useful to show students an example of a situation in which intervention in markets disrupted the key features of the market mechanism. For example, during the oil crises of the 1970s the US government intervened to set price controls and set commands for where oil should be supplied.

The price system was not allowed to function, and it resulted in surpluses of oil in some parts of the country and shortages in others. As a result, long lines for gas stations occurred across the US.

Key takeaways

- Emphasise as strongly as possible that changes in price do not cause a demand or supply curve to shift. Spend time explaining this by showing the effects of changing demand conditions, such as a change in income or changes in the price of a substitute good, *at the same price level.*
- Begin your explanation of supply by introducing students to the idea of production costs. This is likely to be something that they haven't considered before or have direct experience of. A lack of an understanding of production costs is a key barrier to a strong understanding of the supply curve.
- Model the functions of the price mechanism by first showing excess demand and excess supply and how the price mechanism corrects this disequilibrium.
- Label the functions of the price mechanism on one diagram sequentially to show how this works to achieve an equilibrium price and quantity.

Note

1 For stronger classes, you can reference the idea that economists may use ordinal utility to demonstrate this idea. Instead of assigning an arbitrary util value to each bottle, ordinal utility simply requires us to rank preferences. In this scenario, it is easy to see that bottle 1 > bottle 2.

3 The price elasticity of demand

What's the big idea?

Students now understand that demand for products decreases as their price increases and vice versa. However, students will have generally seen and constructed demand curves that suggest this relationship is proportional: a 10% increase in price leading to a 10% decrease in quantity.

We now need to introduce students to the idea that the relationship between demand and price may not be proportional. An increase in price may lead to a dramatic fall in demand, a relatively small fall in demand or somewhere in between. This has important implications for a firm's pricing strategy. If a firm knows that they can increase price without significantly reducing demand, they will be incentivised to do so in order to maximise their revenue. This is seen in the real world. Apple knows that they can increase the price of each new iPhone launched because the quantity demanded is unlikely to fall significantly in comparison to the last release.

There is a lot of technical detail that students need to understand about the price elasticity of demand, but it is important not to lose sight of the point made earlier: this is fundamentally a concept that helps firms making pricing and branding decisions.

A strong understanding of the price elasticity of demand is fundamental to students accessing some of the more challenging concepts later in the course. This is the case for both micro and macroeconomics. For example, the price elasticity of demand is important when considering the kinked demand curve in oligopolistic markets and when understanding the J-curve in international trade.

Why do students find this topic difficult?

Students often find this topic difficult because of the following:

- They find the concept of proportionate change difficult. Students are comfortable with the idea that as price increases demand decreases but they can find it difficult to conceptualise that one may increase or decrease relatively more than the other. This is likely to reflect a broader difficulty in students' comfort with the idea of proportionality.

DOI: 10.4324/9781003724179-3

- They are not confident with mathematical concepts like percentage change or ratio. This often means that students try to memorise elasticity calculations without an understanding of what their answers mean.

Students may also struggle with the level of preciseness required when assessing elasticity. Students will often suggest that if demand for a product is price inelastic, then an increase in price will lead to no change in demand or 'not much' change in demand. They need to be more specific. The law of demand still holds: an increase in price will lead to a fall in demand, but the size of the decrease may be less significant than the increase in price.

Explaining this content

Mistakes to avoid

There is a lot of technical detail that students need to understand about the price elasticity of demand. In my experience reviewing resources and observing lessons, the typical structure of a PED lesson may look something like the sequence in Figure 3.1.

This structure is likely to overwhelm students:

1. New terminology is introduced before students have been given any concrete examples.
2. Examples are limited to one or two examples of products where demand is price inelastic.
3. New terminology, graphs and formulae are all introduced in quick succession without any chunking.

Quite quickly, we can see why students retreat to memorisation tactics in the topic: a steep curve demonstrates inelastic demand, a shallow curve is elastic, a figure with an absolute value greater than one is elastic, and so on.

We need to be careful when labelling demand curves as 'inelastic' or 'elastic'. Elasticity changes along a linear demand curve and so it is not correct to label an entire curve as 'elastic' or 'inelastic'. It may be easier to label these curves in

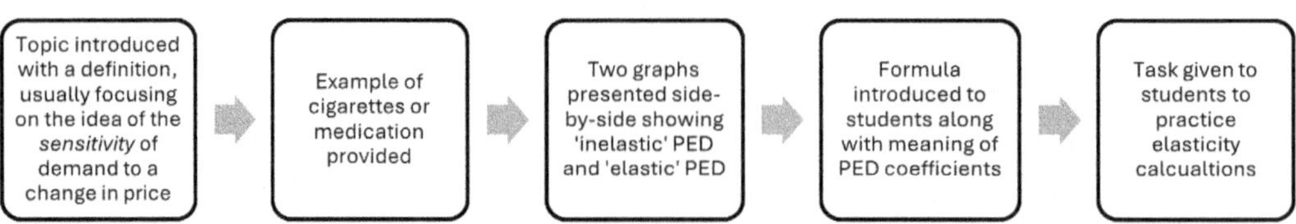

Figure 3.1 A typical price elasticity of demand lesson

this way early in the course to aid understand. However, this can cause confusion for students at later points in the course. We, therefore, need to make sure that we label a curve demonstrating that a product's demand is 'relatively more price elastic' and 'relatively more price inelastic'.

The key implication is that we need to slow down when introducing elasticity: the concept needs unpicking before we rush into any of the more technical details. Elasticity is a cornerstone topic that students need a strong foundational understanding in if they are going to understand other content later on the course. Slow down. If you don't get to the formula until lesson two, that's okay; it will save you time in the long-run.

Explaining this concept

The rest of this chapter will break down the teaching of PED into the following sections:

1. Introducing the price elasticity of demand
2. Factors affecting the price elasticity of demand
3. The price elasticity of demand and revenue
4. The formula for calculating the price elasticity of demand

I do not suggest a particular number of lessons that need to be allocated for the earlier sequence. This will be dependent on the timetable at your school.

Explaining this concept – introducing the price elasticity of demand

Start by recapping the law of demand. Use some MWB questions to check that all students are clear on the idea that an increase in price leads to a fall in demand and vice versa. Then explain that you want to explore this relationship for a product that is addictive, typically something like cigarettes (although current consumer trends are making this a less robust example!). It may go something along the lines of:

> *People are addicted to cigarettes, caused by the nicotine within the product. For many people, this can help to relieve anxiety or stress. What happens when the price of cigarettes increase by 10%? Sure, some people will stop because they may no longer be able to afford the cigarettes, or some people may start smoking less. But do we think 10% of people are going to stop? Probably not – as we've said, they are addicted and feel like they need the product. Maybe the 10% increase in price will lead to a 4% fall in the quantity of cigarettes sold.*

Highlight this change visually on the board or visualiser: a 10% increase in price leads to a 4% decrease in quantity demanded. Accompany this with a large upwards arrow representing the change in price and a small downwards arrow representing the change in quantity. This is sticking with our principle that explanations need live drawing to support the narrative.

> *Okay, so we can see that the size of the decrease in demand is much smaller than the size of the increase in price. Let's have a think about how that may look on a diagram.*

I would then model a demand curve that is more inelastic, clearly labelling the 10% increase in price and 4% fall in quantity demanded. Use arrows to demonstrate the relative changes in price and demand, as shown by the diagram on the right. The process may look something like the diagrams shown in Figure 3.2.

The arrows in Figure 3.2 are a good tool for demonstrating proportionality to students, as hopefully, they can clearly see that the increase arrow is larger than the decrease arrow. Note also that at this point, we are not introducing any technical terminology, such as 'inelastic' or 'sensitivity'. We are just focused on understanding the concept.

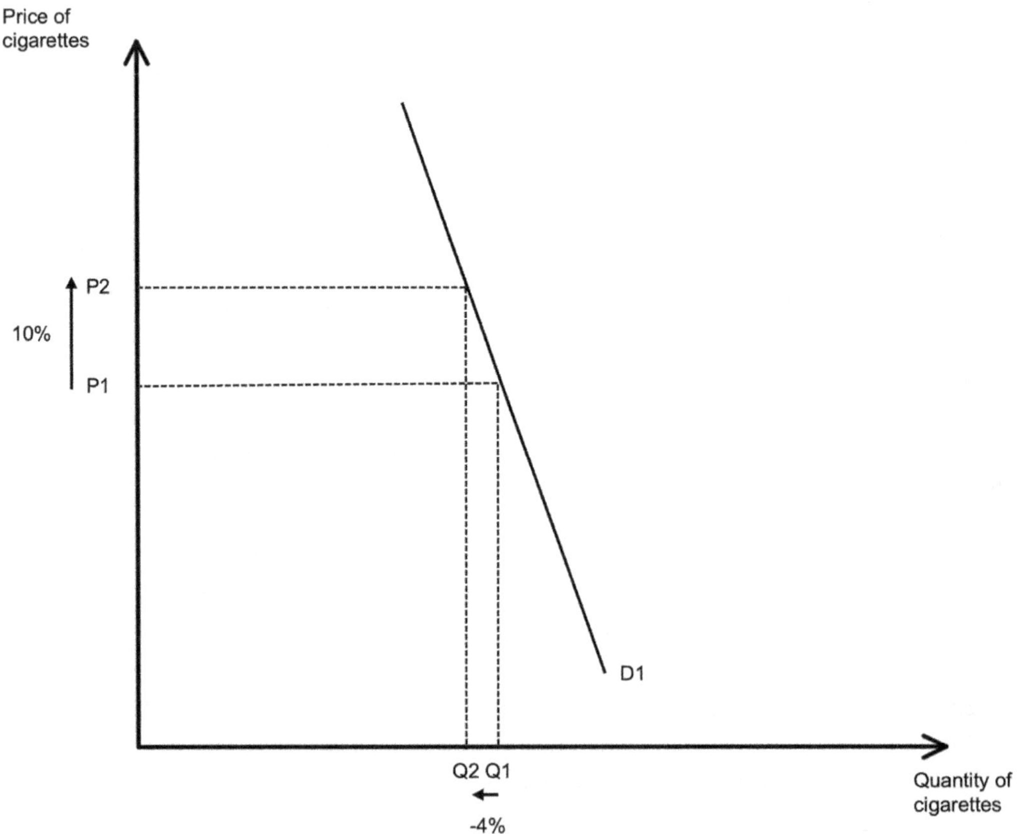

Figure 3.2 An increase in the price of cigarettes

We now need to consolidate this understanding with further examples and the gradual introduction of more specific terminology. The overall sequence may then look something like this:

1. Concrete example of cigarettes, highlighting the addictive/habitual nature of the product and showing what the demand curve for this product may look like.
2. Second concrete example of a product which highlights a different factor impacting the PED of a product. This may be Apple with a focus on branding or petrol for cars with a focus on the lack of substitutes available.
3. Define the concept: price elasticity of demand refers to the responsiveness of demand to a change in price. It is often useful here to refer back to your diagrams at this point, highlighting that the *responsiveness* of demand refers to the change in quantity demand and the change in price obviously refers to the increased price level.
4. Third concrete example that focuses on a product where demand is more price elastic. This may be an own-label can of baked beans or a Mars bar.
5. Fourth concrete example of a product where demand is more price elastic and the price of the product is decreased. This is to demonstrate that PED is not restricted to increases in price.

The sequence earlier ensures students have seen multiple examples of products that have varying levels of sensitivity to price changes and various different examples of factors that affect the price elasticity of demand.

Now is a good time to label each of the graphs that we will have drawn and label them accordingly. For example, you may label the cigarettes example as one in which demand is more price inelastic and the own-label baked beans as one where demand is more price elastic. This helps students to label the concepts that they have learnt correctly but has ensured that cognitive overload has not occurred by introducing technical terms too early. Remember, we don't want to label them as simply 'elastic' or 'inelastic', as this will cause confusion when students come to calculate elasticity at different points of linear demand curves.

At this stage, it is useful to check students' understanding with some MWB questions. These may check their understanding of what relatively price inelastic and elastic demand curves should look like and a check on their understanding of these concepts using some obvious examples that have not been previously introduced. For example, you may ask students to classify prescription drugs/medicine and a specific brand of breakfast cereal. You can also start to bring in questions that hint at the formula that students will use to calculate elasticity. For example, you may ask students: *A product increases in price by 12%. Demand for the product falls by 5%. Is demand for this product price elastic or inelastic?* I like slowly introducing the elements of the formula to students in this manner because it reduces the burden when the formula is introduced.

Explaining this concept – factors affecting the price elasticity of demand

In the next stage of the sequence, introduce students to the various factors that will influence a product's price elasticity of demand. Start this by reminding students of some of the examples used earlier:

1. Cigarettes were addictive, which meant consumers were less sensitive to price changes.
2. Apple has excellent branding which has developed customer loyalty.
3. A Mars bar has a large number of substitutes.

You will then need to introduce new examples based on other factors you teach, such as the example of a car when considering the proportion of income spent and durability (the buyer hopes!). The number of examples you use will be dependent on exam board requirements.

Check students' understanding at this point with questions like the one shown in Box 3.1.

BOX 3.1 MWB CHECK FOR UNDERSTANDING ON PED

MWB check for understanding

Which of the following is a factor influencing the price elasticity of demand of a product? There may be more than one correct answer.

A. A change in the price of substitute goods

B. The number of substitute goods available

C. A change in a consumer's income

D. The size of the price change

E. The habitual nature of the good

Answer B and E are correct.

Answer A and C check that students can differentiate between factors causing a shift of the demand curve and factors affecting the price elasticity of demand. Answer A is a particular distractor because students will know that one of the factors impacting elasticity regards substitute goods, but it is the quantity of substitutes rather than a change in their price which influences elasticity.

Answer D reveals a misunderstanding of the concept itself. It is not the size of the change that influences elasticity; the size of the change is part of the calculation.

Once a MWB check for understanding has been completed, use a knowledge consolidation exercise to ensure that students have a sound understanding of the concept of price elasticity of demand and the factors influencing it. This might include knowledge recall questions on the definition of elasticity, graphical representations of PED that is more elastic/inelastic, examples of products with differing PEDs and factors influencing PED.

Explaining this concept – PED and revenue

Then introduce students to the relationship between PED and revenue. This is one of the key reasons PED is an important concept, as it will help business make decisions to maximise their revenue. Depending on how confident you are with regards to students' understanding of revenue, you could ask them to explore this themselves on MWBs. If you are less sure, I would explicitly model the relationship between PED and revenue. An example of the graphs you may be showing students is shown in Figure 3.3.

It is useful to demonstrate this using curves that are *almost* perfectly inelastic and elastic, as this will ensure the revenue increase when price increase for products where demand is more price inelastic is clear and vice versa. Notice also in the graphs in Figure 3.3 that the size of the price change in each scenario is exactly the same. This makes the sensitivity of the fall in demand extremely clear to students because one variable is staying the same between both graphs.

Again, use some MWB check for understanding questions before moving on. Examples of these questions can be seen in Box 3.2.

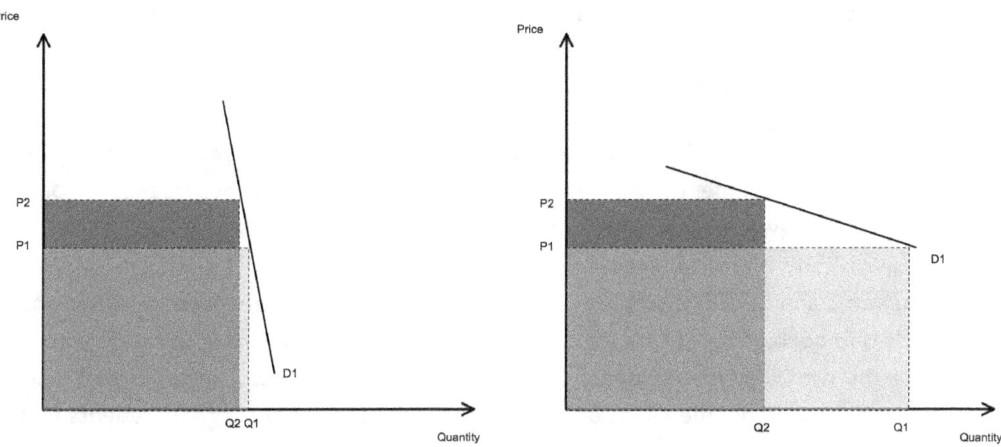

Figure 3.3 Revenue differences between PED that is more inelastic and more elastic

BOX 3.2 MWB CHECKS FOR UNDERSTANDING

MWB checks for understanding

Question one

A firm increases the price of the product. In which circumstances would this lead to an increase in the revenue made by the firm? There may be more than one correct answer.

A. The product is not addictive in nature.

B. A large proportion of individuals' income is spent on the product.

C. There are few substitutes available.

D. The product is effectively branded.

E. There is an increase in consumer incomes across the economy.

The question is testing both students' understanding of factors affecting PED and the relationship between PED and revenue.

Answer C and D are correct.

Answers A and B are factors affecting price elasticity but are likely to signal that PED is more elastic, and therefore, revenue would fall following a price increase.

Answer E would lead to an outward shift of the demand curve.

Question two

Figure 3.4 shows the demand curves of two different products with differing PEDs. Which of the following statements relating to the demand curves is correct? Assume ceteris paribus for each answer. There may be more than one correct answer.

A. Product A is likely to be more addictive or habitual in nature than Product B.

B. Product A is likely to have fewer substitutes than Product B.

C. Product B is likely to take up a smaller proportion of consumers' incomes than Product A.

D. Product A is likely to be an unbranded product.

This question is useful for teaching students' multiple-choice question techniques. Students should first identify the contrasting elasticities of both products before going through each answer one by one.

Answer A and B are correct.

Answer C and D demonstrate an incorrect understanding of the factors influencing PED. It is important to include multiple correct/incorrect answers in this question to reduce the probability of students guessing all answers correctly. In my experience, the proportion of income spent on a product tends to be a factor that students find

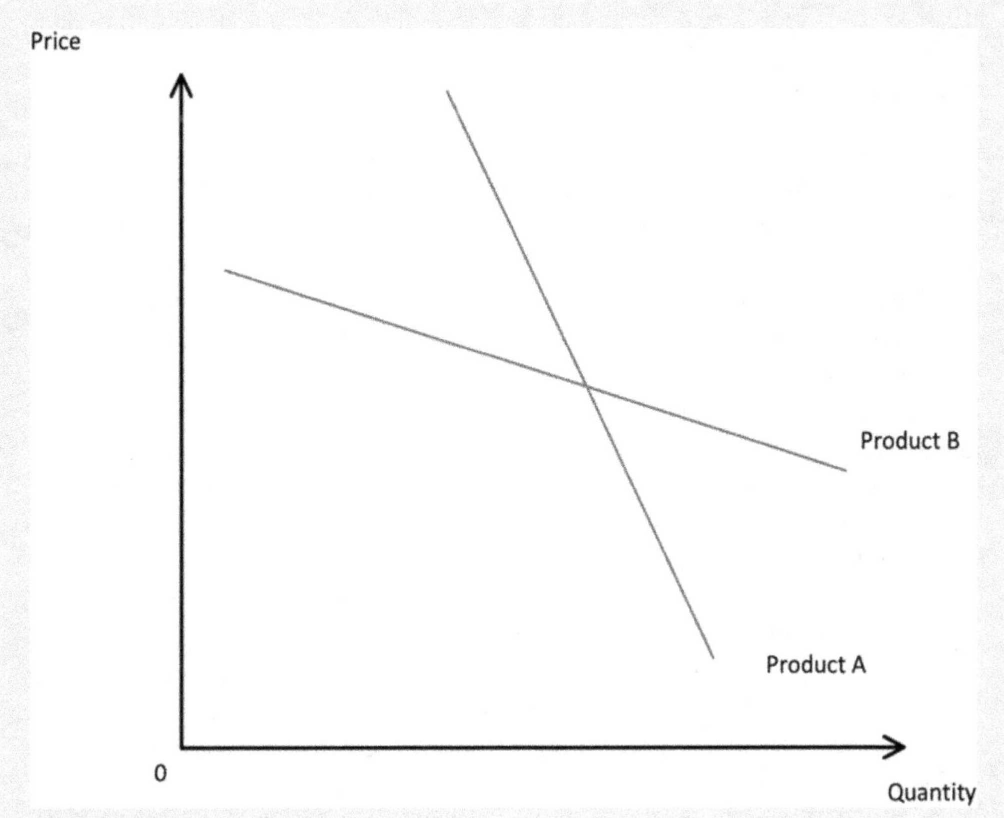

Figure 3.4 MWB PED question

difficult to understand. Take note of those that are answering incorrectly on Answer C, and consider the need for re-teaching.

It is important to emphasise to students after this question that the presence of one factor alone does not determine the PED of a product. This is why students are asked to assume ceteris paribus.

Consolidating with a case study

Students should now have a sound understanding of the concept of price elasticity of demand, the factors influencing it and its influence on revenue. The case study contained in Box 3.3 is a useful way to consolidate students' understanding of the content studied so far. It is also a useful case study for highlighting that a product's PED at any given price point is determined by multiple factors, rather than a single one.

BOX 3.3 CASE STUDY ON PED

Case study – Pret a Manger coffee

Pret a Manger, or 'Pret', is a coffee and sandwich shop. It currently has nearly 500 stores in the UK, with many located in busy cities and town centres. Pret operates in a competitive industry, competing against global rivals Starbucks, Costa Coffee and Café Nero. In comparison to Starbucks and Costa, who have nearly 1,500 and 3,000 UK locations, respectively, Pret is much smaller. Pret also must compete against independent coffee shops and cafés, which are often preferred by local citizens due to their community appeal.

Pret have found that many consumers tend to switch between coffee shops based on convenience. Many customers may have a 'regular' coffee shop because it is in a convenient commuting location, but those customers will be happy to switch to other brands of coffee in other situations. To compete against their rivals and reducing the tendency for consumers to switch, Pret has attempted to market itself as a higher quality producer of fresh food. In 2021, Pret also launched a loyalty scheme to encourage customers to keep coming back to Pret.

Pret have recently experienced an increase in their costs. The cost of purchasing supplies such as milk and coffee beans has increased in recent years. As a result, Pret are considering increasing their prices by 8%. This would increase the average price of their coffee from £3.20 to £3.45.

Pret need to consider the impact that this would have on the demand for their products. They know that coffee is an addictive product and often forms part of a person's daily routine, but the company are concerned the price increase may lead to customers switching to some of their competitors.

Questions

1. Identify and explain factor included in the case study that you think suggest that the PED for Pret's coffee is more price inelastic at the current price level.
2. Identify and explain factor(s) included in the case study that you think suggest that the PED for Pret's coffee is more elastic at the current price level.
3. Based on the factors you have discussed in the previous questions, rank each factor in terms of its influence over the PED for Pret's coffee.
4. Assume that PED for Pret's coffee is more inelastic and the company choose to increase their prices by 8%:
   a. Would the fall in quantity demanded be more or less than 8%?
   b. What would happen to revenue made by Pret from their coffee?
5. Based on your answers in all questions earlier, do you think Pret should increase the price of their coffee or not? Justify your answer.

Explaining this concept – the formula for price elasticity of demand

Finally, introduce the formula for calculating the price elasticity of demand. This is the aspect of the topic that I think many students find the most daunting, and so I think it is key to delay its introduction until students have demonstrated a sound understanding of all other aspects of the concept. It is likely that the sequence earlier will have taken at least two timetabled periods on most school timetables. As a result, the formula can be introduced in a stand-alone lesson after students have had the time to consolidate their understanding of the concept through homework or starter activities.

Start with an example:

Let's imagine a firm increases the price of one of their products by 10% and that this leads to a decrease in demand of 20%. What would this tell us about the price elasticity of demand for this product?

Students should respond that PED is elastic at this point.

What if I wanted to find a mathematical way of representing that? I need to find a way to compare the size of the change in price to the change in the quantity demanded. Well, if I divide the change in the quantity demanded by the change in price, that would tell me how big the change in quantity demanded is compared to the change in price. So, let's do −20 divided by 10. We can see that I get the answer −2: the decrease in quantity demanded is twice the size of the change in price.

Okay, so I can use the formula $\frac{\%\,change\ in\ quantity\ demanded}{\%\,change\ in\ price}$ *to calculate the size of the change in quantity demanded in comparison to the change in price. Let's do another example.*

The key figures from the calculation should be written on the board so that students can see the calculation live. Repeat the process for a product where PED is inelastic and the answer is less than 1. Repeat for one more example where the answer is equal to −1 (e.g. a product where an increase in price by 10% leads to a decrease in quantity of 10%). This can then be highlighted as unitary elasticity, and we can identify that anything with a PED greater than the absolute value of 1 will be elastic and anything between 0 and 1 will be inelastic.

Get the students to practice a few examples on their mini-whiteboards and check that they understand the meaning of the PED values. Then explain to students that in many exam questions, they are usually required to complete another couple of steps to calculate the PED. Provide the students with an initial worked example, as shown by the question in Box 3.4.

The worked examples in Box 3.4 is likely to adequately support students in answering the majority of price elasticity of demand questions that feature in exam papers. However, they may also be tested on their use of the formula in other ways. The second example in Box 3.4 contains a more difficult example of a question that students may be asked.

BOX 3.4 WORKED EXAMPLE ONE

Worked example one

Question: a business increases the price of its product from £10 to £12. As a result, they experience a reduction in demand from 1,200 units per week to 1,100 units per week. Calculate the price elasticity of demand for the product.

Step one: write out the formula for the problem that you need to solve.

$$PED = \frac{\%\,change\ in\ quantity\ demanded}{\%\,change\ in\ price}$$

Step two: check if this information is given to us within the question. If it is not, identify another formula that you will need.

$$Percentage\ change = \frac{(New\ value - original\ value)}{Original\ value} \times 100$$

Step three: calculate the percentage change in quantity demanded.

$$\frac{(1{,}100 - 1{,}200)}{1{,}200} \times 100 = -8.33\%$$

Step four: calculate the percentage change in price.

$$\frac{(12 - 10)}{10} \times 100 = 20\%$$

Step five: insert these figures into your formula for price elasticity of demand.

$$\frac{-8.33}{20} = -0.42$$

Worked example two

Question: in 2023, the average price of a t-shirt at a particular shop was £12. At this price, the product sold 7,200 t-shirts each week. It was estimated that the price elasticity of demand for t-shirts at the shop was −0.6.

Assuming everything else remains unchanged, calculate the change in total revenue if prices were increased by 5% to £12.60.

Step one: write out the formula(s) for the problem that you need to solve.

$$Change\ in\ revenue = new\ revenue - previous\ revenue$$

$$Revenue = quantity\ sold \times selling\ price$$

Step two: check if this information is given within the question. If it is not, identify another formula that you will need.

We can see that we have the information that we need to calculate the old revenue:

$$Previous\ revenue = £12 \times 7,200 = £86,400$$

However, we have the new selling price but not the new quantity sold, and so at this point, we do not know the new revenue. We do have information that will help us calculate the price elasticity of demand, and we know that the percentage change in quantity features in this formula.

$$PED = \frac{\%\ change\ in\ quantity\ demanded}{\%\ change\ in\ price}$$

Step three: use the information that we have to calculate the percentage change in quantity demanded:

$$-0.6 = \frac{\%\ change\ in\ quantity\ demanded}{5}$$

We know that *something* divided by 5 is equal to −0.6. This must mean that whatever this quantity is, it is five times larger than −0.6. As a result, we multiply −0.6 by 5:

$$-0.6 = \frac{-3}{5}$$

We now know that as a result of the 5% increase in price, the quantity of t-shirts sold will fall by 3%.

Step four: calculate the new quantity sold.

We can use a decimal multiplier to reduce a number by a certain percentage. To reduce 7,200 by 3% we multiply it by 0.97:

$$7,200 \times 0.97 = 6,984$$

Step five: we can use this new quantity sold to calculate our new revenue:

$$New\ revenue = £12.60 \times 6,984 = £87,998$$

Step six: we can now solve our problem by inputting this number into our original formula:

$$Change\ in\ revenue = new\ revenue - previous\ revenue$$

$$£87,998 - £86,400 = £1,598$$

We have solved our problem: revenue increased by £1,598.

Figure 3.5 Worked example continuum

Box 3.4 represents a difficult problem and certainly one that will have required some practice of the first type of elasticity question. However, this is likely to be one of the more difficult elasticity and revenue questions that students encounter. If they can complete questions similar to both worked examples, it is likely that they can tackle the majority of elasticity questions that they are asked. If we imagine that the first worked example is near the easier end of the spectrum of questions that students could be asked, and the second worked example is near the harder end of the spectrum, it is likely that most problems will fall somewhere in between. This is represented in Figure 3.5.

In theory, students should be able to use the strategies provided by the worked examples to answer any question that fits within that difficulty spectrum.

Notice how the first two steps are the same. This is designed to ingrain good habits in students: start by writing out the formula that you need to answer the question and then identify whether you have the information that you need. If you do not, you will then need to consider other formulas required to answer the question.

Finish by using the questions in Box 3.5 to check students' understanding of the price elasticity of demand.

BOX 3.5 MWB CHECKS FOR UNDERSTANDING

MWB checks for understanding

Question one

A product has a price elasticity of demand of −0.6. The firm increases their price by 6%. Without calculating the specific answer, which of the following do you know cannot be the firm's corresponding decrease in quantity demanded? There may be more than one correct answer.

A. −2%

B. −4%

C. 12%

D. −6%

E. −7%

Answer D and E are correct.

This should be a straightforward check on students' understanding of price elasticity as a concept. If PED is inelastic, the decrease in demand must be proportionately smaller than the increase in price. Students can then be asked to calculate the change in quantity specifically, which is –3.6%.

Question two

A firm increases prices by 8%. As a result, demand for the product falls by 12%. Which of the following statements is correct?

A. −1.5

B. −0.66

C. PED for the product is elastic.

D. PED for the product is inelastic.

E. The increase in price will lead to a reduction in revenue.

F. The increase in price will lead to an increase in revenue.

Answer A, C and E are correct.

This question ensures that students recognise that if A is correct, C and E must also be correct in this situation. This is because answer A and C essentially tell us the same thing, and answer E must be correct given that the question states that this firm has increased prices for the product.

The question is purposely phrased with price as the first piece of information that students receive. This is to test that students are thinking carefully about the formula and do not mix up the numerator and denominator in the division calculation. If students do mix these up, they are likely to answer B. It is then interesting to note students' other answers if they have initially answered B: Do they then use metacognition strategies to check that this logic holds, given that the reduction in demand is proportionately larger than the increase in price?

Key takeaways

- Take your time teaching price elasticity of demand. The teaching sequence should be clearly chunked to separate the introduction of the concept, graphical representations of elasticity, factors affecting elasticity, PEDs relationship with revenue and the formula used to calculate PED.
- Don't introduce the formula too quickly! Introduce it once conceptual understanding has been embedded.
- Avoid labelling curves as 'inelastic' or 'elastic'. Elasticity changes along a linear demand curve, and so this is likely to cause confusion.
- Use multiple worked examples to help students with some of the more challenging elasticity calculation questions. These worked examples should show the range of questions students can be asked.

4 Price elasticity of supply

What's the big idea?

An increase in the demand for a product will cause market prices for that product to rise. Firms would like to respond by increasing supply, which enables them to maximise their revenue. However, firms cannot always respond by increasing their supply. This may be because they lack the factors of production or raw materials required to increase quantity supplied sufficiently to meet the increase in demand. The price elasticity of supply measures firms' ability to respond to changes in the price of a product.

A sound understanding of the price elasticity of supply provides the platform for students to access other areas of the specification. Whenever students need to consider a firm's response to an increase in demand, they need to be able to evaluate their price elasticity of supply. For example, when studying the j-curve in macroeconomics, students will need to consider the price elasticity of exporting firms to evaluate the impacts of a currency depreciation.

The concept can also be linked to the price-signalling function of the market mechanism that students have previously studied. If the PES is inelastic at a given price point, an increase in price will lead to a less-than-significant increase in quantity supplied. The signalling function of the market mechanism is thus not working efficiently. This point can really help embed students' understanding of the market mechanism!

Where may misconceptions or misunderstanding arise?

As with the price elasticity of demand, students find this a difficult concept to understand because of the following:

1. They have a difficulty understanding the idea of proportionate change.
2. A confusion between the numerical meaning of PES figures, both in terms of the sign and magnitude. Students tend to try to learn these by rote, rather than understanding the mathematical logic. For example, students may try to

DOI: 10.4324/9781003724179-4

memorise that PED calculations produce a negative number while PES calculations produce a positive number.

3. A confusion between the factors affecting PES with factors affecting supply.

The earlier factors have all been discussed in greater depth in *Chapter 3: The price elasticity of demand*. They are all valid reasons that students may find learning about the PES difficult. However, treating the PES as the same as the PED is likely to ignore a key cause of students' difficulty to understand PES. Students often quickly understand the idea of PED because they have real-life experience of their purchasing response to a change in price. However, students typically lack real-world experience of PES. Students are often introduced to PES before they have studied the theory of the firm. As a result, students have a limited understanding of production processes and decisions. This may be one of the first times that students have considered ideas such as capital- or labour-intensive production. It is likely that they have not yet considered firms' productive capacity or the level of inventories that they may hold. These are aspects of foundational knowledge that students need to understand if they are to gain a firm grasp of the price elasticity of supply.

Explaining this concept

Mistakes to avoid

Like PED, do not introduce students to the definitions of PES or the formula for calculating PES before they understand the concept itself. The definitions of elasticity can feel wordy and make the concept sound extremely technical. As a result, students struggle to see that what they are really thinking about here is this: Can a firm increase the quantity supply when demand (and, therefore, price) increases? Start with this question, and consider the answer in relation to a specific example first.

As with PED again, we don't want to label curves as 'inelastic' or 'elastic' because the price elasticity of supply will vary along a linear supply curve (except in circumstances where the curve passes through the origin!).

Explaining this concept

I often find the following example useful to get students thinking about production processes at firms:

> *Imagine you run a company that produces bespoke wedding cakes. You employ 10 members of staff who produce these cakes by hand. These members of staff have been specially trained in the techniques required to make these*

cakes. This training process usually takes around six months to complete. You do not currently use machinery in your production process as you cannot find a piece of machinery that produces the same cakes at the required quality. At present, you generally work at maximum capacity most weeks – the number of orders you receive is approximately the number of cakes you can produce each week.

Pause there and consolidate the information that you have been through. I would have the following information displayed on the board and would check that students understand:

- The firm produces a bespoke product that is made by hand, without any machinery.
- Labour has been trained to make these bespoke products. This is a lengthy training process.
- The firm is currently producing at its maximum capacity.

Now let's imagine that some of your competitors in the local area unexpectedly shut down. As a result, there is a sudden surge in demand in the number of customers who order cakes from your business.

Follow this example with two questions:

1. *What would you* ***like*** *to happen to your supply of cakes in response to the change in demand?*
2. *Why would you not be able to increase the quantity supplied significantly?*

The example may be a simplified example that reduces the complexities of production decisions at firms. However, it introduces students to the idea that firms may not be able to respond to a change in demand (and, therefore, price signals) as much as may be desirable. This is because of constraints in the resources that they have available to them. This should help to address one of the key drivers of a superficial or weak understanding of the price elasticity of supply because it provides students with examples of constraints on production.

Once this has been discussed and students have demonstrated an understanding of the earlier factors, students can be shown how this may be shown on a graph. This is shown in Figure 4.1. As with the price elasticity of demand diagrams, make sure you highlight the size of the change in price in comparison to the size of the change in output. As with PED, I like to do this by drawing the arrows on each axis and clearly pointing out to students the different sizes of these arrows.

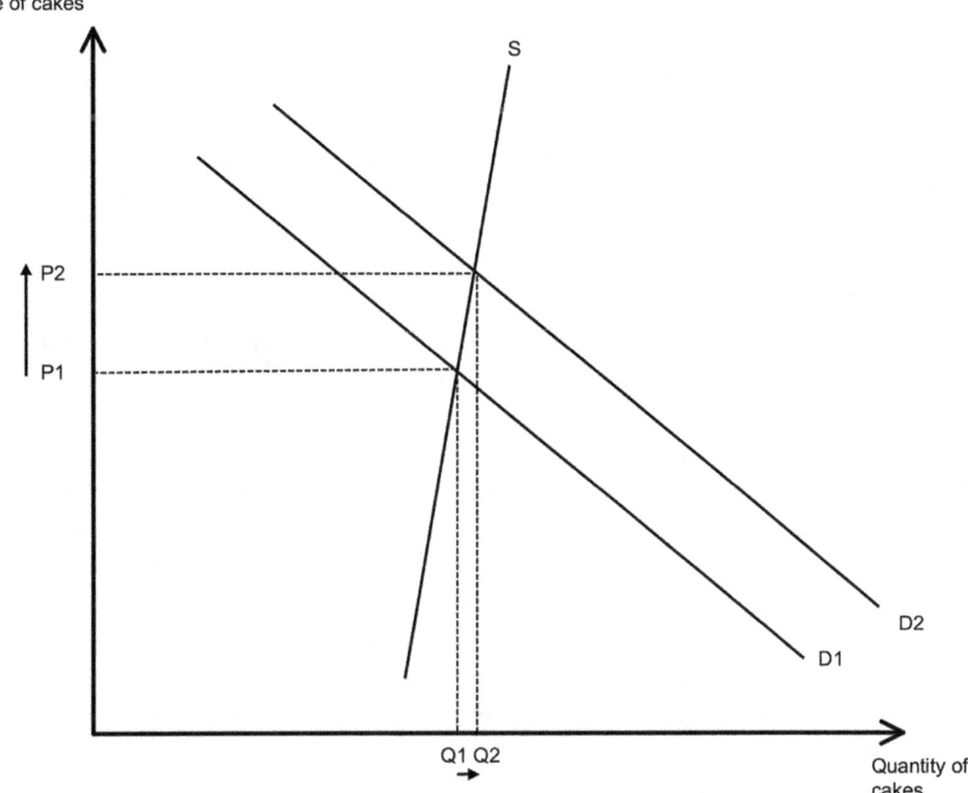

Figure 4.1 The price elasticity of supply

Continue your example to demonstrate a change in the production potential at the cake shop:

> *Now imagine that a piece of technology has been invented that can help in the production process of these cakes. This piece of machinery is brand new and can replicate the unique, hand-made nature of your current labour. Not only that, but the machinery can produce cakes more quickly. How would this change your ability to respond to the increase in demand?*

Students can then be shown that the supply schedule of the cake producer is becoming flatter. Emphasise now that the change in quantity produced is larger than the increase in the price of the product.

As with our explanation of the PED, we have not yet used terms like 'elasticity' or 'responsiveness' to explain what we are showing. These are technical terms that can often overload students' working memory while they try to understand the concept. It is likely that lots of students' 'brain power' will be taken up with trying to understand proportionate change and production processes at firms, so it is useful not to complicate this further with technical terms before students are ready.

Once both curves have been shown to students, you can now start to introduce the more technical terms. You can revisit both curves that you have drawn and explain that these demonstrate the price elasticity of supply, with one situation demonstrating the firm being less able to respond to a change in demand and one being more able. Remember, we don't want to label each curve as 'inelastic' or 'elastic' because elasticity will vary at different points on a linear supply curve.

At this point, add one more example of a change that will impact the production processes at the firm. For example, you may introduce the idea that there is a shortage in eggs across the country as a result of a disease outbreak in farms. You want to draw out that these are key ingredients in the cake-making process and cannot be easily substituted for other raw materials. Add a further layer of detail by comparing the significance of this impact if the cake shop currently has very limited stock of eggs in comparison to a scenario where they do have some eggs in storage. In the first scenario, the cake shop is going to be very unresponsive to an increase in demand, and prices charged will increase significantly, whereas in the second scenario, they may be able to service the increase in demand for a short period of time. Check students' understanding by asking them to show you each scenario on a supply-and-demand diagram for the cake shop.

Once this is complete, bring this all together, and summarise the factors that are going to impact the responsiveness of supply to a change in demand. Make this explicit on your whiteboard:

1. The level of spare capacity a firm has (the cake shop was working at maximum capacity)
2. The ease of switching between factors of production (the new machine made this easier for the cake shop)
3. The availability of raw materials and the ease of switching raw materials (the egg shortage caused a problem!)
4. The level of stock a firm has (the firm had some eggs left but not many)

Certain exam boards may require students to know others, and it is worth checking the specification list here.

Finish this sequence with a comprehension activity. An example of this is shown in Box 4.1.

BOX 4.1 COMPREHENSION TASK ON FACTORS AFFECTING PRICE ELASTICITY OF SUPPLY

Comprehension task

The demand for avocados has increased significantly over the past decade. They have become extremely popular in Western culture as part of 'brunch' menus in cafés. However, despite the increase in demand for the product, supply is constrained by several factors.

Firstly, avocados require very specific conditions for their growth. Avocados require a 'Goldilocks climate', meaning that they need to be grown in areas that are not too hot but also not too cold. They also require a specific type of soil to be grown in. Many farmers will often try to change the crops grown on their land at different times during the year, but this is often not possible for avocados because they require a specific type of land. As a result, it is difficult to easily switch the use of land for farmers that have chosen to grow avocados. This also means that avocado farmers also like to use the land available for avocados to its maximum capacity. Given that there is limited land available, farmers need to ensure that they are maximising the use of any land that is available.

Linked to this is the fact that avocados require a significant amount of water and zinc to grow. Given that avocados are generally grown in hot countries like Mexico or Peru, droughts can sometimes reduce the amount of water available. Secondly, if the soil being used to grow avocado lacks zinc, farmers must buy fertilisers and inject these minerals into irrigation lines. These zinc fertilisers are generally accessible for farmers.

Thirdly, avocados are perishable. Farmers are not typically able to store avocados because they have a limited shelf life. Avocados can typically be stored for around six weeks, but part of this storage time will also be taken up by delivery requirements. For example, many avocados are grown in Mexico but are consumed in Europe. Farmers, therefore, need to allow for at least a week to deliver the products to retailers or wholesalers in their destination country.

Finally, avocados take a long time to grow. A typical avocado tree will take approximately ten years to grow. However, farmers generally use something called a 'grafted tree' to reduce this timeframe. This means that farmers cut off some branches from the top-half of a fully grown avocado tree and put these onto the trunks of different trees. This generally reduces the time taken to grow an avocado tree to around five years – which is still a long period of time!

Questions

1. With reference to each factor that impacts the responsiveness of supply, explain whether you think the supply of avocados is likely to be relatively price elastic or inelastic. The factors you need to consider are as follows:
   a. The level of spare capacity farmers have
   b. The ease with which farmers can switch raw materials
   c. The availability of raw materials and the ease of switching raw materials
   d. The level of stock farmers have
2. How does the time it takes to grow avocados impact the responsiveness of supply to a change in demand?
3. Use a supply-and-demand diagram to show an increase in the demand for avocados and the likely change in price and quantity of these products
4. With reference to question 3, how may this impact consumers in the UK who wish to eat avocados with their breakfast?

The questions attached to the task in Box 4.1 are not designed to be *too* challenging. This is designed to be a quick task that helps students consolidate their understanding of price elasticity of supply and the factors that influence it.

Finish this sequence by checking students' understanding with some MWB questions. Examples of the kinds of question that you could ask are shown in Box 4.2.

BOX 4.2 MWB CHECKS FOR UNDERSTANDING

MWB checks for understanding

1. Which of the following will influence the responsiveness of supply to a change in the price of a product? There may be more than one correct answer.
   A. A decrease in the cost of raw materials
   B. An increase in the minimum wage
   C. A decrease in the amount of inventory a firm holds
   D. An increase in the availability of raw materials
   E. An increase in the demand for the product

Answers C and D are correct. A and B are included to check that students are not confusing factors affecting the position of the supply curve and the elasticity of the curve. E is included to ensure that students have not concluded from the examples if levels of demand influence the PES.

2. The price of a product increases and a firm would like to respond by increasing the quantity that they supply. In which circumstances are the firm more likely to be able to increase the quantity supplied at a proportionate level to the change in price? There may be more than one correct answer.

   A. The firm has a large amount of stock available.

   B. The firm has limited spare capacity available.

   C. The firm buys cheap raw materials.

   D. The firm produces a product that can be produced by labour only.

   E. The level of corporation tax is reduced.

Answers A is the only correct answer. B and D are factors that will influence the PES, but these answers would suggest PES is inelastic. Answer C may be a misconception – just because raw materials are cheap does not mean they are readily available for firms to increase the quantity supplied. The key here is that firms can afford their raw materials *and* the raw materials are available.

Explaining this concept – the formula

Students then need to know and apply the formula for price elasticity of supply. As with price elasticity of demand, I would recommend working through an example *before* spending too much time on the formula. So the steps here may be as follows:

> *Now, throughout this explanation I have been talking about the 'responsiveness' of supply to a change in the level of demand. You can probably guess already that we are going to refer to this as the 'price elasticity of supply'.*
>
> *Okay, so we now want to see if we can measure elasticity mathematically. To do this, we want to compare the size of the change in quantity to the size of the change in price.*
>
> *So, let's imagine that a product has increased in price by 10%. In response, a firm increases their quantity supplied by 20%. We could compare the proportional size of this response by using the formula:*
>
> $$\frac{20\%\ \textit{increase in quantity supplied}}{10\%\ \textit{increase in price}} = 2$$
>
> *We can see that this would give us the answer 2. This tells us that the increase in quantity supplied is twice the size of the increase in price. Notice that the number is positive: that is because supply increases as price increases, and so we are completing a division calculation with two positive numbers*

We can therefore see that our formula for calculating the price elasticity of supply is:

$$\frac{\%\,change\,in\,quantity\,supplied}{\%\,change\,in\,price}$$

Repeat this process for the following:

1. A 5% increase in supply in response to a 10% increase in price (0.5)
2. A 15% increase in supply in response to a 15% increase in price (1)

This will mean that students have seen examples of supply that is relatively price elastic, inelastic and unitary.

As with the price elasticity of demand, key aspects of this explanation are as follows:

- The numbers are kept simple. Students' working memory is not being used up for different calculations.
- The explanation focuses on proportionality *before* the formula is introduced. This should give students the 'why' and ensure that they understand the meaning behind the price elasticity figures.

Case study

Once this sequence is completed, use the case study in Box 4.3 to consolidate students' understanding of the price elasticity of supply.

BOX 4.3 CASE STUDY ON THE PRICE ELASTICITY OF SUPPLY

Case study

Donatello's is a local pizza restaurant. The firm currently has a small kitchen with one pizza oven. *Donatello's* employ three chefs in the kitchen who prepare the pizzas before putting them in the oven. At the moment, this production process enables the restaurant to produce a maximum of 40 pizzas per hour. This is enough to meet the current demand for the restaurant's pizzas.

At the back of the kitchen, there is a small storage room and fridge where the company is able to keep enough stock to store produce for two days' worth of raw materials. The restaurant sources its raw materials from a local supplier. If orders are made before 12 p.m., this supplier can deliver raw materials the next day.

The owner of *Donatello's* has recently paid for the company to sell their pizzas on the delivery app *Just Eat*. On top of this, a local competitor has recently shut down. As a result, the owner of *Donatello's* is forecasting a 20% increase in the demand for their pizzas. The owner is concerned about the restaurant's ability to respond to this level of demand. At present, the owner is preparing to increase prices by 10% and believe the restaurant could increase the quantity supplied by 4%.

In an attempt to increase the restaurant's responsiveness to the change in market conditions, the owner of *Donatello's* is planning to build an extension to expand the size of the kitchen. This will give the owner the following options:

1. Increase the storage room to enable the restaurant to store raw materials for up to five days.
2. Purchase a second pizza oven which would increase the number of pizzas that could be made each hour
3. Purchase a piece of machinery that would automate the preparation of the pizzas before they are required to be put into the oven
4. The owner can currently afford to implement *two* of these options. They believe that this would enable them to increase the quantity supplied by 8% in response to a 10% increase in price.

Questions

1. For each of the options provided, explain why they would increase the restaurant's price elasticity of supply.
2. Calculate:
   a. The firm's initial and forecasted price elasticity of supply
   b. The percentage change in the initial and forecasted price elasticity of supply
3. Draw a supply-and-demand diagram that shows the following:
   a. The change in price and quantity as a result of the increase in demand *before* the proposed changes
   b. The change in price and quantity as a result of the increase in demand *after* the proposed changes
4. Recommend which two options the owner of the restaurant should choose. Justify each option, and explain why you are not recommending the third option.

Finish off the sequence with some final MWB checks for understanding. An example of the kind of question you could ask is shown in Box 4.4.

BOX 4.4 MWB CHECKS FOR UNDERSTANDING

MWB check for understanding

A firm's price elasticity of supply is relatively inelastic. The firm increases its price by 8% in response to changes in the market. Which of the following *cannot* be the firm's corresponding increase in quantity supplied? There may be more than one correct answer.

A. 6%

B. 10%

C. 12%

D. 8%

E. 4%

Answers B, C and D are correct answers here. This is a good question for checking students' understanding of the price elasticity figures and helps to check that students are not just learning the formula by rote. Students should recognise that for a firm's PES to be relatively inelastic, the increase in quantity must be lower than the increase in price. If unitary PES has not yet been discussed with students, answer D may lead to some interesting discussions.

The sequence earlier does not introduce students to the idea of perfect price elasticity or inelasticity of supply. I typically save these until the end of the sequence and students have a fundamental understanding of the concept. You can introduce this by asking students about a real-world example, perhaps a Taylor Swift concert where customers are willing to pay hundreds of pounds for a ticket but the supply of a stadium is fixed in the short run and so cannot increase.

Key takeaways

- Introducing the topic by giving an example of a firm with certain production processes that constrain their ability to respond to an increase in demand for their product. This means that factors that impact a firm's production process become inextricably linked in students' minds with the price elasticity of supply. As a result, students will not treat the price elasticity of supply as some abstract concept that has factors that influence it. Instead, students will see that those production factors determine the extent to which firms can increase the quantity supplied in response to a change in demand.

- Starting with these production processes also familiarises students with production processes at firms. As was laid out at the beginning of this chapter, this is something that many students will not be familiar with.
- Ensure students understand the concept of the price elasticity of supply before they are introduced to the formula. The formula doesn't mean anything if students don't fully understand what they are even trying to measure!
- Emphasise that PES is not static; it is highly dependent on the time period. PES becomes more elastic in the long run as all factors of production become variable. It is important to emphasise this because of its implications for PES but also introduces students to the idea of the 'long run' in economics, which is useful later in the course when students study concepts like average costs.

5 Externalities and representing them graphically

What's the big idea?

Free markets do not always produce the 'optimal' allocation of goods and services. At this point in the curriculum journey, students are likely to assume that the forces of supply and demand determine the allocation of resources and that this method of allocation is always efficient. In many instances, this assumption will be implicit and will not have been explicitly taught to students; they simply have not come across anything that questions this assumption.

The big idea that students need to grasp is that in many instances the free market produces too many demerit goods and too few merit goods in comparison to the 'socially optimum level'. As a result, governments may feel it is necessary to intervene to adjust the allocation of merit and demerit goods within the market. This introduces students to arguments about the role of free markets and the extent of desirable government intervention. A sound understanding of externalities equips students with the knowledge necessary to then make links when they learn about free markets, mixed economics and government intervention.

Why do students find this topic difficult?

Students often demonstrate a sound understanding of the concept of private costs/benefits, external costs/benefits and social costs/benefits. However, students struggle with the graphical representation of these concepts. This is because of the following:

- Rather than seeing market equilibrium as the sum of individual choices made by consumers and firms, students see the free market level of output as some abstract force. As a result, the 'free market' level of output can seem like a nebulous concept, and students struggle to understand why the market 'fails' to account for external costs and benefits.
- The 'socially optimum' level of output is also seen as an abstract concept. Students struggle to see how this can be understood or quantified.

DOI: 10.4324/9781003724179-5

- The distinction between production and consumption externalities requires shifting different curves. Without an accurate understanding of why a specific curve shifts, students instead resort to memorising what the graph 'looks like', instead of a deeper conceptual understanding.

Explaining this concept

Mistakes to avoid

To minimise the likelihood of some of the earlier misconceptions occurring, avoid the following:

- Focusing on a narrow range of examples that all share similar costs or benefits. For example, if you only use cigarettes and alcohol as examples of products with negative externalities, then students may only associate the concept with products that have some sort of negative health effect.
- Introducing students to a negative externalities diagram by plotting private costs, private benefits and social costs all at once often leads to cognitive overload. The diagram is new, students have not considered externalities before, and the concept of a 'socially optimum' level of output is nebulous. Trying to combine this all on one diagram at once can be confusing. The method shown later will break up the teaching of the graph more effectively.
- Using mnemonics too early within the sequence to memorise the position of curves or where the net welfare loss 'triangle' should be. These can be handy as memory aids, although the initial focus should be on deep comprehension before these aids are introduced. As a general rule, if it feels like the students may use the mnemonic to short-cut understanding, then avoid introducing it.
- Using values to plot cost and benefit curves. I have done this many times because I thought using actual figures and getting students to plot the curves makes this easier for students to understand these curves. However, in practice, I think this means students spend a lot of time thinking about plotting the graph accurately, rather than what the graph is showing them. I think the following method helps to avoid this tendency.

Explaining this concept

Teach the sequence in the order shown in Figure 5.1.

This sequence is likely to take at least a double period in a standard timetable, if not more. Once the consolidation has been complete, you should then follow a similar sequence for positive production and consumption externalities.

Figure 5.1 Sequence of teaching externalities

Step one: private costs and benefits

Start by explaining to students that you are going to be considering all the 'costs' involved with the production and consumption of goods and services. We first need to understand the idea of private costs. Start with the production of cigarettes:

> *A firm producing cigarettes has a number of costs when they produce the product. They need to pay for the raw materials that produce the cigarettes. They need to pay rent for the factory where they produce the cigarettes. They need to pay the salaries of their employees. These are all costs experienced by the firm when producing cigarettes.*
>
> *We can also think about the private costs for the consumer. The consumer has to pay money for the cigarettes, which is a cost to them. The consumer will also experience negative impacts on their own health as the result of smoking.*
>
> *These are all costs that are incurred by the economic agents involved in the transaction – the firm and the consumer. We refer to these kinds of costs as 'private costs'.*

Then give another example of private costs, such as the purchase of a pair of trainers. As previously discussed, it's useful to use an example where there is not a negative impact on the individual's health so that students do not assume this is a key component of private costs.

Then use the same two examples to highlight the private benefits gained by both firms and consumers. For example, you can highlight the revenue gained by firms and utility from consuming the product for consumers.

Check students' understanding with some quick MWB questions. You want to be confident that students understand the following:

1. The difference between private costs experienced by firms and those experienced by consumers.
2. The difference between private benefits experienced by firms and those experienced by consumers.
3. If students can correctly define and identify examples of private costs and benefits.

You could use the earlier examples by showing them different private costs and benefits and asking them to categorise them and whether they would be experienced by the firm or consumer.

Finally, finish this sequence by demonstrating private costs and benefits on a graph.[1] We need to be careful with our explanation of the upward sloping marginal private cost curve, as students are unlikely to have studied the law of diminishing marginal returns. I think it is okay to let students know that this is something we will explore in more depth later in the course, but at this point, they simply need to understand that the production of each additional unit will increase firms costs more and more.

Explain that equilibrium occurs at the point at which marginal private costs and marginal private benefits meet. As with supply and demand, this determines the free market output of the good or service.

The overall sequence will look like this:

1. Concrete example of cigarettes, highlighting the private costs of production and consumption
2. Definition of the concept: private costs are costs experienced by economic agents involved in the transaction
3. Concrete example of a pair of trainers, highlighting the private costs of production and consumption
4. Concrete examples of private benefits, using both cigarettes and trainers again
5. Definition of the concept: private benefits are benefits experienced by economic agents involved in the transaction
6. MWB check for understanding
7. Teacher modelling of private cost-and-benefit diagram and emphasising that this is the point at which the free market will choose to produce

Many A-level students tend to find these concepts straightforward. It is important to find the right balance of keeping this sequence pacey without neglecting key technical details.

Step two: social costs

Now start to introduce the idea of negative production externalities. The explanation may go something along the lines of:

> *Let's take the example of a burger at McDonald's that is purchased by an individual. To produce the burger, McDonald's will experience private costs – raw materials, rent, salaries etc. But the production of that burger will also create some costs that are experienced by economic agents other than McDonald's or the individual that purchases the burger. For example, it has been shown that cattle farming*

creates methane emissions which contribute to global warming. Similarly, when McDonald's transport that burger from the farm to the restaurant, their delivery van creates carbon emissions. All citizens experience the costs of global warming, not just those that have been involved in the transaction for the burger.

We can think of another example: the production of products that contain palm oil, such as a shampoo, results in deforestation in countries like Malaysia and Indonesia. This has environmental impacts on the local community. Again, we can see that citizens that were not involved in the initial transaction are experiencing negative costs because of the production of this good.

We can see that the production of goods have spillover effects because they can have a negative impact on one or more parties outside of the transaction.

Provide the students with another example of negative production externalities, such as the production of steel requiring the use of iron ore furnaces. At the end of this example, categorise these as 'negative production externalities', and provide students with a definition. This sequence ensures we have taken students from the concrete to the abstract and have not introduced technical terms too early. We also haven't overloaded students because we have separated the concept from how it looks diagrammatically.

Following this, use a MWB check for understanding to ensure students can differentiate between examples of private costs and negative production externalities.

Step three: negative externalities diagram

Start this sequence by asking students to draw a private cost-and-benefit diagram for a McDonald's burger. Check that students have got this correct and then draw the same diagram as a base on your whiteboard or visualiser. Reiterate that this level of output reflects the market output because firms and consumers only take into their private costs and benefits.

Then slowly go through the following explanation step-by-step as shown in Box 5.1.

Pause your explanation at this point and check for understanding. For example, tell students to turn over any notes and ask them to draw a graph on their MWB that shows the marginal private costs and benefits of McDonald's burgers. Then set a sequence of tasks along the lines of:

1. Identify two negative production externalities associated with producing these burgers.
2. On your boards, add a curve that shows the marginal social costs of producing burgers.
3. Explain why this curve is above the marginal private cost curve.

BOX 5.1 EXTERNALITIES EXPLANATION STEP ONE AND TWO

Explanation	Diagram
Now, we know the free market will produce where marginal private cost is equal to marginal private benefit. As a result, the costs associated with this level of output are equal to C1. *However, we have just seen that there are some costs to society on top of these private costs. For example, the methane caused when producing burgers. We haven't taken this into account in within that market output!* *What is the total level of cost produced with this market output if we did take into account all those societal costs? Well, we know it is going to be higher. So, let's go up from the market output and show that societal costs are actually going to be higher.*	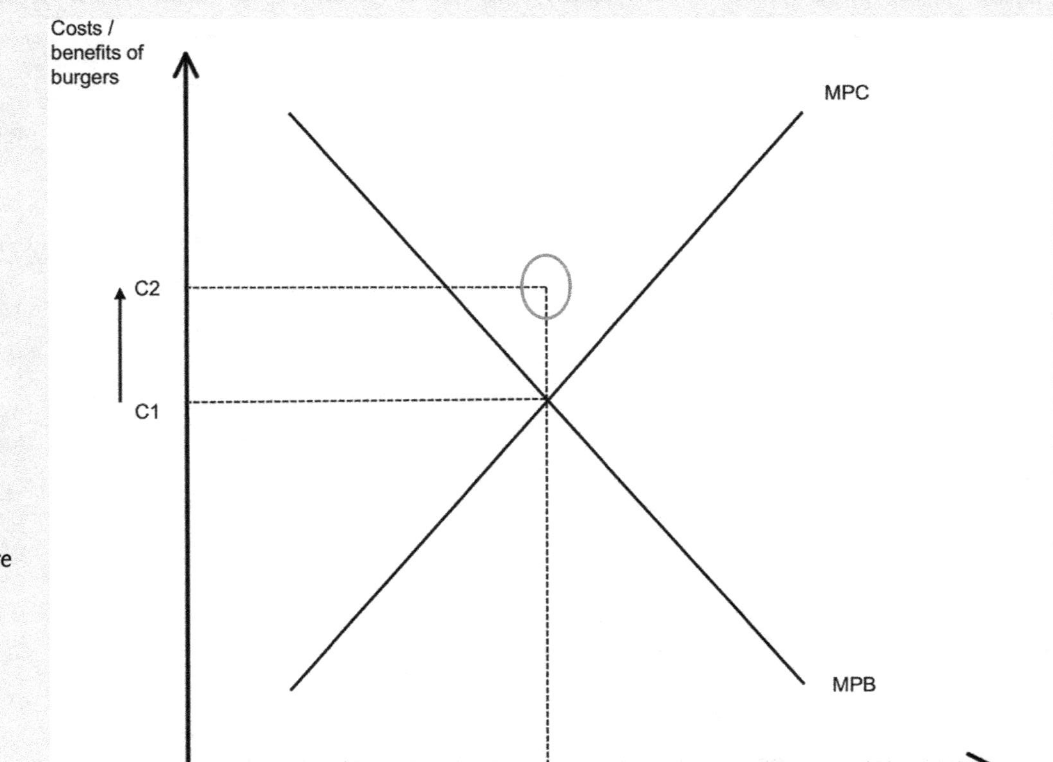 **Figure 5.2** Negative externalities diagram step one

Explanation	**Diagram**
We can see that the marginal cost to society is higher at every level of output than the marginal private cost. We can show this by adding the marginal social cost curve like this . . . *That marginal cost to society can be thought of as:* *Marginal private costs + externalities*	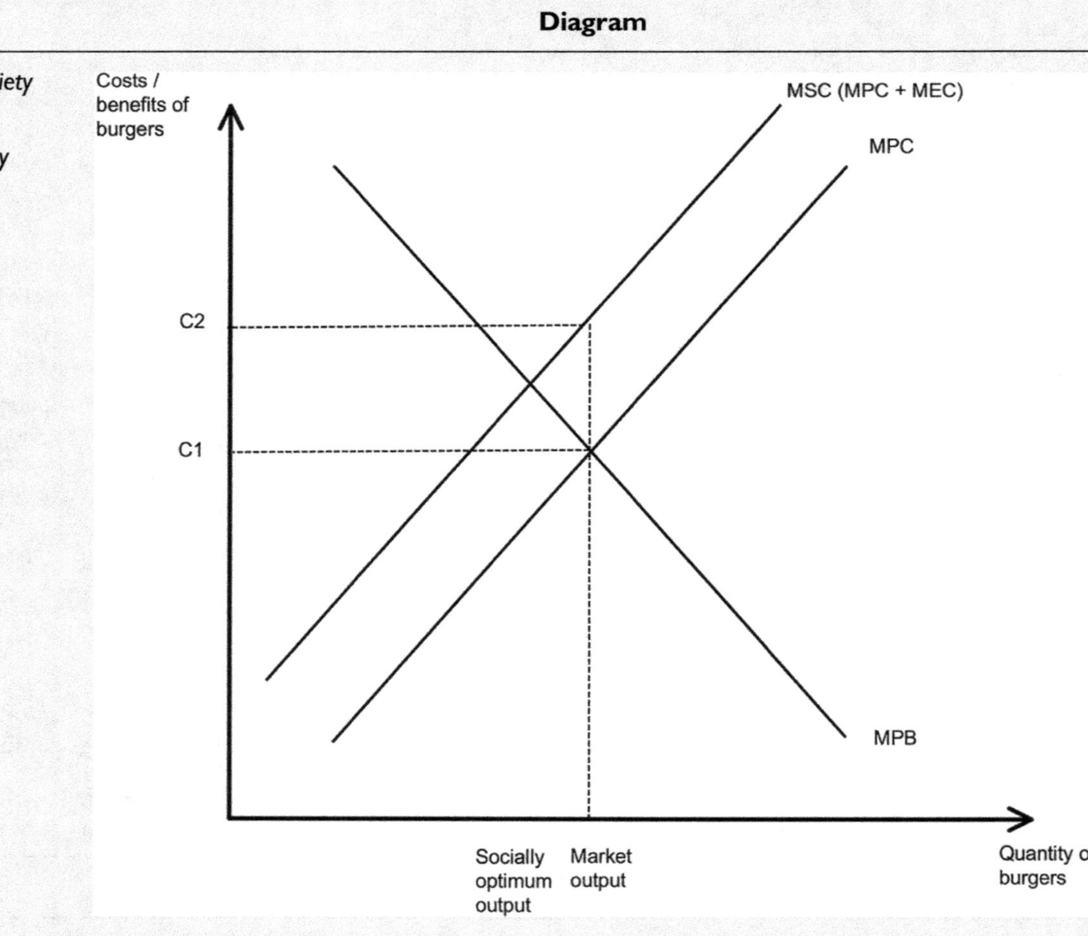 **Figure 5.3** Negative externalities diagram step two

Explanation	Diagram
Now, we may notice there is a new equilibrium point ***if we took into account social costs.*** *At this equilibrium, the output of burgers would be lower than the market output.* *We can therefore see that this is a product that is over-produced by the free market.* *We just need to be clear here: without any sort of government intervention, the market is still going to produce the market output of this product because the price mechanism does not take into account social costs.*	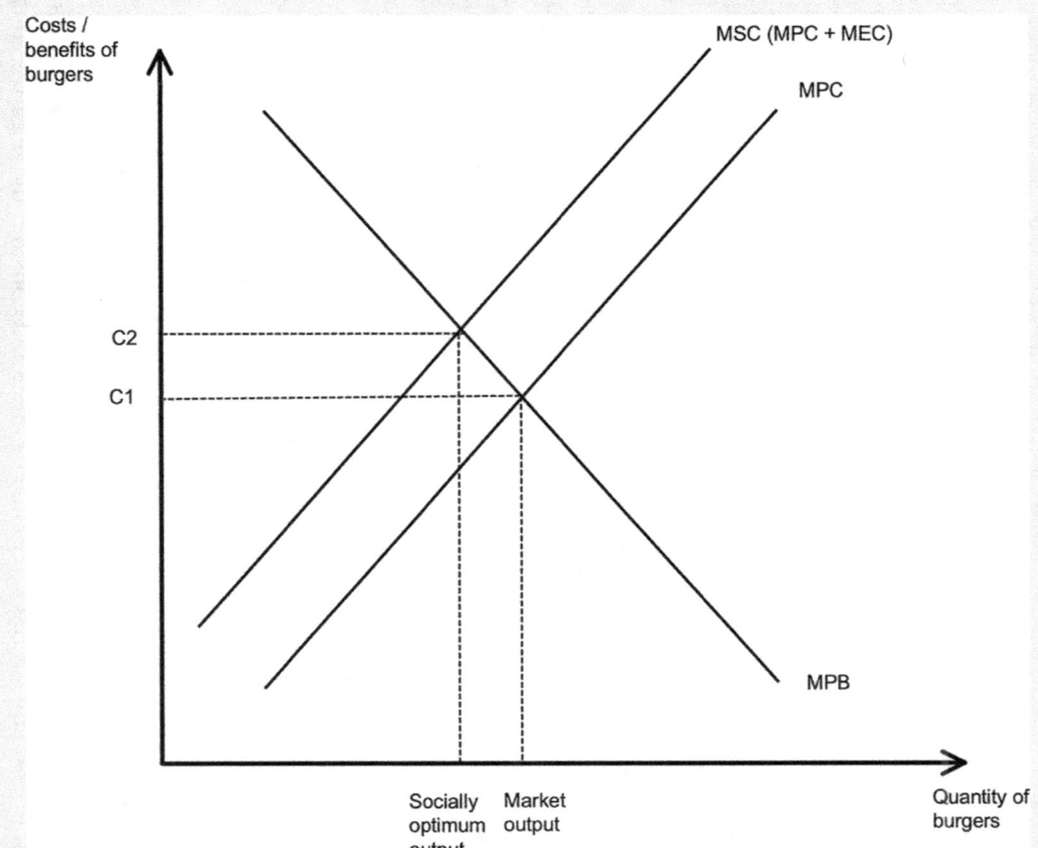 **Figure 5.4** Negative externalities diagram step three

4. Label this curve using the formula for marginal social costs.
5. On this graph, circle the market output of burgers.
6. On this graph, circle the socially optimum output of burgers.
7. Explain why the market does not produce at the socially optimum level.

The range of questions included in the list above should check students understand what is being shown, rather than simply memorising what the graph looks like.

Finish your explanation by bringing in the area of net welfare loss as shown by the explanation in Box 5.2.

This explanation in Box 5.2 places a real focus on the reasoning behind the shape of the net welfare loss triangle. It relies on the intuition that the free market will produce a greater quantity than the socially optimum level, and so we can accumulate the losses of each unit produced above this level. Without explicitly referencing it, it is showing students the intuition behind marginal analysis. This is likely to be much more effective than trying to get students to remember a mnemonic to explain the shape of the net welfare loss.

Consolidation task

Students are likely to need a consolidation exercise to bring this content together and to see a new example of negative production externalities. The case study in Box 5.3 will be useful at this point.

Negative consumption externalities

A similar sequence can now be used for negative consumption externalities. I would revisit the example of the McDonald's burger and consider the negative consumption externalities of this product. For example, non-recyclable packaging may have a negative environmental impact, and public service pressure related to obesity can be discussed. An extension of the case study earlier can also be used to consolidate students' understanding of negative consumption externalities. For example, students can consider the social costs of increased pollution and traffic as a result of the car purchase.

In a separate lesson, students can then be introduced to positive production and consumption externalities. A similar sequence can be used when teaching this topic.

Checking students' understanding

The questions in Box 5.4 can be used during various points of the teaching sequence to check students' understanding of externalities and their diagrams.

BOX 5.2 EXTERNALITIES EXPLANATION STEP THREE AND FOUR

Explanation	Diagram
We can demonstrate the overall welfare loss as a result of the over-production of these burgers by the free market. *Remember we've just said that without any sort of government intervention, the market is going to produce the market output quantity of burgers. I therefore want to consider the costs to society of producing that level of burgers.* *Now, let's start at the socially optimum level of output and then show the impact of producing one more burger. I'm going to label that as 'S+1'. Then I'm going to go up from my X axis and see what my social cost is at that level of output . . .* *We can see that my marginal social cost is above my marginal private benefit by the distance shown by the thick line.*	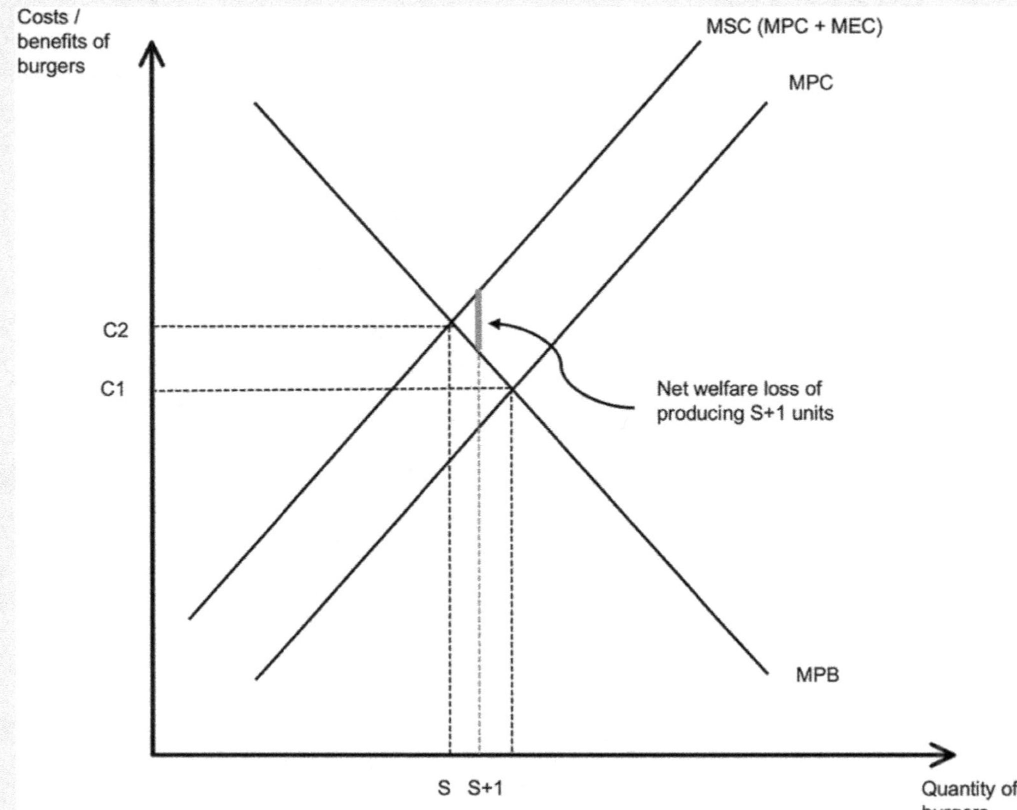 Figure 5.5 Negative externalities diagram step four

Explanation	Diagram
Now I could keep adding units until I reach the market level of output – this is the level of output we know that the free market will produce at. *We can see that the accumulation of our thick lines creates us this triangle. This 'triangle' represents the net welfare loss to society of producing at the free market level of output. It shows us the loss occurred because each unit produced above the socially optimum level has a greater social cost than it does private benefit.*	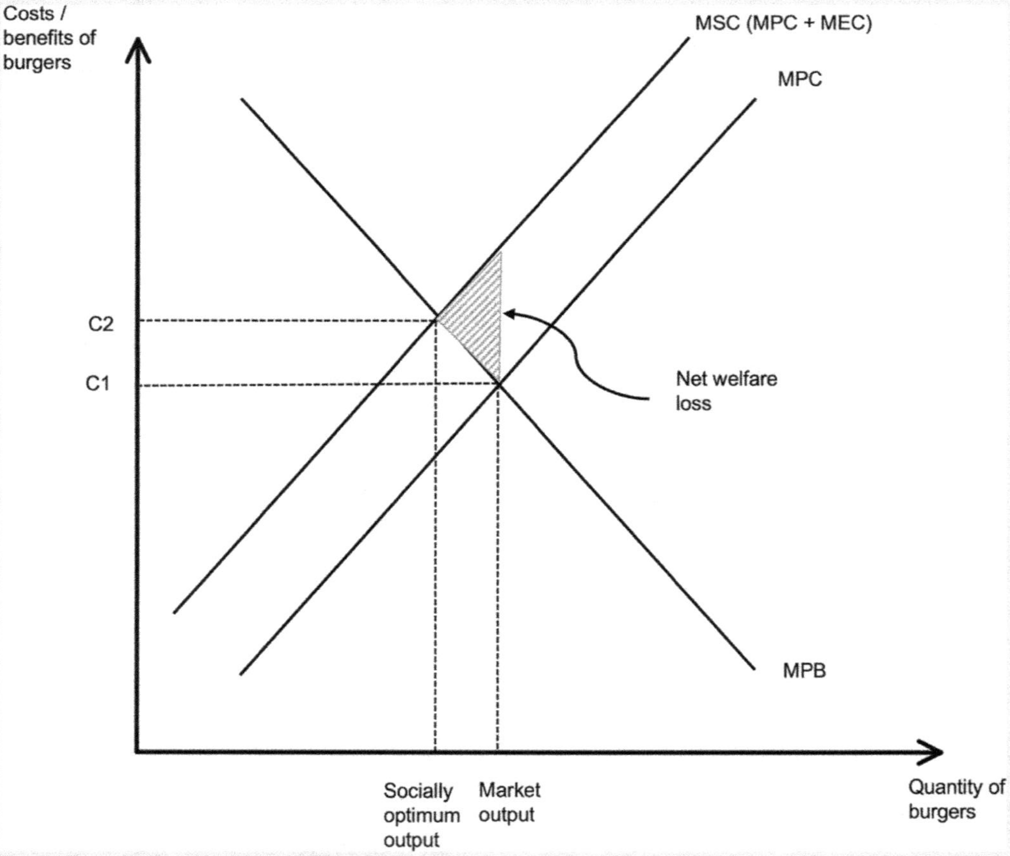 

Figure 5.6 Negative externalities diagram step five

BOX 5. 3 CASE STUDY

Case study – the car market

An individual in the UK travels a lot for work. They have typically used public transport, but this isn't always ideal, particularly when they need to travel to locations where there are few public transport options. As a result, the individual decides to purchase a car from a manufacturer in the UK. This will make work travel much more convenient. The price of the car is £12,000.

The car manufacturer has three production facilities in the UK, for which it pays a land rent of £42,000 each year. Other expenses for the manufacturing include salaries and raw material costs. The car manufacturer purchases its aluminium from a producer in China. They pay $2.50 for each kilogram of aluminium that they purchase and pay transport costs of $0.70 per kilogram.

Aluminium production is particularly energy intensive. The smelters used to produce aluminium emit powerful greenhouse gases that are damaging for the environment. Further, sulphur dioxide is released during the production of aluminium, and this has a negative impact on air quality in surrounding areas. The impact on air quality can have negative health effects for individuals, such as respiratory problems. Further, the transport of aluminium from China to the UK will also cause pollution. Shipping from China can cause air and water pollution, while the use of fossil fuels will also have negative environmental impacts.

Having said this, aluminium is often portrayed as a 'green metal', as it is recyclable. Shipping is also considered the most energy-efficient way to transport large amounts of cargo, and in recent decades, great efforts have been made to improve the sustainability of transport via shipping.

Questions

Using information from the case study, answer the following questions:

1. What private benefits is the consumer likely to experience as a result of purchasing the car?
2. What private costs is the consumer likely to experience as a result of purchasing the car?
3. What private benefits is the car manufacturer going to experience as a result of selling the car?
4. What private costs is the car manufacturer going to experience as a result of selling the car?
5. Identify and explain two negative production externalities involved in this transaction.
6. Use a negative production externalities diagram to show the following:
   a. The output of cars sold by the manufacturer
   b. The socially optimum output of cars sold by the manufacturer
   c. The net welfare loss associated with this manufacturer

BOX 5.4 CHECKING FOR UNDERSTANDING

Question one

An individual purchases a t-shirt from a shop. Categorise the following list as follows: private costs/benefits from the individual, private costs/benefits for the firm, negative production externalities, negative consumption externalities.

A. The cost of the raw materials used to make the t-shirt

B. The utility gained from wearing the t-shirt

C. The price paid for the t-shirt

D. The revenue gained from the t-shirt

E. The pollution caused by the factory that produced the t-shirt

Answers:

A – private cost for the firm

B – private benefit from the consumer

C – private cost for the consumer

D – private benefit for the firm

E – negative production externality

There is no negative consumption externality in the list earlier.

Question two

Figure 5.7 shows negative externalities related to air travel.

What can be concluded from this diagram? There may be more than one correct answer.

A. Without government intervention, air travel is overproduced.

B. Air travel has negative consumption externalities.

C. Air travel has negative production externalities.

D. Private firms will produce at the socially optimum level.

E. If price is increased to P2, then there will be no social cost of air travel.

Answer A and C are correct.

Many students are likely to put B. This is because B is a correct statement regarding air travel. However, it cannot be concluded from the diagram that air travel has negative consumption externalities, as there is no marginal social benefit curve drawn.

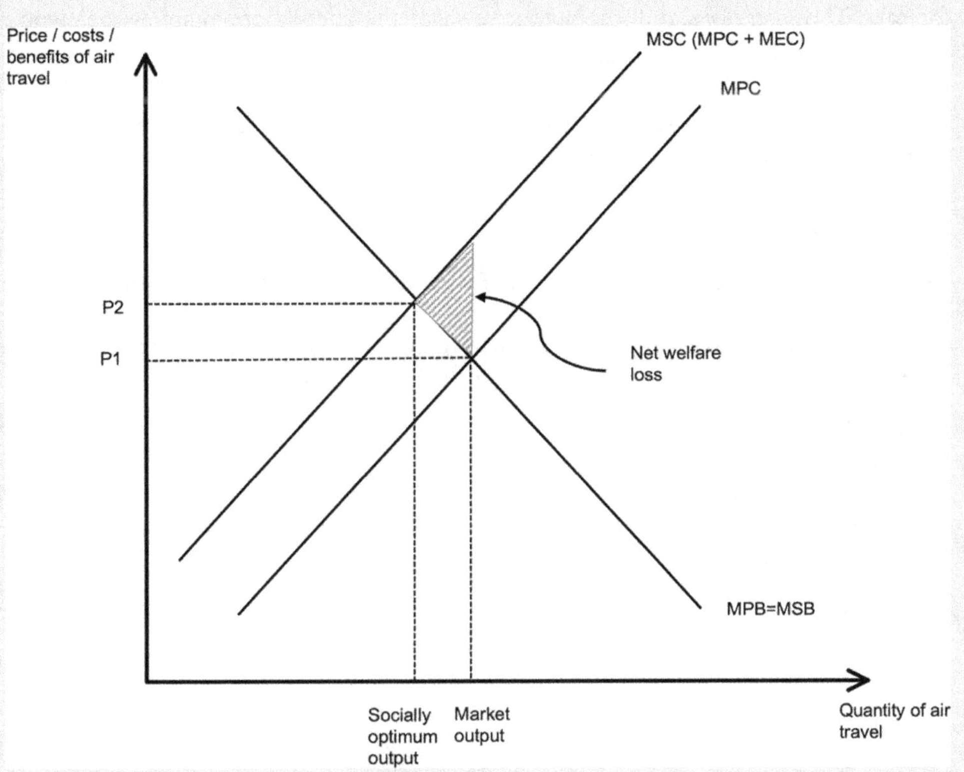

Figure 5.7 Air travel externalities diagram

Students may also incorrectly put E because they believe at the social optimum output, there will be no deadweight loss. However, this does not mean that social costs do not exist.

Question three

Consider the market for car travel. Which of the following changes is likely to move market output closer to the socially optimum level of car travel? There may be more than one correct answer.

A. A decrease in the cost of fuel

B. A decrease in the price of alternative transport methods

C. A decrease in the costs of production for car manufacturers

D. The discovery of a new energy source that does not release carbon emissions

This is a useful question to introduce, as it should force students to plot graphs to help them answer the question, which is an important metacognition skill in economics.

Answer B and D are correct. B would reduce the private benefit associated with car travel relative to alternative transport measures, which would reduce the demand for cars. This, therefore, reduces output towards the socially optimum level. D would reduce the external cost associated with car travel and, therefore, increases the socially optimum output, bringing it closer to the market output.

Answer A would decrease the private cost of car travel, and C would reduce private costs of car production. Both would lead to a greater market output.

Question four

Figure 5.8 shows the private costs and benefits and social costs and benefits of production of a particular good.

Assuming that there is no government intervention, what measure shows the difference between the free market level of output and socially optimum level?

A. A to B

B. A to C

C. B to C

D. B to D

E. C to D

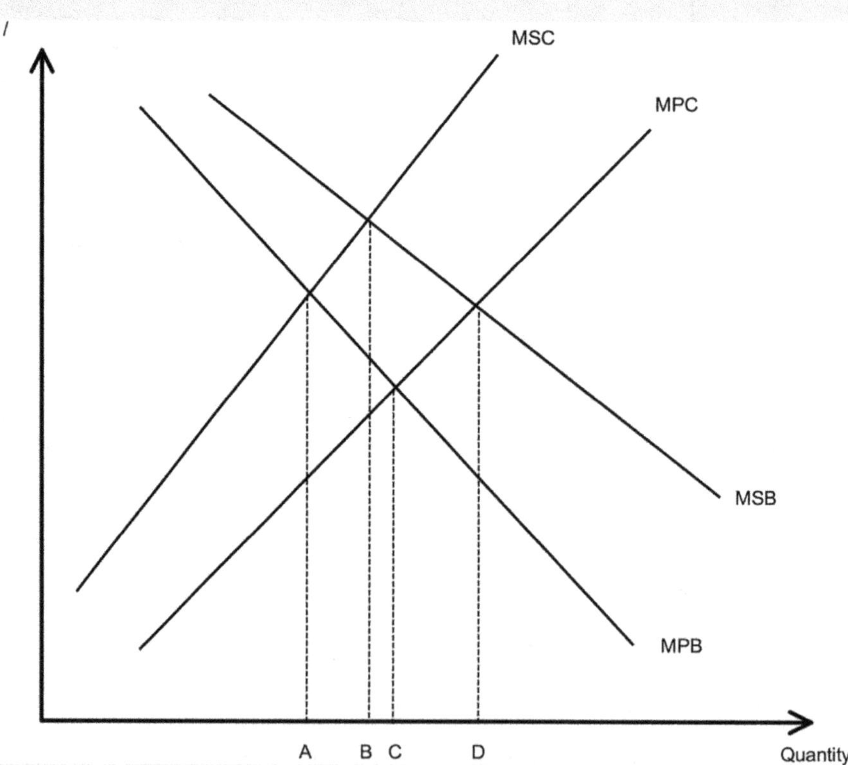

Figure 5.8 Externalities diagram

C is the correct answer, as this is the difference between equilibrium output of MPB = MPC and equilibrium output of MSB = MSC.

This question could also be asked without the multiple-choice options given to students, depending on their mathematical reasoning skills.

Key takeaways

- Use multiple examples that contain different features when teaching students about externalities. If all examples cause individual's health problems and put pressure on a nation's health services, then students will have a narrow view of externalities.
- Teach students the graph for private costs and benefits before adding social costs/benefits curves in a separate teaching sequence. This is likely to result in a stronger conceptual understanding of each concept and their corresponding curves.
- Teach net welfare loss by adding units at the margin above the socially optimum level of production. This will help students understand *why* the triangle represents a net welfare loss, rather than trying to remember what the diagram 'looks like'.

Note

1 A note on the graph: strictly speaking this should be labelled as 'Price/costs/benefits'. This can sometimes cause confusion, as students will ask why the axes can have each label. I have taught classes where I have gone ahead with this label and provided students with a brief explanation as to why, and I have taught classes where I have just labelled the axis as 'Costs/benefits'. I think either can work at A-level; you will need to make the decision based on your understanding of your class.

The law of diminishing marginal returns and short-run cost curves

What's the big idea?

The effective management of the factors of production helps firms to maximise their profitability. Analysis of the law of diminishing marginal returns should help to determine the optimal balance of factor inputs and identify the most efficient output for a given production process.

The big idea here is that adding an increasing amount of labour to a fixed amount of capital will eventually lead to total output falling. This is because, in simple terms, there is not enough capital to spread out amongst the increasing levels of labour. An analysis of the law of diminishing marginal returns will guide firms in deciding the most efficient amount of labour to employ. This analysis can be furthered by considering the impact on the average costs of production in the short-run.

The law of diminishing marginal returns and short-run cost curves represent a fundamental topic in microeconomics and one that links to several other areas in A-level specifications. An understanding of this content underpins the shape of the long-run average cost curve, and this understanding is used when analysing output decisions of firms in different market structures.

Why do students find this topic difficult?

At a surface level, this is a topic that students will be familiar with: the idea is somewhat similar to the idea of *too many cooks spoiling the broth*. However, students need to add sophisticated technical detail to this surface-level understanding:

- The definition of the law of diminishing marginal returns requires students to understand that total output will reduce as increasing amounts of a variable factor are added to a fixed factor. This definition requires students to join together some technical concepts (total output, variable factors and fixed factors) and understand the impact of changing and constant variables. This is cognitively demanding because there is a significant element interactivity!

DOI: 10.4324/9781003724179-6

- Students then need to recognise the link between the law of diminishing marginal returns and average cost to be able to construct the short-run cost curve. This involves multiple complex concepts (the law of diminishing marginal returns, average costs, graph drawing, etc.). Again, element interactivity is high.

If we consider the various pieces of technical information that students need to understand, it's easy to see how cognitive overload can occur. It is useful to think of some of the questions that students may be thinking when trying to understand this topic:

1. Why are we saying that capital is a 'fixed factor'?
2. Why are we saying that labour is a 'variable factor'?
3. Why is total output increasing as more labour is added?
4. Why does the rate of increase in total output reduce at a certain point?
5. How is total output linked to average cost?
6. What does average cost actually mean?
7. Why is the law of diminishing marginal returns linked to average costs?

I am sure you can think of more questions, but clearly, we can see that may be a lot going on here in the student's mind! In particular, that last question is one that students tend to find really difficult. This a topic that necessitates careful thinking and the effective use of examples.

On top of this, the relationship between marginal cost and short-run average cost can cause confusion. Many students generally find thinking at the margin difficult at first, and combining this with trying to understand the law of diminishing marginal returns can lead to cognitive overload.

Explaining this concept

Mistakes to avoid

This is often a topic where teachers try to get creative by getting students involved in a demonstration. Typically, a teacher may give a student some paper, scissors and some pens and ask them to produce a particular product. The teacher will then ask more and more students to join the demonstration and model what happens to output as increasing amounts of labour are added to the fixed amount of capital.

I have seen this approach work well, and I understand some teacher's motivation to 'get students involved' in a topic that can become quite technical. However, I advise caution. I think with explicit signalling, this demonstration can be effective at helping students answer questions 1–4 listed earlier. It takes a little more careful planning to make sure that questions 5–7 can be answered clearly following the demonstration. For example, you may need to assign each unit of labour a wage and live model the calculations on the board as students are doing the demonstration. However, the meaning here can sometimes be lost as students try to split their attention between the demonstration and the numbers displayed on the board.

I am also cautious about these approaches because it is difficult to control what students will remember about the demonstration. In *Why don't students like school?*, Daniel Willingham suggests that 'memory is the residue of thought'.[1] Essentially, we remember best the things that we are thinking carefully about. During the diminishing marginal returns demonstration outlined earlier, some students are likely to be thinking about how rubbish their peer is at cutting out the design instead of fixed factors and variable factors of production. How do we make sure this doesn't become remembered as 'the lesson where we got to make paper cranes and Alex was rubbish at cutting out the design'?

I am not saying you shouldn't give this a go! I've used it in the past, and I know that some of my students have enjoyed the change in delivery style. However, I am going to present a different way of teaching the topic that I think ensures students are able to answer the questions earlier with a greater degree of clarity.

Finally, I recommend separating the teaching short-run average cost and marginal cost. Given the interrelated nature of these concepts, I had previously always taught them and their curves at the same time. However, the cognitive overload that this causes often leads to a superficial understanding of both concepts. Students resort to learning the shapes of each curve and 'what they look like', rather than gaining a more robust conceptual understanding.

Explaining this concept

I now always use the example of a pizza restaurant to explain this topic. I find the process of making a pizza has a few distinct stages of production that means it lends itself well to the division of labour required to make this topic accessible students. It might go something like this:

> *Imagine that you are the manager of a pizza restaurant. You have one kitchen that has a fixed amount of equipment: you have one counter for making the base, one counter for assembling the ingredients, one pizza oven and a hot counter where finished pizzas are placed to be served to customers. All of this equipment, which we are going to call your 'capital', cost you $100.*
>
> *Now, as the manager, you are trying to decide how much labour you should employ. You are trying to find the 'optimal' amount of labour. 'Optimal' means the best or most favourable situation.*[2]

It will be difficult to follow if we just present this as a vocal narrative, so we need something visual to help them. At this stage, use the visualiser or board to draw the restaurant's kitchen.

The explanation carries on in Box 6.1. As you go through the explanation, annotate your visual on the board with key information.

BOX 6.1 EXPLANATION OF THE LAW OF DIMINISHING MARGINAL RETURNS

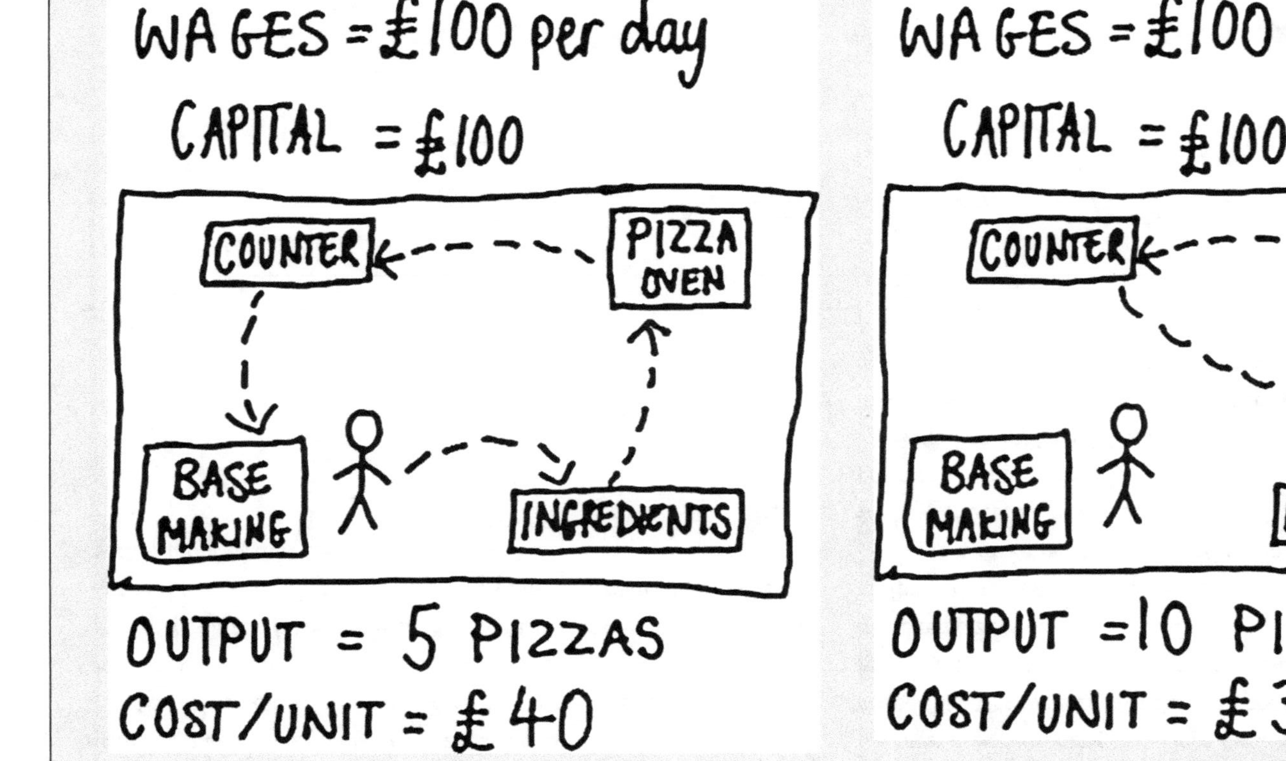

Figure 6.1 Law of diminishing marginal returns step one

Your restaurant pays workers $100 a day. This means that if you employ one worker, your total cost will be the cost of wages and your capital. $100 + $100 = $200 total cost.

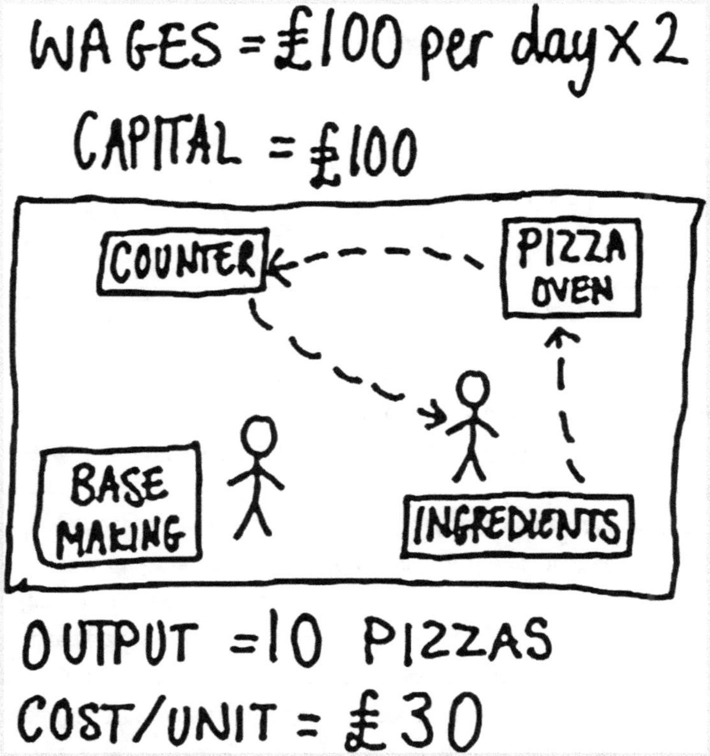

Figure 6.2 Law of diminishing marginal returns step two

What if we get Alisha some help now and employ a second worker – let's say its Tom. We are going to also pay Tom $100 per shift. What will our total cost be now . . . Serita?

Now, let's say you employ Alisha as your worker. Poor Alisha has to do everything – she has to make the base, then run over to put the ingredients on top of the base, then put the pizza in the oven and lastly leave it on the hot counter to be served. Poor Alisha is pretty stressed with this and can only make five pizzas each shift this way.

We can use this information to work out your cost per pizza. Remember we said our total cost was $200, and we have managed to make five pizzas. If we divide our total cost by our number of pizzas, we get $40 per pizza. Quite expensive! It's going to be difficult to make any sort of profit at that cost.

Yes, $300, great – our capital is $100 and we have two workers that we are paying $100 each.

Now, Tom and Alisha can be a little bit more efficient in their production. Maybe Alisha spends all of her time making the base because this is the most time consuming part. Once the base is done, Tom puts on the ingredients, puts the pizzas in the oven and then onto the hot counter. As a result, Alisha and Tom can make more pizzas each shift – maybe they can make ten pizzas now.

Remind we how we calculate our cost per pizza . . . Jo?

Great, we take our total cost and divide it by the number of pizzas we have made. So let's do $300 divided by 10. It is now costing us $30 per pizza being made.

What has happened to our cost per pizza . . . Ade?

Exactly – the cost per pizza has gone down. Our ***total*** *cost has gone up to $300 because we have to pay more labour, but our* ***cost per pizza*** *has gone down – interesting!*

Notice the elements in bold. These are key parts to highlight to students: total cost is increasing because we are employing more labour, but our average cost is decreasing. These will help clarify answers to some of the questions I listed at the beginning of this chapter.

Carry on going adding a third and fourth unit of labour that continue to reduce the cost per pizza. For example, the third unit of labour can be in charge of the oven and putting pizzas on the counter. The further unit of labour can split the base making, as we have previously said that this is the most time-consuming aspect of the process.

It is useful to be constructing a table on the board at the same time. This may look like Table 6.1.

All the time you want to be highlighting to students that as you add more units of labour, the total costs of the restaurant go up because more wages have to be paid, but the cost per pizza continuously reduces, as each unit of labour is adding efficiencies to the production process.

Notice we are trying to keep the numbers as 'clean' as possible. This isn't always possible, but wherever you can, you want to avoid lots of decimal places to round or recurring figures; these take students' working memory away from the key messages we want to be giving.

Now we get to our fifth and sixth unit of labour. This explanation continues in Box 6.2. Now we get to our fifth and sixth unit of labour. This explanation continues in Box 6.2 The final cost table that you will have completed by the end of this explanation is in Table 6.2.

Table 6.1 Average costs decreasing

Labour	Total cost	Number of pizzas	Cost per pizza
1	£200	5	£40.00
2	£300	10	£30.00
3	£400	20	£20.00
4	£500	35	£14.29

Table 6.2 Average costs decreasing and then increasing

Labour	Total cost	Number of pizzas	Cost per pizza
1	£200	5	£40.00
2	£300	10	£30.00
3	£400	20	£20.00
4	£500	35	£14.29
5	£600	60	£10.00
6	£700	62	£11.29

BOX 6.2 EXPLANATION PART TWO

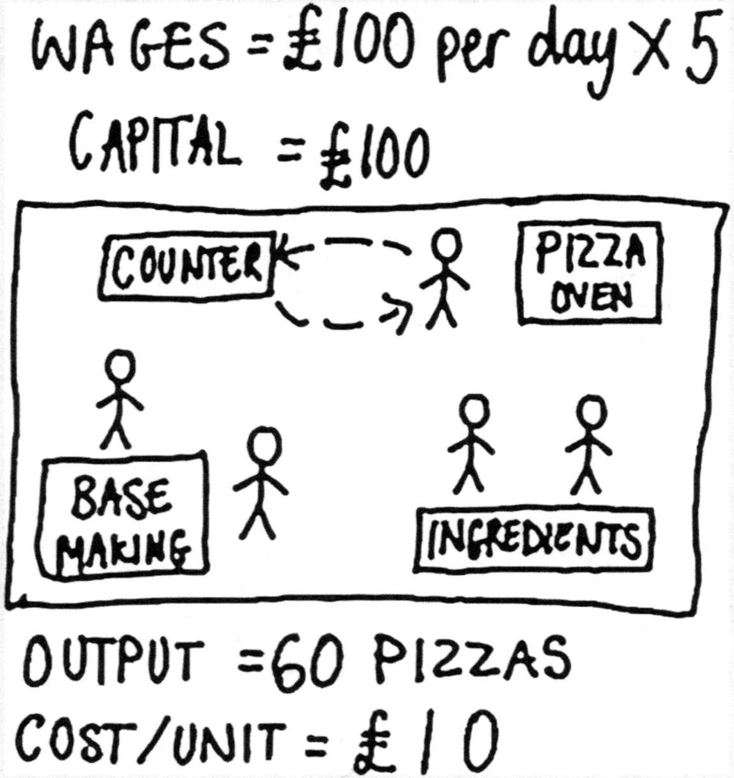

Figure 6.3 Law of diminishing marginal returns step five

Okay, now we are going to employ Lucy. What is our total cost going to be now please . . . Lizzie?

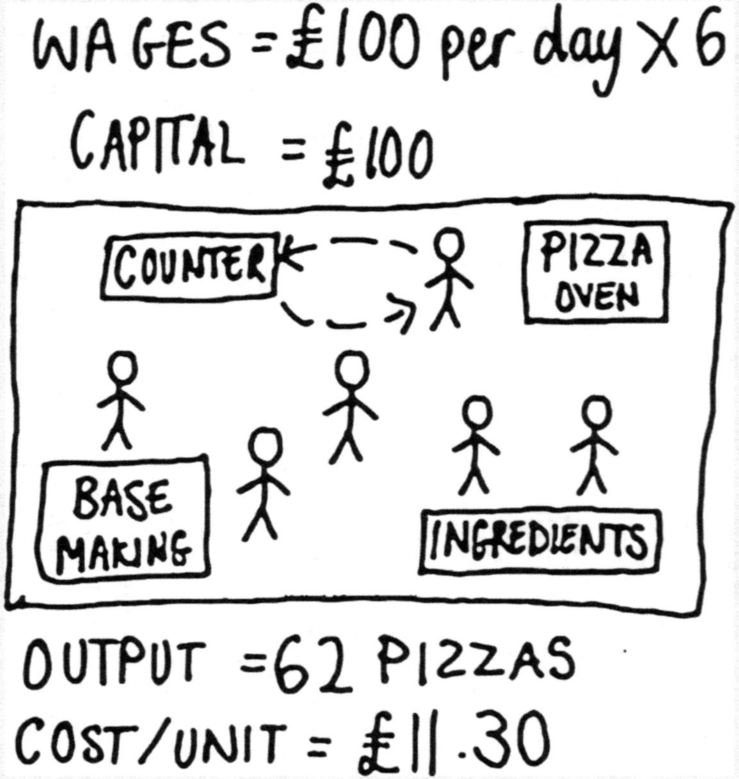

Figure 6.4 Law of diminishing marginal returns step six

Now we have employed Billy. But we have a bit of a problem . . . there isn't really any work for Billy to do, sorry Billy! We only

Perfect – £600 now.

Lucy is going to work with Tom on the ingredients counter. This is going to make us even more efficient – remember those pizza bases that were piling up on Tom's counter? Well now Lucy is going to help Tom get those pizzas ready for the oven super quickly.

As a result, our total production is going to go up to 60 pizzas – this is 25 more than our previous production!

That is going to reduce our cost per pizza to $10. Every time we add more labour into our kitchen we can see that our cost per pizza is falling. Can you remind me why we said that was the case please . . . Adam?

Excellent explanation – each unit of labour that we add is making our production process more efficient and helping us to make more and more pizzas, so even though our total costs are going up our cost per pizza is going down.

Now, let's add a sixth worker. Some of you might have already guessed we are going to have a bit of a problem here. have a fixed amount of equipment – we've still got the same amount of counters and ovens and they are all being fully used. As a result, Billy is just standing around twiddling his thumbs and getting in people's way.

Maybe Billy can be a little bit helpful. He could help Alisha and Tami clean their base making counter for example, but he's not really adding much value. As a result, our total production ***only*** *goes up to 62 pizzas.*

Let's see what happens to our cost per pizza now. When we divide £700 by 62 we can see that we get £11.30. What was our average cost last time, Ella?

Exactly – it was only £10 before. We can see that our cost per pizza has actually gone up after we've employed Billy.

Finish the scenario by asking what may happen if we had a seventh unit of labour. At this point, the kitchen is going to become so busy and crowded that perhaps production of pizza actually *goes down* to 58 units. More labour is simply getting in the way!

Pause here and check students' understanding of this table through some MWB and think-pair-share questions. You want to make sure that students are completely comfortable with the concept before we start introducing some technical terms and extrapolating definitions from what we have taught. Consider asking the following questions:

1. What happens to total cost as we continuously add more units of labour?
2. What happens to the total number of pizzas produced as we add our first five workers? (We want students to recognise that production is going up at an increasing rate.)
3. At what point does total production start to decrease? Why does this happen?
4. What happens to our cost per pizza as we add our first five workers?
5. What happens to our cost per pizza when we add the sixth worker?
6. Why did cost per pizza increase when we added our sixth unit of labour?

Now you can start to add some technical terms and definitions. For example, you may label your 'cost per pizza' column as your average cost and reiterate that these two terms mean the same thing. You can also explain that 'marginal product' is the units that each additional worker adds.

You can then draw out the idea of diminishing marginal returns by emphasising what is happening to the number of pizzas as we add more and more units of labour. As we add increasing numbers of a variable factor (labour) to a fixed factor (capital), total production, at first, increases, then increases at a decreasing rate and then starts to decrease. Finally, show that diminishing marginal returns lead to average cost initially decreasing and then starting to increase again.

Before moving on to the short-run average cost curve, I would consolidate understanding through the use of a case study resource, like the one shown in Box 6.3.

The first three questions in this case study should be routine, and you may find that students go through them quickly. You may think: 'Why not skip those questions and jump straight to the table? It requires pretty much the same processing'. This may seem logical, but I think it is a mistake to jump straight to the table for the following reasons:

- Tables can be intimidating for some students: even if they require a simple repetition of the same process, suddenly, there are ten gaps to fill in with answers. The first few questions break this down into one question at a time.
- When students go to the table, we want their cognitive processing to be focused on *what* the table is showing them, rather than *how* to calculate each answer. Giving the students some quickfire questions beforehand should mean that they are more able to do this.

BOX 6.3 CASE STUDY

Case study

Amber opened a café in her local town two years ago. Amber's café currently has a large serving counter, two coffee machines and two ovens for preparing food for customers. This equipment cost Amber £1,500.

Over the past two years, Amber has been experimenting with how many employees she needs to have working during the café's most busy shifts on a Saturday. Amber has collected some data based on differing numbers of staff employed. The data can be seen in Table 6.3.

Table 6.3 Amber's café meals sold

Labour	Meals sold
1	60
2	120
3	240
4	290
5	300
6	305

Amber pays her staff £80 for a full-day shift on a Saturday.

Amber noticed that when she had six members of staff working, the café's serving area often became quite chaotic. The employees working on the tills were serving customers too quickly for the employees who were making coffee and food. The employees who were making food and coffee also seemed to be getting in each other's way.

Amber would like to use the data she has collected to analyse her average costs and make a decision about how many employees to have work a Saturday shift.

Questions

1. What is Amber's cost of capital?
2. How much will Amber need to pay in wages if she employs the following:
   a. One member of staff
   b. Three members of staff
3. What will Amber's total cost be if she employs the following:
   a. One member of staff
   b. Four members of staff

4. What is Amber's marginal product of employing the following:
   a. The second member of staff on a Saturday
   b. The third member of staff on a Saturday
   c. The sixth member of staff on a Saturday
5. Based on the information contained within the case study, complete Table 6.4. The first row has been completed for you.

Table 6.4 Calculation question

Labour	Total cost	Meals sold	Cost per meal
1	£1,580	60	£26.33
2	£ -	120	£ -
3	£ -	240	£ -
4	£ -	290	£ -
5	£ -	300	£ -
6	£ -	305	£ -

6. Based on the information in the table:
   a. How many staff should Amber employ on a Saturday?
   b. Explain your reasoning for the previous question.
7. What do you think may happen to meals sold if Amber employs a seventh unit of labour?

Questions to deepen your understanding

1. How will the information provided in this table help Amber make decisions about what prices to charge consumers?
2. How could Amber increase the marginal product of the fifth and sixth members of staff? What may she need to consider doing?

Short-run average cost

Once you have completed this task, you can then move on to deriving the short-term average cost curve from the data provided. You may wish to continue the example of Amber's café or provide a new example to give students a different context. Whichever way you choose to use, hopefully, students have a sound understanding of the content they are looking at, and this becomes a fairly routine task of plotting a graph.

When introducing the short-term average cost curve to students, I recommend reminding them of what average cost means: it is the cost per pizza, or meal, or unit. I usually get a few different students to repeat this to me before we move on. With this done, I will take the data points from the example I am using and plot the short-run average cost curve. I do not plot this perfectly to scale, but I do use the numbers to provide a rough scale on the graph. As discussed in the previous chapter, we don't want students to expend working memory on plotting things perfectly to scale. Instead, we want their focus on conceptual understanding.

Once its drawn, you can annotate the diagram with key points. For example:

Point 1: *We can see that as we move from producing 60 meals to 120 meals, our average cost falls from approximately £26 to £18. This occurred when we employed our second unit of labour and became more efficient because the café could divide labour more efficiently.*

Point 2: *We can see that when we sell 290 meals the café is at the lowest point on the average cost curve. This is when we were most efficient: our employees could be divided into separate tasks but we didn't have so much labour that it was all getting in each other's way.*

Point 3: *We can now see that our average costs are starting to increase. Clearly we have got too many employees in our café and we are becoming inefficient.*

This might look something like the following:

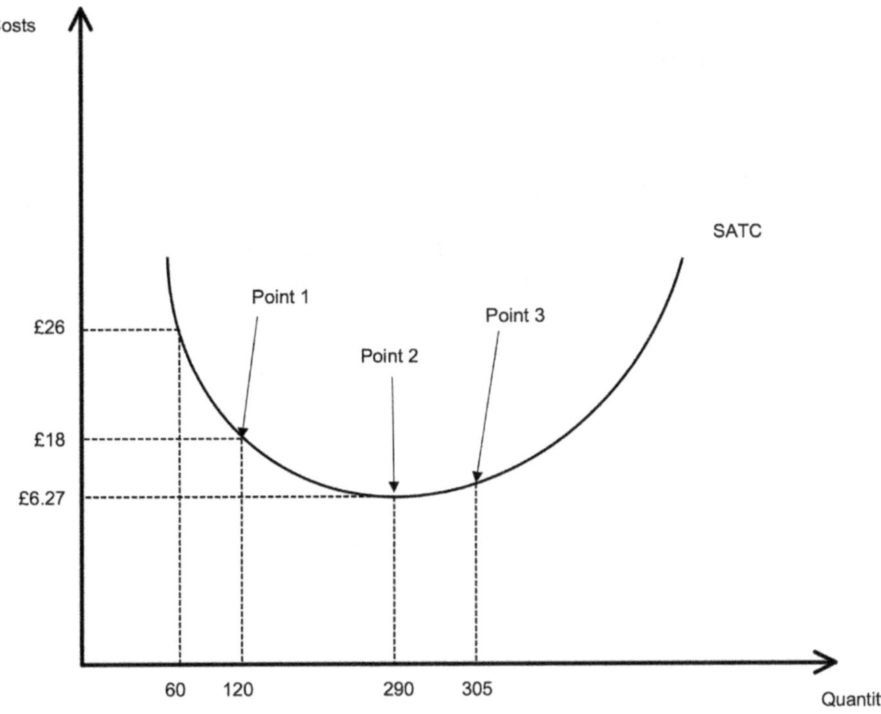

Figure 6.5 Short-run average cost curve overview

The graph in Figure 6.5 may look busy. However, if you label each point incrementally (rather than displaying it to students already fully labelled), then the demands on working memory should not be overbearing. This demonstrates the importance of live drawing as you go through your explanation with students.

Explaining marginal cost

As has been discussed at the beginning of this chapter, I always previously taught marginal cost at the same time as teaching short-run average cost. Table 6.2 would have had an additional column where I would have shown students the calculation for marginal cost. Then when we constructed the short-run average cost curve, we would have also plotted on the marginal cost curve. In hindsight, this led to significant cognitive overload.

Instead, I now spend a lot of time consolidating students' understanding of the short-run average cost curve before introducing the marginal cost curve. As much as possible, I aim to be introducing marginal cost at a point where students no longer have any questions about the short-run average cost curve.

Use the 'checking students' understanding' questions later to help you assess whether students are at this point.

Once you've done this, you can either revisit Amber's café and use this to demonstrate the calculation of marginal cost, or you can introduce students to a new case study. This decision may depend on the time elapsed since initially looking at the Amber's café case study. If it is part of the same 'double period', then Amber's café is fine, but if there has been a break in between, then I would suggest moving to a new case study.

Checking students' understanding

The questions in Box 6.4 can be used during various points of the teaching sequence to check students' understanding of the law of diminishing marginal returns and short-run average costs.

BOX 6.4 CHECKING FOR UNDERSTANDING

Question one

Table 6.5 shows information regarding a car mechanic shop.

Table 6.5 Car mechanic production costs

Cost of capital	Mechanic wage	Number of mechanics	Total cost	Cars fixed	Average cost
2,000	150	1	£2,150	18	£119.44
2,000	150	2	£2,300	40	£57.50
2,000	150	3	£2,450	80	£30.63
2,000	150	4	£2,600	98	£26.53
2,000	150	5	£2,750	104	£26.44
2,000	150	6	£2,900	102	£28.43

Answer the following questions:

1. What is the marginal product of the fourth employee?
2. Which employee has a negative marginal product?
3. At which point do diminishing marginal returns set in?
4. How many employees should the car mechanics employ?
5. Plot the short-run average cost curve for the car mechanics.

Question two

Which of the following statements is correct regarding average costs? There may be more than one correct answer.

A. Average cost is the price paid per unit by the customer.

B. Average cost is the cost per unit for the firm.

C. Average cost is calculated by the following formula: $\frac{\text{Total quantity}}{\text{Total cost}}$.

D. Average cost is calculated by the following formula: $\frac{\text{Total cost}}{\text{Total quantity}}$.

E. A lower average cost may mean that firms will make a larger profit per unit if price is kept the same

Answers B, D and E are correct.

Students will often use the terms 'price' and 'cost' interchangeably and need frequent reminders that these have specific meanings in economics. Answer A is an opportunity to provide this reminder to students.

Answer E is important to ensure that students see the big picture of this topic: if firms are maximising their efficiency, then they are able to maximise their profit per unit.

Question three

Figure 6.6 shows the short-run average cost curve for a firm.

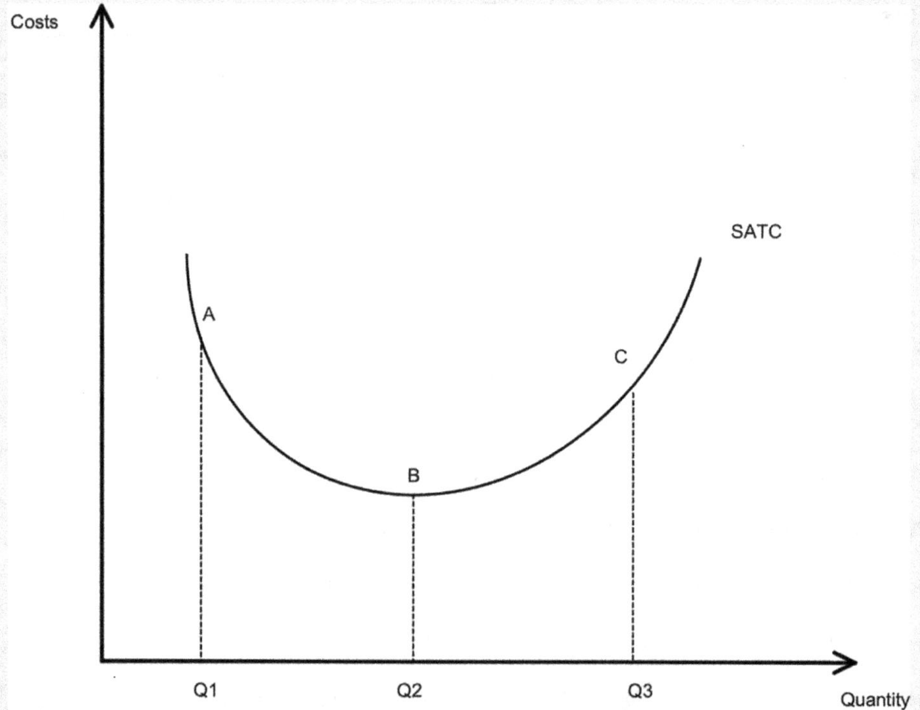

Figure 6.6 Short-run average cost curve multiple-choice question

Which of the following statements regarding the diagram can we say are definitely correct? There may be more than one correct answer.

A. Production at Q3 means the firm will make more profit as they are selling a greater quantity of products.

B. Production at Q2 is less optimal then Q1.

C. The firm's cost of capital is lowest at Q2.

D. The firm's average total cost is lowest at Q2.

D is the only correct answer. Students would require more information to know if A is correct. B is incorrect. C is incorrect as capital remains fixed when considering short-run average costs.

Key takeaways

- Explain one example of the law of diminishing marginal returns and average costs to students slowly and deliberately. Plan carefully the elements that you wish to highlight, and make sure you support this by live drawing the example for students.
- Pause your explanation at appropriate points to check students are with you. I would recommend doing this first before your example shows the increase in marginal product slowing down. This means that the initial check for understanding can focus on students' comprehension of fixed factors and variable factors.
- Separate the teaching of marginal cost from your explanation of short-run average costs.

Notes

1 Willingham, D. T. (2010). Why don't students like school? A cognitive scientist answers questions about how the mind works and what it means for your classroom, pg. 54, Jossey-Bass.
2 The text here is using 'optimal' to mean productively efficient because students are unlikely to have encountered this term before.

7 Economies of scale and long-run average costs

What's the big idea?

In the long-run, all factors of production are variable. This means that firms are no longer constrained by fixed capital. In the long-run, our pizza restaurant from the previous chapter could expand by extending the size of their kitchen. As such, they would no longer be constrained by their one pizza oven and one base-making counter. This has implications for a firm's most efficient level of output.

This becomes an important aspect of strategic planning. If Firm X wants to produce 10,000 units, how many factories should they operate? The minimum efficient scale represents the point where the firm have fully exploited economies of scale. This supports students' understanding of market structures. For example, a natural monopoly is going to reach their minimum efficient scale much later than a firm in perfect competition.

Why do students find this topic difficult?

The idea of returns to scale can seem quite obscure, particularly for students who have not stepped foot in a production facility or experienced 'real-world business'. It can be difficult for students to grasp the idea that unit costs reduce if a firm is able to maximise the use of their transport or because a firm orders more from their supplier. I think this is one of the main reasons that students find this topic difficult, and it is one that again requires the use of explicit examples.

I also think students can become confused because the long-run average total cost curve is the same shape as the short-run curve. As such, students can fail to see the distinction between the two. I have certainly been guilty in the past of not making these distinctions clear enough to students.

Finally, a strong understanding of economies of scale requires a strong understanding of average cost. Many students struggle to clearly understand that average cost represents the cost per unit produced, which then inhibits them fully understanding economies of scale. A failure to understand that average costs can decrease even as total cost increases can reveal that students don't truly understand what these terms represent. This is one of the reasons I focus on getting students to repeat the definition in the previous chapter.

DOI: 10.4324/9781003724179-7

Explaining this concept

Mistakes to avoid

I had always started teaching economies of scale by explaining purchasing economies. For example, I may start by comparing the price of a single can of Coke in the supermarket compared to a multi-pack. I would draw the comparison shown in Figure 7.1.

This is a concrete example of a unit price falling as quantity increases. It is also an example that students have direct experience of and so can comprehend easily. A perfect example to introduce economics of scale, I thought!

However, the example has two limitations:

1. It doesn't explain *why* it is cheaper to buy the multi-pack. Purchasing economies occur because of an interdependence of economies of scale. A supplier is able to provide a lower unit cost for bulk orders *because* the bulk order enables them to achieve other economies of scale. The example leaves open the possibility that a student asks: 'But why does selling the multi-pack enable the supermarket to charge a lower price?'
2. A slightly lesser limitation is that the example is tied to a consumer purchasing a product, as opposed to a firm purchasing from a supplier. While the analogy can be transferred to a firm easily enough, I think we can start the sequence with a better example that doesn't require this transfer.

Figure 7.1 Price of a single can against a multi-pack

I also previously would explain a couple of economies of scale to students and then set them a comprehension task that explained the other types. I had assumed that students would 'get the gist' from the first two examples and be able to apply this to the others independently. This completely ignores the fact that each type of economy of scale is distinct and occurs for different reasons. As a result, my students often had a fairly secure understanding of the two that I had explained and a fairly weak understanding of the rest. They'd often forget them and have to resort to some mnemonic to remember each different types (*Really Fun Mums Try Making Pies* was the one I remember). The mnemonic was great in helping them remember the names of each economy, but they would struggle to explain how each occurred.

Explaining this concept

Start this topic by recapping students' understanding of average cost. Students should be familiar with this, as it is likely that they will have only just finished covering short-run costs in the scheme of work. However, it is worth using the beginning of the lesson to check their understanding here. It is also worth checking students' understanding of total cost and their ability to differentiate between average total cost and total cost. Start with a simple question like the following:

> *A firm produces 20,000 units of a good. At this output, the firm has fixed costs of $60,000 and total variable costs of $80,000.*
>
> 1. *What are the firm's total costs?*
> 2. *What are the firm's average costs?*
> 3. *If the firm sells their product for $10,*
>   a. *What will their profit per unit be?*
>   b. *What will their total profit be?*

At this stage of the course, this question shouldn't be too difficult but should confirm for you that students can distinguish between averages and totals. Depending on the strength of your class, you may wish to run through a series of questions like this. Once you are confident that students understand, you can begin teaching economies of scale.

Explaining economies of scale

As discussed earlier, I now try to avoid starting this sequence with purchasing economies. Instead, start with technical economies of scale at a manufacturing business. I find this the easiest for students to understand in terms of average costs.

Okay, I want you to imagine a business that produces parts for bikes. Let's say they produce the brake pads that are used on the bike. The business is run by a lady called Tanya. It is quite small at the moment – it has a fairly small factory and Tanya employs four full-time members of staff.

Tanya's business produce brake pads for two small national bike manufacturers. In total, Tanya sells around 10,000 brake pads per year. Tanya's business uses a piece of machinery that she purchased at the beginning of the year for £5,000. It is a fairly basic piece of machinery and requires a significant amount of manual operation to cut each brake pad.

We can think about the cost per unit in terms of the amount of money Tanya spent on this machinery and the amount of units it is producing [Figure 7.2]:

We can work the average cost for Tanya here: she sells 10,000 brake pads a year and the machinery cost her £5,000 – the cost per unit here is therefore £0.50. We just need to be a little bit careful here – this isn't Tanya's total cost per unit, it is just the cost per unit of the machinery.

Now, let's fast forward to next year. Tanya has managed to secure a contract with a larger bike seller. As a result, Tanya's output is going to increase to 50,000 units – her business is growing!

As a result, Tanya needs a more advanced piece of machinery. She decides to invest in a laser cutter which is going to help her produce brake pads more efficiently. The machinery is more expensive than her old piece of machinery – it is £20,000. We can work out Tanya's average cost now [Figure 7.3]:

We can see that the unit cost of the machinery has actually decreased. The cost per unit is now £0.40, which is £0.10 lower than her previous piece of machinery. ***As Tanya's output has grown, her cost per unit has actually decreased.***

We need to notice something important here: ***Tanya's total cost will have increased as she has purchased a more expensive piece of machinery. However, the increase efficiency of this better piece of machinery has enabled her to reduce her cost per unit.***

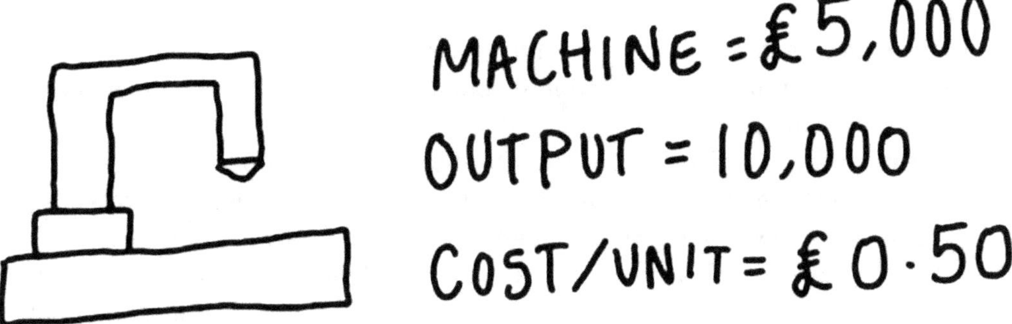

Figure 7.2 Initial machinery for Tanya's business

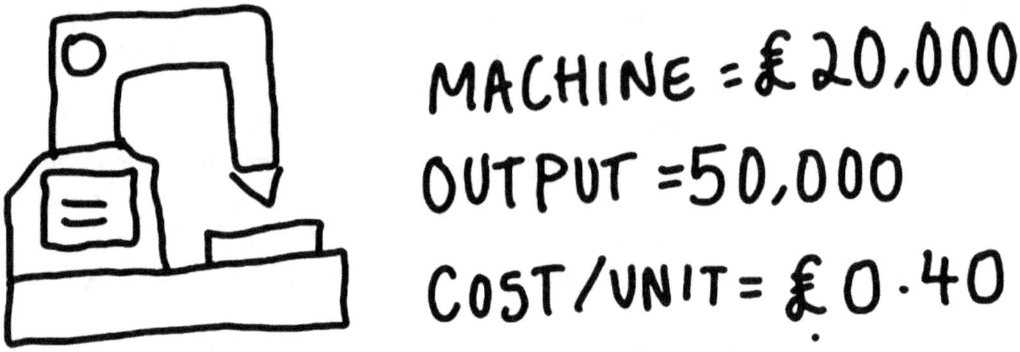

MACHINE = £20,000
OUTPUT = 50,000
COST/UNIT = £0.40

Figure 7.3 Laser cutter machinery

As with previous examples that have been shown, keep the numbers nice and clean here to avoid any unnecessary confusion over calculations. The bold elements of explanation are really important. These are essentially the definition of economies of scale, but the explanation plants that idea in students' minds without necessarily labelling it as a technical definition at this point.

Then move on to managerial economies of scale:

At the moment we have said that Tanya employs four members of staff to work in the factory. Tanya has to run all the functions of the business herself: she does the stock ordering, she does the meetings with potential buyers and she does the accounting.

This can sometimes be quite inefficient. Tanya is not a specialist in any of these areas and so they often take her a long time. Last month she made a mistake when making a stock order and it increased her costs significantly.

Now, fast forward a year and Tanya has grown significantly. She has secured an additional two large buyers of her brake pads and is now forecasting an output of 80,000 units this year. As part of her expansion, Tanya has been able to move to a new factory and has been able to hire a finance manager who is able to handle her accounts and also runs the stock ordering system. This has allowed Tanya to focus on marketing and speaking with customers.

Hiring this extra manager may have increased Tanya's total costs, but it has enabled her to become much more efficient. As a result, the cost per unit that she actually produces has decreased.

We can see again that as Tanya's output grows, her cost per unit decreases.

We can refer to this as 'economies of scale'. ***Economies of scale occur when average costs decrease as the output a firm produces increases.***

Our first example there was what we call a 'technical economy of scale': as a firm's output grows it can spread the cost of capital over a greater number of units. Our second example was what we call a 'managerial economy of scale': a larger firm is able to hire specialist managers, which in turn makes the company more efficient and therefore reduces average total cost.

There are two useful things to emphasise about this example. Firstly, Tanya has been able to move to a new factory: she does not have a fixed amount of capital available to her. It is really important to stress this to students, as this is a key differentiating factor between short-run and long-run average costs.

Secondly, notice that that we haven't made Tanya's business grow too large; she hasn't suddenly turned into a global supplier of brake pads. This is to ensure we don't run into issues later down the line when thinking about diseconomies of scale, or when we discuss the minimum efficient scale in different market structures. Instead, we are tracking the business's journey as its output gradually grows.

At this point, to avoid overloading students with each different type of economy of scale, I would pause and do a quick check for understanding. This might include asking students to explain the difference between transport and managerial economies, or to answer a series of mini-whiteboard questions like the one in Box 7.1.

BOX 7.1 MWB CHECK FOR UNDERSTANDING

MWB check for understanding

1. A clothing store has expanded from running two local stores to eight stores within a region. As a result, the store can now afford to hire a specialist finance manager. This is not a position that the firm has previously had. Up until this point, the owner has run the finance department themselves, but they are not an expert in this area. The owner of the clothing store expects that the finance manager will help the business to more efficiently manage their financial resources.

   Which of the following statements is correct? There may be more than one correct answer.

   A. The firm's total costs will increase.

   B. The firm's total costs will decrease.

   C. The firm's average total cost should increase.

   D. The firm's average total cost should decrease.

   E. The firm is likely to experience transport economies of scale.

Answers A and D are correct. This is a good question for checking that students can effectively differentiate between total costs and average costs and highlights why it will have been useful to recap both average and total costs at the beginning of the lesson.

I purposely leave out the 'correct' economy of scale from this question. Given that the word 'manager' is in both the question and the type of economy, students are likely to simply match these two words if they see it as an option in the answers. This doesn't necessarily demonstrate that students *understand* managerial economies. To try to do so, I would then cold-call the following questions:

1. Which type of economy of scale is being experienced here?
2. Why is the firm's average total cost likely to decrease?

Once you are confident that students have a good grasp of what we mean by economies of scale and the two types that we have introduced, you can then move on to examples of other economies. Typically, I follow this with transport economies and then purchasing economies. Purchasing economies can be fully understood at this point because students have an understanding of other economies that suppliers may experience when they receive a bulk order.

The overall sequence may look something like this:

1. Example of technical economies
2. Example of managerial economies
3. Introduction to definition of economies of scale
4. Check for understanding on initial part of sequence
5. Example of transport economies
6. Example of purchasing economies
7. Examples of marketing economies
8. Examples of risk-bearing economies
9. Check for understanding on whole sequence

Finish this section off by considering how this may look on an average cost curve. This is shown in Figure 7.4.

You may not wish to add every single economy of scale on the diagram; it may become a little busy. Add enough to ensure that the narrative is clear: as a firm increases its output, its average costs are falling for the various reasons that you have explained. It's really important to stress to students that this is possible because capital is not fixed. Tanya has been able to move to a new café, and she has been able to purchase better equipment, which has led to technical economies of scale. This is the key distinction between short-run and long-run average costs.

Diseconomies of scale

Students often find this a little easier to understand, perhaps because they will have first-hand experience of something becoming a little chaotic or difficult to manage because it has got 'too big'. Again, though, we need to make sure we lead with an example:

> *Okay, so we have seen that as firms grow larger they experience economies of scale. This means that their average costs fall as the firm's output gets bigger. But will this go on forever? Do we think a firm could ever get too large?*

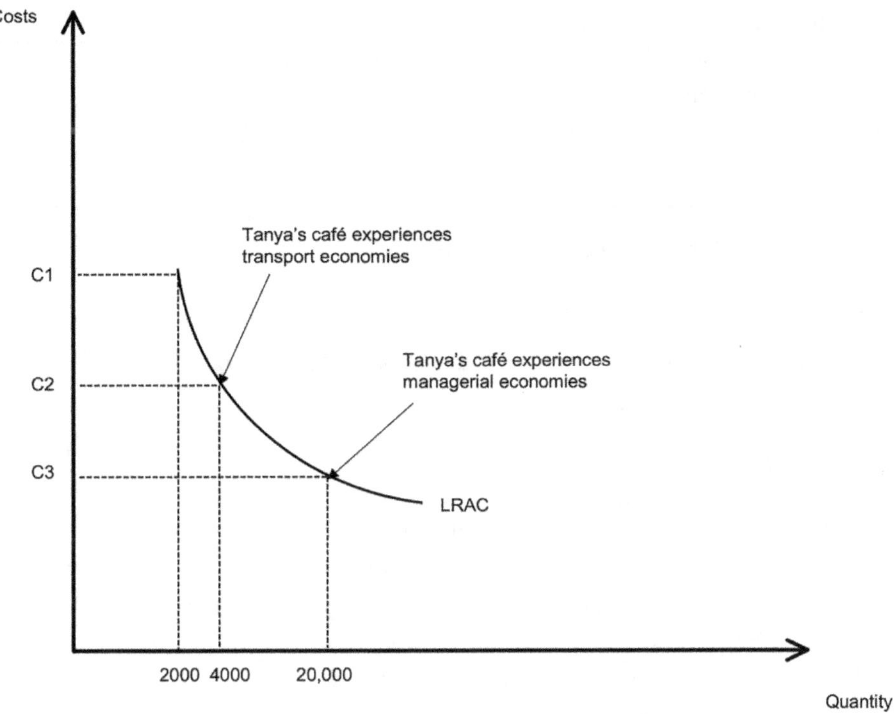

Figure 7.4 Long-run average costs and economies of scale

> *Well, let's imagine Tanya's business expands further and becomes a global supplier of brake pads. Over the space of a few years, it starts supplying bike manufacturers in Europe, the USA and Asia. To reduce costs, Tanya opens a factory in Vietnam but continues to run the rest of her operations from the UK. The size of the company expands from five employees to 3,400 employees. Many of these employees are working in different countries, on different time-zones and speaking different languages. Suddenly the management of the company is finding it difficult to co-ordinate all their different locations – perhaps efficiencies are starting to reduce. Maybe it is difficult to find a convenient time to speak to the heads of manufacturing in Vietnam and the marketing team in the USA because of the time zones and language barriers. Maybe it is difficult to get the same quality of raw materials in different locations around the world. Suddenly we see that the firm has possibly become too large and it is starting to become inefficient. As a result, as they continue to grow larger, the firm's average costs are actually going to start increasing. We refer to this as a diseconomy of scale.*

We may then go onto give another example, perhaps highlighting a declining employee motivation, increased bureaucracy or transport costs becoming so large due to the increased scale.

You can then revisit the long-run average cost curve and add on the diseconomies of scale section. Students will now have a complete long-run average cost curve plotted and should understand the reasons for its shape.

Consolidate students' understanding with the task in Box 7.2.

BOX 7.2 CONSOLIDATION TASK

Consolidation task

You have been given information about three different restaurant businesses, which is detailed next.

Restaurant one

Restaurant one is a local Italian restaurant. It has one location in the local community and is run by Alex, who has run the restaurant with his wife for the past 30 years. Alex is an excellent chef who learned to cook at a cookery school in Italy. However, neither he nor his wife have any formal business knowledge; he has learned much of this while 'on the job', but this has occasionally lead to mistakes.

Many locals love Alex's restaurant, particularly because of the large menu that he offers. The menu contains over 20 different types of pastas and over 10 different types of pizzas. While Alex can order some ingredients, such as tomatoes and pasta, in bulk, he has to order many ingredients in much smaller quantities because they only feature in one or two dishes.

Restaurant two

Restaurant two is a national Italian restaurant called *Zaza's*. *Zaza's* has over 50 locations in the UK. The restaurant offers customers a small range of menu items and orders a small range of raw materials in bulk. The average cost of their raw materials has fallen as they have grown. For example, when they had 20 locations, the average raw material cost for *Zaza's* to produce one meal was £4.10. Now that they have 50 locations, the average raw material cost for *Zaza's* for one meal is £3.35. This has enabled them to charge lower prices, which has helped them to grow their market share across the country.

Zaza's have also planned new restaurant openings carefully to make sure they always have a 'cluster' of two to three restaurants that are within 10 miles of each other. This ensures that they are able to have raw materials delivered by the same courier company, which has also helped to minimise costs.

Zaza's also benefits from the purchase of high-quality equipment. Each restaurant's kitchen is fitted with state-of-the-art ovens and kitchen utensils. Two years ago, the company replaced the pizza ovens in every single restaurant, which has enabled the firm to double the amount of pizzas they make per hour.

Restaurant three

Fratelli's is an Italian restaurant that has 110 locations in the UK. It recently expanded to open its first international locations in Paris, New York and Tokyo. However, the expansion has had complications. The management of *Fratelli's* have found it difficult to hold meetings where employees from every country can attend due to time differences. This has led to some inconsistencies in strategies, which has led to some mistakes in decision-making, particularly in the Tokyo location.

The company has also found it difficult to reduce the average cost of their raw materials. Each country currently only has one restaurant in each location and, therefore, needs a limited amount of raw materials. This has meant that the average cost of raw materials in Paris, New York and Tokyo is significantly higher than the raw material costs in the UK.

Finally, some employees in the UK office have started to become demotivated. They have felt that their manager's focus has been distracted by the international expansion, and it means that they are spending less time focusing on the UK operations. As a result, some employees are finding their work has less purpose than it did before. The company has noticed that the number of days employees in the UK take off sick has increased by 12% over the past year, and the number of employees leaving the company has increased by 7%.

Questions

1. The text suggests that Alex's restaurant is finding it difficult to achieve two types of economy of scale.
   a. Which types are they failing to achieve?
   b. Why is Alex's restaurant failing to achieve each type?
   c. Can you think of a recommendation to provide Alex to help achieve economies of scale in one of these areas?
2. The text suggests that Zaza's has been able to lower their raw material cost per pizza.
   a. Which economy of scale has helped them achieve this?
   b. What was the total raw material cost of Zaza's producing 100 meals when they had 20 restaurants?
   c. What is the total raw material cost of Zaza's producing 100 meals now they have 50 restaurants?
   d. Why have Zaza's been able to charge lower prices to customers?
3. What economy of scale do Zaza's achieve by locating restaurants near to each other?
4. What economy of scale do Zaza's achieve by purchasing high-quality equipment?

5. How has high-quality equipment helped Zaza's reduce their average costs?
6. Identify and explain three reasons why Fratelli's are experiencing diseconomies of scale.
7. Can we say for certain whether average costs at Fratelli's are higher than Zaza's? Explain your answer.
8. How may Fratelli's try to delay the onset of diseconomies of scale?

Question 8 in box 7.2 is important to facilitate discussion that demonstrates to students that the point at which diseconomies of scale occur can change. Businesses can make decisions which delay the onset of diseconomies of scale.

Once the consolidation task is complete, check students' understanding with the questions in Box 7.3.

BOX 7.3 CONSOLIDATION TASK

MWB check for understanding

Finish off this whole sequence by ensuring that students are clear on the distinction between the short-run and long-run average cost curve. Use questions like the ones later to test this:

1. A small factory currently has two pieces of machinery and does not have room to expand. The factory expands its labour force by employing an additional member of staff, who increases production by a greater amount than the previous staff member employed. As a result, the firm's average costs fall.

   Which of the following statements is correct?

   A. The firm has experienced managerial economies of scale.
   B. The firm is experiencing increasing marginal returns.
   C. The firm experiences a movement along their short-run average cost curve.
   D. The firm experiences a movement along their long-run average cost curve.

Answers B and C are correct here. Answer A is a good distraction between students may see that average costs are falling as a result of hiring an extra employee and confuse this with managerial economies.

2. The firm expands by opening five new factories. As a result, communication between each factory becomes difficult, and the firm finds that average costs increase. Which of the following statements is correct?

   A. The firm is experiencing diseconomies of scale.
   B. The firm is experiencing economies of scale.
   C. The firm is experiencing diminishing marginal returns.

D. The firm experiences a movement along their short-run average cost curve.

E. The firm experiences a movement along their long-run average cost curve.

Answers A and E are correct. Students may not identify E, as they may consider a 'movement along' the curve as a positive thing, and yet the firm's average costs are increasing.

The two questions earlier should not be too difficult for students. However, they will also quickly reveal if students are struggling to understand the difference between the short-run and long-run average cost curve.

Putting the two curves together

Finish off the overall sequence by showing them the 'envelope curve' relationship. This demonstrates that the long-run average cost curve 'wraps around' all hypothetical short-run average cost curves.

Start by introducing a firm in manufacturing that has a fixed amount of capital. It initially expands by employing additional members of staff and experiencing increasing marginal returns. Eventually, diminishing marginal returns kick in. As a result, the firm moves to a new, larger factory. This means the firm operates on a new, lower, short-run average cost curve. You then repeat the process again by showing the firm initially experiencing increasing returns, then diminishing returns and finally deciding to move to a new factory. Keep repeating the process until eventually, the firm gets so large that it is difficult to coordinate all the different factories it now owns. As a result, they start operating on higher short-run average cost curves. Eventually, you can connect all these short-run average cost curves to show the shape of the long-run average cost curve.

Key takeaways

- Use one consistent example of a business for each economy of scale. For example, in this chapter, we used the example of Tanya's factory. This ensures students aren't switching focus between different businesses and can instead concentrate on the reason that average costs are falling.
- Don't begin your sequence with an example of purchasing economies. Delay the introduction of purchasing economies until at least two other types of economy of scale have been introduced.
- Consistently reiterate to students during your explanation that Tanya's capital is not fixed: she is able to change the amount of capital that she is employing. This highlights the key distinction between short-run and long-run average costs.
- Check students' understanding with questions that relate to either the law of diminishing marginal returns or economies of scale, and check that students can then differentiate between which curve this applies to.

8 Oligopoly and the kinked demand curve

The big picture

In most curriculum sequences, students will be taught monopoly and perfect competition as the first two market structures. These can seem overly theoretical, with various assumptions set out that make the models seem unapplicable in many real-world scenarios. Students often ask: 'Why do we need to study this if these theoretical markets very rarely exist in reality?' I often explain this to students by saying that we need to understand the extreme ends of market structure theory to be able to understand what markets within the continuum may look like. Throughout this sequence of learning, I constantly begin lessons by drawing the market structure continuum shown later. A good, regular recall activity for students is to draw the continuum from memory and list the assumptions and the implications of each market structure. This helps students start to build the picture of why it is important to study the extremes. This continuum is shown in Figure 8.1.

In understanding the extreme ends of the competition, we gain a better insight of the conditions in the middle.

Oligopoly is often the first market structure taught after monopoly and perfect competition and is, therefore, the first opportunity to examine the 'middle' of the continuum. Firms in oligopoly have market power but not as much as those in monopoly. As a result, they need to consider the actions and responses of their competitors when they make decisions. This interdependence lies at the heart of decision-making in oligopolies. A sound understanding of oligopoly provides the basis for students' understanding so much of the commercial world around them, from the smartphone market to the supermarket industry.

Figure 8.1 Market structures

DOI: 10.4324/9781003724179-8

Why do students find this content difficult?

Students typically demonstrate a good initial understanding of the kinked demand curve. Real-world examples that students are familiar with often make this a topic that they can access well. However, students often get confused when depth is added by looking at the shape of the marginal revenue curve in the kinked demand model. This is because this *is* a difficult concept to understand. The marginal revenue curve is discontinuous, and students will not have encountered this before. It is also because students' understanding of marginal revenue is typically a little bit shaky to begin with. As such, students are layering a difficult concept onto a weak foundation.

Explaining this concept

Mistakes to avoid

A sound conceptual understanding of the discontinuous marginal revenue curve is typically only required to gain the most 'difficult to get' marks on an exam paper. Typically (although not always!), students are tested on their understanding of changes in demand based on a firm's pricing decision. Students who are able to confidently discuss the discontinuous marginal revenue curve are likely to be those students that are getting the top marks. As such, it can be tempting to brush over it fairly quickly. Students can be told to remember that the gradient of the marginal revenue curve is always twice as steep as a linear demand curve and so the marginal revenue curve is simply 'following' the demand curve. Students will still wonder why the curve is discontinuous, but hopefully, they won't need to know why!

This is wrong primarily because it limits the access to knowledge for students. It is also wrong because it shies away from teaching students some of the trickier content and deepening their understanding of the subject discipline.

A second mistake to avoid is using the smartphone market too early in your menu of examples! I used to always introduce this topic by giving Apple, Samsung and (at the time!) Motorola. However, the combination of Apple's market dominance and students' acute understanding of differentiating features of Apple and Samsung phones can often lead to difficulty in making the concept initially clear. I would keep the mobile phone example until later in the sequence, when you want to critique the kinked demand model.

Explaining this concept – the kinked demand curve

There is a lot to teach within oligopoly. I would teach the topic in the following order sequence:

1. Concentration ratios and the definition of oligopoly
2. Interdependence and the kinked demand curve

3. Critiques of the kinked demand curve
4. The prisoner's dilemma and game theory
5. Pricing strategies and collusion

The rest of this chapter will focus on points 2 and 3 in the list earlier.

Start by recapping marginal revenue with students. I would recommend giving students several marginal revenue calculations and scenarios in which they have to explain how marginal revenue is changing in each instance.

Then begin your explanation on the kinked demand curve. Start with the use of an example. I use low-cost airlines:

The low-cost airline market is an example of an oligopoly. EasyJet and Ryannair are the two largest firms, but Jet2 and Wizz Air also have significant market share in the industry. Customers in this market aren't particularly loyal – ***the majority of customers happily switch between these airlines based on whichever is offering the cheapest flights to the destination that they want to go to.***

This last bit of the explanation is really important; it is customers' willingness to switch between airlines that makes this a good example for introducing the kinked demand curve. It also demonstrates why Apple and Samsung aren't a good example because there is strong brand loyalty in this market.

Now, let's assume that you are all bosses at EasyJet. You are considering your pricing strategy. Let's imagine we can easily assign an 'average price' for your flights in Europe, and let's say that it is currently £60. You are considering decreasing your prices. If you do this, how do you think Ryannair would respond?

This is the sort of question that I would think-pair-share. The majority of students at this stage of their studies should be able to think through Ryannair's response. You then draw out from discussion that Ryannair are likely to also reduce their price because they would be worried that customers would switch to EasyJet. Live draw this response on the board by drawing a simple matrix that shows if EasyJet decreases their price, you expect Ryannair to follow suit. Introducing a simple matrix at this stage helps reduce some of the cognitive overload when introducing game theory payoff matrixes a little bit later because students are already familiar with the idea of representing decisions in this way.

Okay, so how many customers are EasyJet going to gain from reducing their prices below £60? Probably not many, because Ryannair and Jet2 and Wizz Air are all probably going to reduce their prices as well and so EasyJet doesn't gain from the lower price. Interesting!

Now, you are then considering whether you should increase your prices. What do you think Ryannair and your other competitors may do in response?

Unlike the first think-pair-share question, this one sometimes gets some different responses. Some students assume that competitors will price match so that everyone benefits from higher profit margins. Make sure you are really clear and live drawing as you go along:

Ryannair would probably be quite happy if EasyJet increase their average price to £70. There will be lots of unhappy customers that will probably now switch to Ryannair (or Wizz Air or Jet2). As a result, EasyJet increasing their prices seems a bit of a silly decision because their competitors won't follow suit and suddenly EasyJet will lose lots of customers.

This example identifies two really important features of oligopolistic markets:

1. *Prices are often 'rigid' in these markets – they don't tend to change much*
2. *When firms in oligopolistic markets are making a strategic decision such as changing price, they have to think about their competitors responses. We refer to this as interdependence. This is because the strategy choices of a firm are somewhat 'dependent' on the choices of their competitors.*

Pause and check students' understanding of these key concepts with some MWB questions. This may be as simple as giving them a scenario in which Ryannair is considering increasing or decreasing their prices and students need to correctly identify the ways in which their competitors are likely to respond.

Then slowly draw the kinked demand curve with the students on the board or visualiser. Narrate the story that the diagram is telling: start with a price point of £60, and show the slope of the demand curve at prices above and below this point.

Finish this section by checking students' understanding with a few basic comprehension questions. An example of the kind of question you could use is shown in Box 8.1.

BOX 8.1 MWB CHECK FOR UNDERSTANDING

MWB check for understanding

The UK petrol station market is dominated by large global companies such as Shell, BP and Esso, as well as supermarket petrol stations like Tesco, Sainsbury's and ASDA. This market is an oligopoly.

Shell is considering whether to change the price of the petrol that they sell. They are currently operating at point A in Figure 8.2.

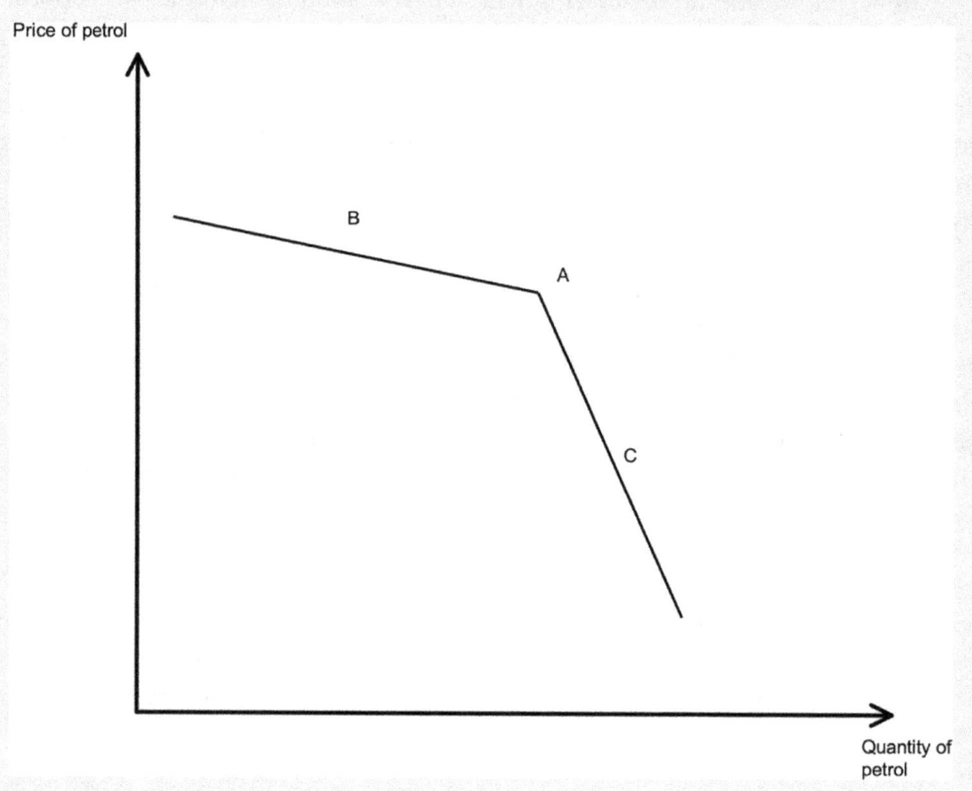

Figure 8.2 Kinked demand MWB question

Which of the following statements is correct?

A. An increase in price will lead to a less-than-proportionate fall in quantity demanded for Shell, as most competitors will also increase their prices.

B. A decrease in price will lead to a less-than-proportionate increase in quantity demanded for Shell, as most competitors will also decrease their prices.

C. Many competitors are unlikely to also increase their prices if Shell choose to do so.

D. The kinked demand theory would suggest Shell should keep their price at point A.

E. Shell can maximise revenue made by increasing their price, as long as other competitors do not follow.

Answers B, C and D are correct. Correctly identifying these three answers as correct should highlight that students have understood the concept of the kinked demand curve.

Answer A is purposely designed to be 'double wrong', as an increase in price will lead to a more than proportionate fall in quantity demand, and this is because most competitors will not follow. This can be used as an opportunity for further questioning of students.

Explaining marginal revenue and marginal cost curves

Once you are confident that students have grasped the concept of the kinked demand curve, move on to adding marginal revenue and marginal cost curves to the diagram. This can be particularly difficult for students to grasp, particularly if they are not studying A-level maths. The following explanation focuses on some simplified math, which should help students understand, rather than a focus on the discontinuity of marginal revenue at the kink.

The graph gets quite busy, so it is really important that you take students through this step-by-step and use a deliberately slow explanation. Again, draw live as you go along.

> *Now, we want to think about the shape of the marginal revenue curve that corresponds with the kinked demand curve. This is tricky, so we are going to walk through it step-by-step [as shown in Box 8.2].*

Students will need you to spend time interrogating this discontinuous marginal revenue curve. For example, marginal revenue would be higher than $14 if the firm could sell 10.1 units, but of course this isn't possible.

Once this is complete and you have checked students' understanding with some comprehension MWB questions, you can then introduce the idea of marginal cost. Show that as long as the marginal cost curve intersects the discontinuous section of the marginal revenue curve, then the firm will be incentivised to operate at the price and quantity that coincides with the kink. Reducing price below this point will result in marginal revenue falling below marginal cost, and therefore, marginal profit becomes negative.

Once this done, check students' understanding with some MWB comprehension questions. Examples are shown in Box 8.3.

Once this sequence is complete, use the case study example in Box 8.4 to introduce the students to critiques of the kinked demand curve theory. This is now a good point at which to introduce Apple and the smartphone market.

BOX 8.2 STEP BY STEP EXPLANATION OF THE KINKED DEMAND CURVE

Step one: *Now, let's imagine a company selling a widget in an oligopolistic market. I've drawn the kinked demand curve and the corresponding marginal revenue curve for all quantities 'to the left' of the kink.*

Let's imagine the firm sells their widgets for £82 and at this price they sell 9 units. This would mean that their total revenue would be £738.

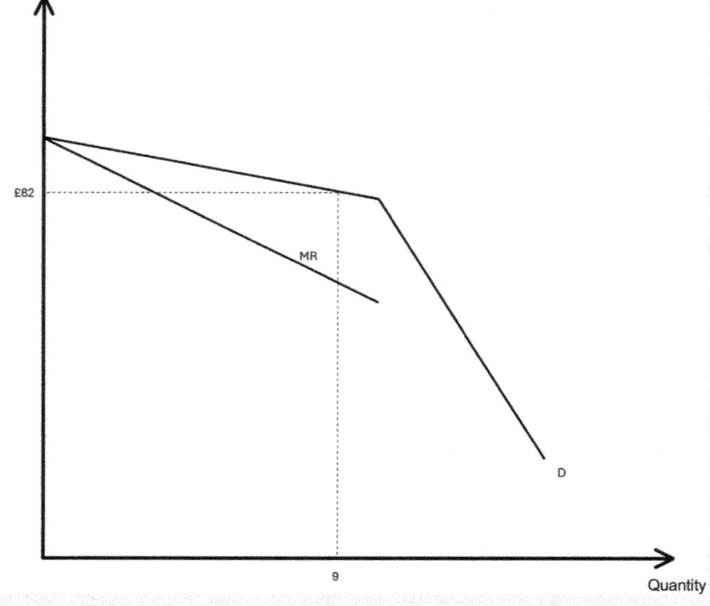

Figure 8.3 Kinked demand explanation one

Step two: *Let's imagine the firm then reduces their price to £80. This increases quantity demanded to 10 units, which coincides with the 'kink' in their demand curve.*

As a result, revenue increases to £800.

The 'extra total revenue' they have generated from selling this 10th unit is £62. Therefore, the firm's marginal revenue is £62.

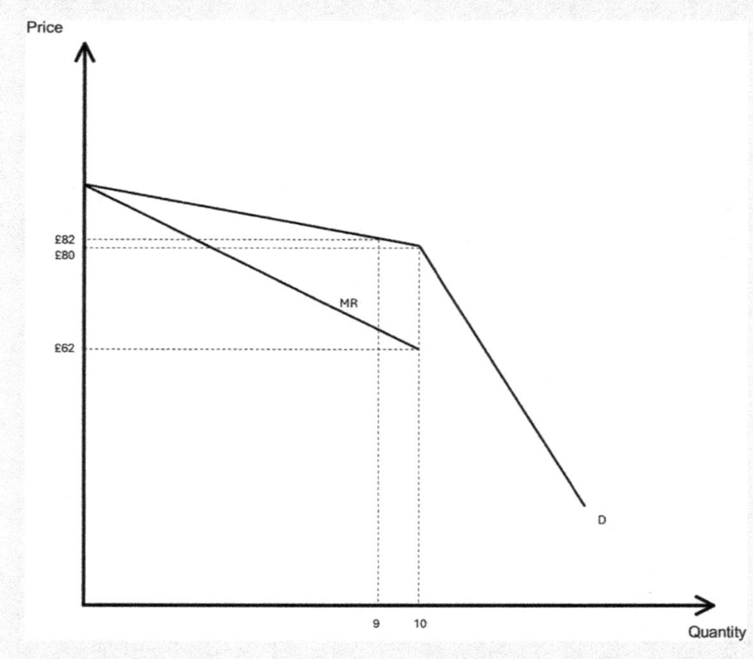

Figure 8.4 Kinked demand explanation two

Step three: *what if the firm wants to sell an 11th unit? Well, according to the kinked demand curve theory, if the firm reduces their price below £80 then their competitors will follow them because they are worried about losing market share. As such, the firm is going to have to reduce price by a lot to make that extra one unit sale.*

We can see that the firm has had to reduce price to £74 to make this sale.

Step four: *what does this mean for marginal revenue? Well, total revenue at this point is going to be £74 x 11, which is £814. This means marginal revenue is now only £14 – much less than the previous marginal revenue. So what is this going to look like?*

We get a disconnected or 'discontinuous' marginal revenue curve that looks a bit like this:

We can see that the marginal revenue of the 11th unit is way down at £14.

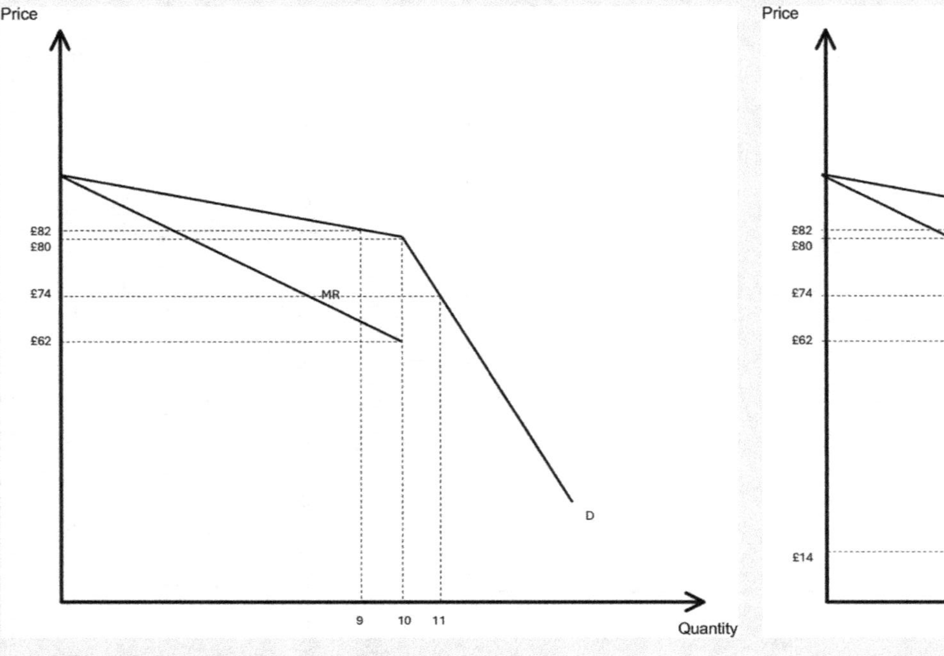

Figure 8.5 Kinked demand explanation three

Figure 8.6 Kinked demand explanation four

BOX 8.3 MWB CHECKS FOR UNDERSTANDING

MWB checks for understanding

Question one

Figure 8.7 represents the demand curve for a firm operating in an oligopolistic market. The marginal cost curves show possible curves that the firm could operate on. P1Q1 and P2Q2 show possible pricing and output decisions.

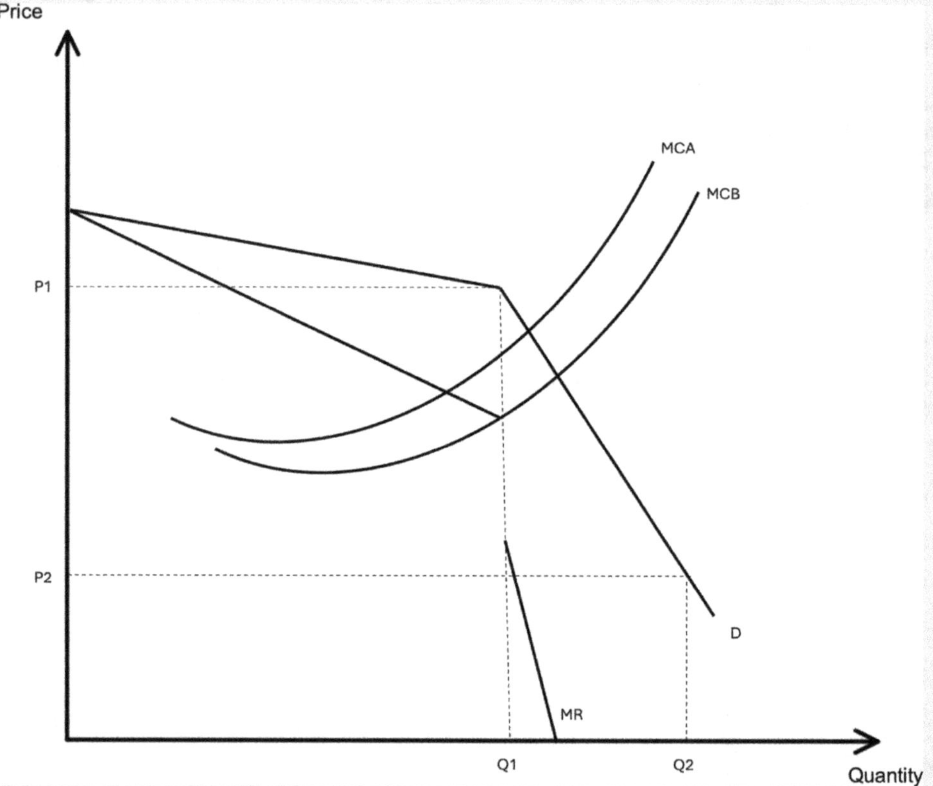

Figure 8.7 Kinked demand MWB question one

Which of the following statements is correct? There may be more than one correct answer.

A. At P1Q1, the firm will only be profit maximising if it is operating on marginal cost MCA.

B. At P2Q2, the firm will be profit maximising as it is maximising the quantity sold.

C. At P1Q1, the firm will be profit maximising if it is operating on marginal cost MCB.

D. The firm should increase its price above P1 to maximise its profit.

Answer C is the only correct answer. If the firm is operating on MCB when Q1 is being sold, then marginal revenue will be equal to marginal cost. This is the profit maximising output for a firm.

Question two

Figure 8.8 represents the demand curve for a firm operating in an oligopolistic market. The marginal cost curves show possible curves that the firm could operate on. P1Q1 shows a possible pricing and output decision.

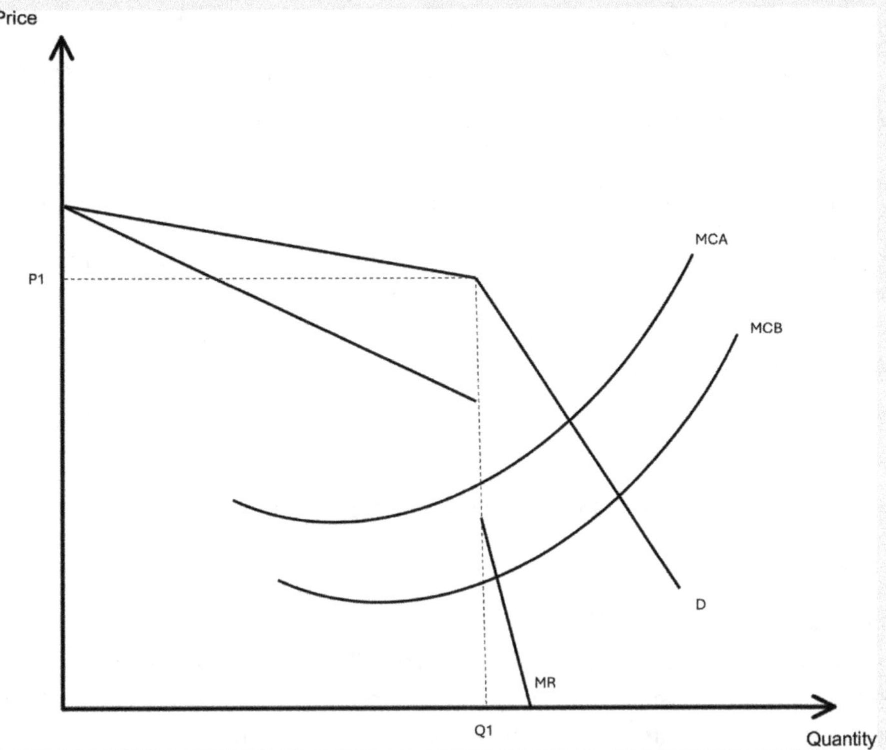

Figure 8.8 Kinked demand MWB question two

Which of the following statement is correct? There may be more than one correct answer.

A. At P1Q1, the firm will only be profit maximising if it is operating on MCA.

B. At P1Q1, the firm will be profit maximising if it is operating on either MCA or MCB.

C. The firm could charge below price P1 and increase its profit as long as it is operating on MCB.

D. The firm should always produce P1Q1, even if it is operating on MCB.

Answers A and C are correct. Answer B is a really important learning moment for students: while marginal revenue would be above marginal cost at P1Q1 if the firm is operating on MC2, they could still increase total profit in this scenario by increasing output. Answer D is also important to demonstrate the boundary of the kinked demand theory: a firm in an oligopolistic market can charge a price below the 'kink' if marginal cost is sufficiently low enough.

Question three

Which of the following statements are correct with regard to oligopolistic markets?

A. There are always two dominant firms in an oligopoly.

B. Firms are interdependent in terms of quantity but make pricing decisions independently of their rivals' actions.

C. The kinked demand curve suggests prices are relatively stable in oligopolistic markets.

D. The conclusions of the kinked demand curve theory relies on the assumption that firms in these markets are interdependent.

E. Firms in oligopoly should reduce their prices in order to gain market share.

Answers C and D are correct. This is a good 'finishing' question to ensure that students have taken the key learnings from this sequence of learning: the kinked demand curve rests on the idea of interdependence between firms and, if this holds, suggests prices in these markets will be rigid.

BOX 8.4 CASE STUDY ON OLIGOPOLY

Case study

Apple holds an estimated 26% share of the smartphone market, followed by Samsung with around 21%. Chinese firms like Xiaomi and Vivo trail with approximately 10% each. While exact figures vary based on measurement methods, these numbers broadly reflect the market structure and its dominant players, demonstrating that the smartphone industry is an oligopoly.

According to the kinked demand theory of oligopoly, this should demonstrate that there is price rigidity in the market. We would expect there to be little incentive for firms to change the price of their products in this market. However, there tends to be fluctuations on prices. The price of an iPhone has increased steadily over recent years, with other iPhones initially retailing at around £500 and new models being sold for over £800. Similar trends can be seen with regard to Samsung phones.

The reason that there is a differentiation in prices is based on the concept of non-price competition. Smartphone producers will try to differentiate themselves in different ways to customers. For example, Apple has invested significantly to innovate and improve each iteration of the iPhone that they launch. This enables them to sell the products at higher prices without significantly losing customers. Apple also invest significantly into branding and advertising, which creates customer loyalty. This is another reason that Apple are able to increase prices without losing significant numbers of customers.

The earlier factors mean that both the producer and customer believe that the phone is worth a higher price than their competitors. This enables Apple to increase prices and means that the price of phones in this market is not rigid. This demonstrates an important concept in oligopolistic markets: products can be differentiated from their rivals.

It should be noted that the degree to which firms compete on non-price factors varies between markets. The smartphone market is one in which there is significant levels of non-price competition. In contrast, the market for consumer goods, such as tinned food, tends to exhibit less non-price competition.

Questions

1. Based on the approximate figures provided in the case study:
   a. What is the two-firm concentration ratio of the smartphone market?
   b. What is the four-firm concentration ratio of the smartphone market?
2. Assume that the conditions of the kinked demand theory do hold. Show the impact on demand for Apple phones if the company chooses to produce higher than the price set by the market.
3. Provide evidence from the case study that the smartphone market does not represent the kinked demand model of oligopoly.
4. Identify three ways in which Apple differentiates themselves based on non-price factors.
5. Why does customer loyalty mean Apple can 'increase prices without losing significant numbers of customers'? Refer to the price elasticity of demand in your answer.
6. Based on your reading, do you think the kinked demand model is an effective way to describe behaviour of firms in an oligopoly? Justify your answer.

Key takeaways

- Use multiple examples when teaching students about the kinked demand curve and oligopoly, but don't start with the smartphone market. Avoid the trap of rushing to the example that students will know best. This will actually reduce the usefulness of the example when trying to explain the kinked demand curve. Instead, use the smartphone example later on when you are seeking to critique the kinked demand model.
- Don't shy away from the discontinuous marginal revenue curve. Make sure you start the sequence by recapping marginal revenue. Then teach the discontinuous marginal revenue curve slowly and using live drawing to help make it clear for students.

9 Long-run aggregate supply

What's the big idea?

Long-run equilibrium in the macroeconomy differs between schools of thought. Monetarists believe the economy will always adjust back to the natural rate of full employment (NRU). In contrast, Keynesians argue the economy can operate below full capacity for a prolonged period. This lies at the heart of the arguments between each school on the ways in which they believe governments and policymakers should respond to macro phenomena, like a recession.

This topic is often students' first introduction to rival macroeconomic schools. It is an essential opportunity to establish an ongoing narrative contrasting Monetarist and Keynesian positions. While specific exam boards vary in required depth for concepts like the NAIRU, the long-run Phillips curve and the quantity theory of money, I highly recommend introducing these concepts where feasible. A stronger grasp of these debates leads to deeper critical thought and significantly enriches students' understanding of economics as a subject.

This is an opportunity to return to the idea of economics as a social science. There is not necessarily a 'right' or 'tested' method. Instead, we have competing theories based on different assumptions made about the real world and human behaviour. I love teaching this topic precisely because it gets to the heart of these debates!

Please note that this chapter will focus on the economic debate regarding the shape of the long-run aggregate supply curve, rather than factors that would cause the long-run supply curve to shift outward. This would come after the following sequence of learning.

Why do students find this topic difficult?

Students can fall into a trap of believing that economics is mono-theoretic. I often represented the subject in this way earlier in my career. Given time constraints and the complexity of content, school economics' curriculums are somewhat necessarily limited to providing a neoclassical economic perspective. I am sure there are many teachers who do not teach the subject in this way, but to a large extent, exam board specifications do not necessitate that they do.

DOI: 10.4324/9781003724179-9

I don't say this as a criticism of exam board specifications. School curricula must always be modified versions of the subject discipline as a whole. However, it is important to recognise such modification because it impacts the perspectives that our students will have of the subject. For example, while government intervention is taught, exam boards do not necessitate that students understand the degree and scope of government intervention may be dependent on the school of thought to which an economist belongs. Government intervention could be interpreted as something that 'just happens', and it will have advantages and disadvantages. As a result, students can find it difficult when introduced to seemingly valid competing arguments, such as that of the classical and Keynesian long-run aggregate supply curve.

Part of the problem outlined earlier can be negated by investing time in considering the nature of economic theory at other points within the curriculum. For example, I like to introduce content around economics as a social science a little later in the course, rather than at the beginning of the specification. I typically introduce this once students have looked at the market mechanism and as an introduction to behavioural economics. I find that students find these discussions more fruitful once they have seen a little 'economics in action'.

The other reason that students find this topic difficult is because they fail to see *why* Monetarists and Keynesian's disagree about the economy's capacity to self-correct. In my own experience, this was because I had not explained clearly the assumptions and contexts in which these economists were making their arguments.

Explaining this concept

Mistakes to avoid

One of the fundamental differences between the Monetarist and Keynesian school is whether or not the economy will naturally adjust back to its original full employment level in the long-run. From the Monetarist perspective, this will occur if there is no government intervention in labour markets. Without spending time to explain this assumption, students can find the model unrealistic. Don't skip past these assumptions; spend time talking them through with students. While a position of 'no government intervention' in labour markets may seem unrealistic, understanding of those extreme ends of a continuum enrich our understanding of the arguments in the middle.

Explaining this concept – the Monetarist school

Start by explaining the idea of a full employment level in an economy. Draw macroeconomic short-run macroeconomic equilibrium and then, as you go through the explanation, plot on the full employment level. This process is shown in Box 9.1.

BOX 9.1 STEP ONE OF THE EXPLANATION OF THE MONETARIST SCHOOL

Step one

We can see I've drawn macroeconomic equilibrium with our aggregate supply and aggregate demand curves as we have done in previous lessons.

I am then going to add on this dotted line, which I am going to say represents the 'full employment' level in the economy. This is the maximum potential output the economy could produce if all possible factors of production were employed.

Now, we need to be a little bit careful – for now I am going to say that this assumes all factors of production are 'sustainably' employed. For example, it assumes our economy's machines are working as hard as they can but takes into account they may need some period of time for maintenance. It is assumes my labour is also working 'sustainably'. For example, workers aren't doing 24 hour shifts that clearly couldn't be sustained.[1]

You will notice that this economy is currently operating below this 'full employment' level. The currently macroeconomic equilibrium is below the full potential of the economy if all its resources were being fully utilised. Perhaps this is because there is a lack of demand to 'use up' all these resources.

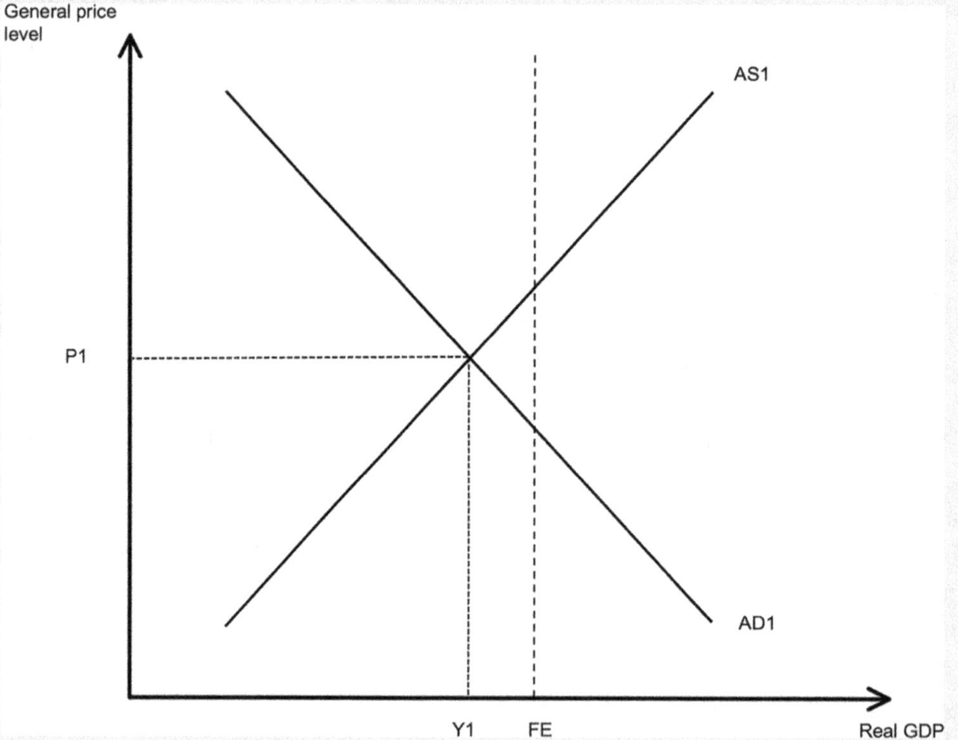

Figure 9.1 An economy operating below full employment level

I then help students to make the link between this diagram and production possibility curves (PPCs), which they will already be familiar with. With some classes, I may explicitly show this; with others, I may ask them to do some whiteboard work to see if they can make the link themselves between what is shown on this diagram and the PPC. This will depend on the strength of your students' understanding of PPCs.

Then use some MWB comprehension questions to check three things:

1. That full employment represents the maximum output of an economy, assuming all resources are fully employed.
2. Full employment does not necessarily represent '100% employment'. Capital may require maintenance, and labour is being used in a sustainable way.
3. An economy can operate at an equilibrium below its full employment level.

Now set the scene for students that over the next couple of lessons, you are going to consider how the economy responds in a position such as the one that you have set out. Explain that you are going to be looking at some competing arguments on this.

Start by explaining how the economy would adjust according to Monetarists. This is shown in Box 9.2.

BOX 9.2 STEP TWO OF THE EXPLANATION OF THE MONETARIST SCHOOL

Step two

Let's imagine we have an economy where there is no ***external intervention in labour markets****. For example, a government has not imposed a minimum wage and does not pay unemployment benefits to those that do not have a job. There are also no trade unions in existence to help protect the rights of workers. These assumption are really key for what we are about to think about!*

If we have an economy operating below its maximum capacity then we have spare resources in our economy: there is some labour that is not employed and there is capital that is not being fully utilised.

Let's think about how some of that unemployed labour may react. Remember, this labour will not be receiving any employment benefits and so their income is set to zero. That labour is going to be keen to get a job as quickly as possible! As such, unemployed labour may be willing to accept wages below those that they would have previously been willing to accept.

This means that firms are going to be able to offer wages that are lower than the market rate that they had previously been paying. As a result, this reduces firms' costs of production.

So, what do we see? We see that when we have unemployed resources in our economy and there is no government intervention, the 'cost' of those resources will adjust downwards and therefore reduces firms' costs of production.

We know from previous lessons how a reduction in firms' costs of production will impact short-run aggregate supply. What will happen . . . Saira? Absolutely, SRAS will shift outwards.

We can see in Figure 9.2 *that SRAS will shift outwards until there is no spare resources left in our economy because any spare resources will be willing to reduce their price demands in order to be minimised. The macroeconomy has 'cleared' and equilibrium now occurs at the full employment level. Interesting!*

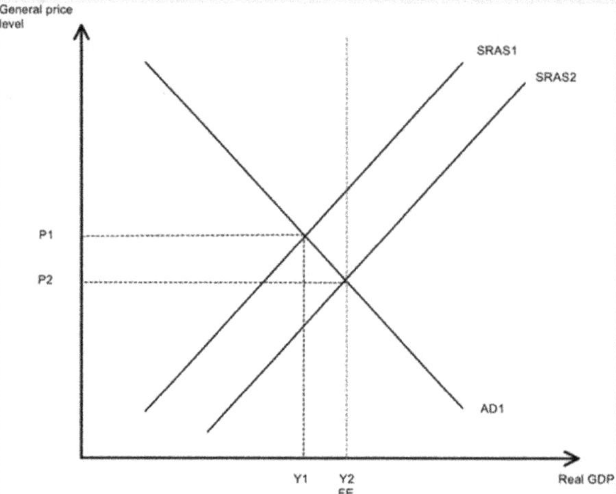

Figure 9.2 An economy adjusting back to full employment level

Use a series of MWB consolidation questions to check that students have an understanding of the assumptions that underpin this theory. A simple question like the one in Box 9.3 helps you check students' understanding while also consolidating the key ideas for students at this early stage. Notice that the question should be straightforward because we are looking to consolidate students' understanding here, rather than challenge or deepen it.

BOX 9.3 MWB CHECK FOR UNDERSTANDING – MONETARIST SCHOOL

MWB question

Adam was previously willing to work for £15 per hour. However, he has recently become unemployed and is searching for a job. He is now willing to work for £10 per hour.

Which of the following statements are correct regarding this scenario?

A. Adam is likely to be willing to work for less than before because the quality of jobs available have decreased.

B. Adam is likely to be willing to work for less than before because he will not be receiving any employment benefit and therefore needs a job.

C. The fall in Adam's wage demands will increase firms' costs of production.

D. The fall in Adam's wage demands will decrease firms' costs of production.

Answer B and D are correct. The question doesn't stipulate that answer B is correct specifically according to the Monetarist school. While this is an important caveat, at this point in the sequence, we haven't even introduced students to the Monetarist school or any competing schools.

Then ask students to show you on their MWBs how this scenario would impact macroeconomic equilibrium. Make sure that all students are comfortable with the idea that the economy would eventually shift back to full employment level.

Then use an example where initial equilibrium is above full employment level. Explain that the economy can operate above full employment level for a short-period of time because existing labour can work overtime and downtime of capital can be minimised. However, in the long-run, this will push up the prices of factors of production and cause SRAS to shift inwards. For example, labour working overtime will start to demand higher wages and capital that has been overused will require maintenance, which pushes up business costs. The end point of this explanation is shown in Box 9.4.

Then ask students to demonstrate their understanding of this on MWBs. For example, give them a scenario of an economy operating under full capacity and ask them to show how the Monetarists believe the economy would adjust in the long run. After a few of these scenarios, test students' understanding further with a MWB question like the ones shown in Box 9.5.

So far, students are likely to be under the impression that Monetarists believe that any sort of government intervention will stop an economy operating at full employment level. It is important to point out here to students that government intervention will stop the economy returning to its *initial* full employment level. With government intervention present, Monetarists do believe that an economy can operate at full employment level. However, that full employment level will be lower than it could be if government intervention was not present. In other words, government intervention reduces the size of the productive potential capacity of the economy. It's important that students understand this if they are then going to have a secure understanding of the natural rate of unemployment later in the course.

Explaining this concept – the Keynesian school

Now it is time to introduce students to the opposing school of thought. Start by making clear to students that you are now looking at an opposing school of thought and that the assumptions of this model will be different. I often like to prefix this by briefly introducing Keynes and explaining that much of this theory was developed after World War I and during the Great Depression. This bit of 'hinterland' knowledge

BOX 9.4 STEP THREE AND FOUR OF THE EXPLANATION OF THE MONETARIST SCHOOL

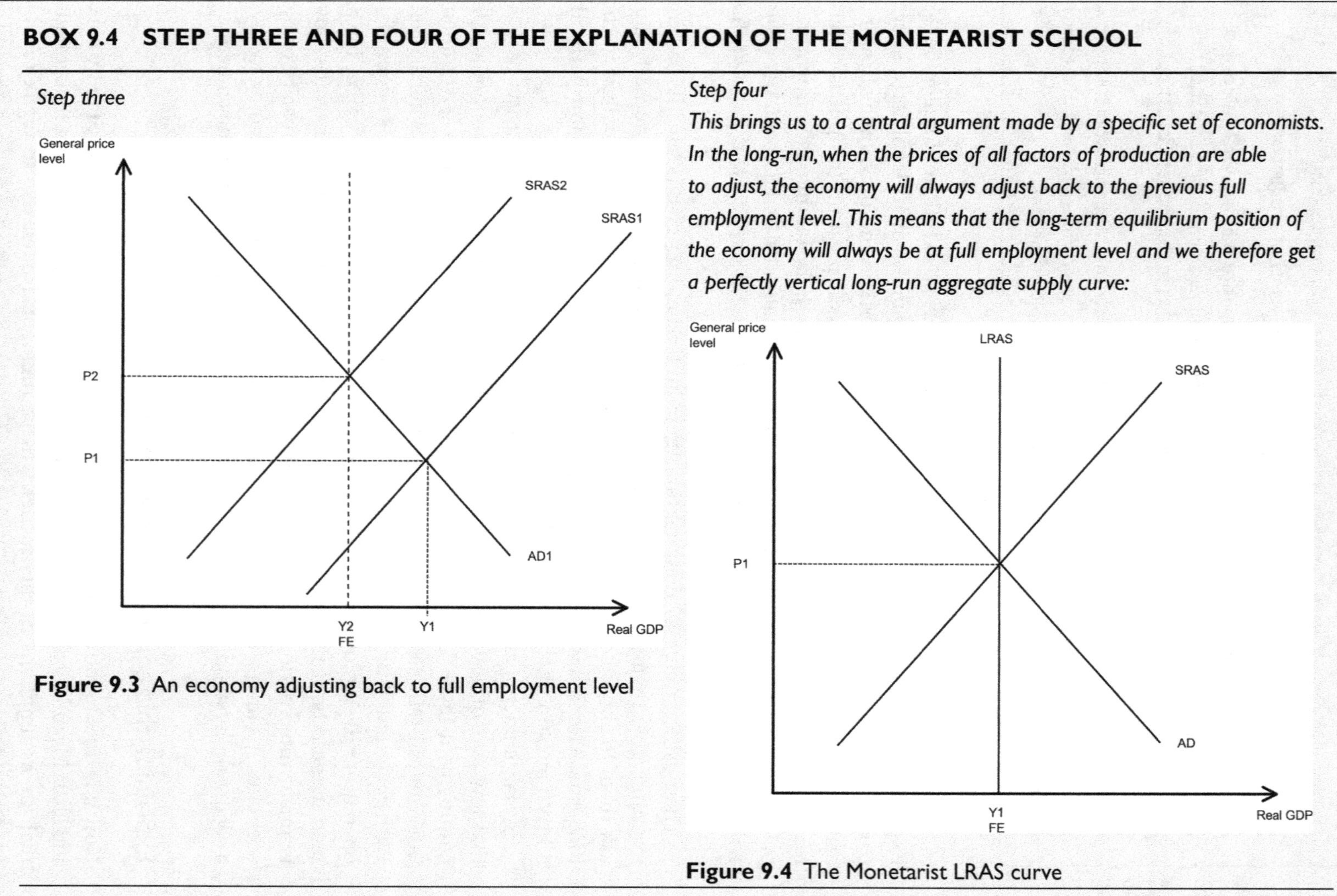

Step three

Figure 9.3 An economy adjusting back to full employment level

Step four

This brings us to a central argument made by a specific set of economists. In the long-run, when the prices of all factors of production are able to adjust, the economy will always adjust back to the previous full employment level. This means that the long-term equilibrium position of the economy will always be at full employment level and we therefore get a perfectly vertical long-run aggregate supply curve:

Figure 9.4 The Monetarist LRAS curve

We can see that higher costs of production have shifted SRAS1 to SRAS2. What do we notice about the new equilibrium position? It has adjusted back to the full employment position in the long-run. Interesting – this is similar to our situation before!

We refer to this long-run aggregate supply curve as the Classical or Monetarist LRAS. This is because it is economists who belong to these schools of economics that believe the LRAS curve is shaped this way. These schools are different, but for the sake of your A-level you just need to recognise that they have similar views on the shape of the LRAS curve.

BOX 9.5 MWB CHECKS FOR UNDERSTANDING OF THE MONETARIST SCHOOL

MWB check for understanding

1. An economy is currently operating below its full employment level. Which of the following statements would be correct according to the Monetarist or classical school?
   - A. Assuming there is no government intervention, existing workers can bargain for higher wages, which will lead to an increase in aggregate demand.
   - B. Inactive workers will be able to negotiate for higher wage rates, which will encourage them to join the workforce.
   - C. Assuming there is no government intervention, firms will be able to attract workers at lower wage rates and so firms' costs of production will fall.
   - D. The price paid to factors of production will increase, which will result in firm's costs of production increasing and short-run aggregate supply shifting inwards.

C is the only correct answer.

A and C begin with the same phrase to check that students understand the reason why a lack of government intervention leads to a long-run adjustment.

D would reveal that students are confusing the ways in which an economy adjusts when it is below or above full employment level.

2. An economy is currently operating above its full employment level. Which of the following statements would be correct according to the Monetarist or classical school?
   - A. Capital may not be sustainably maintained, and significant amounts of labour may be working overtime.
   - B. The economy is likely to be in this equilibrium position in the long run because the prices of factors of production are not flexible.
   - C. The economy will adjust back to the initial full employment level in the long run as a result of reduced aggregate demand.
   - D. The prices paid to the factors of production are likely to rise.

A and D are correct answers.

B is incorrect according to these schools of economic thought. Students may erroneously answer C because they see that the first part of the answer is correct. However, C is incorrect because the economy will not return to full employment as a result of adjustments in aggregate demand.

3. The following answers represent a chain of analysis. At which point does the FIRST mistake appear?
   - A. An economy is operating below full employment level.
   - B. This means that there are unemployed workers that will not be receiving unemployment benefit.

C. To increase their incomes, these workers demand higher wages in order to work.

D. This results in higher incomes and an outward shift of AD.

E. As a result, the economy adjusts back to full employment level.

F. There are no mistakes in the chains of analysis earlier.

I like these types of question, as they play a dual role of checking students' understanding but also implicitly showing them how to build chains of reasoning. This is then helpful for exam writing.

Answer C is the correct answer, as it erroneously states that unemployed workers can demand higher wages to become employed. Instead, these workers will need to accept lower wages.

demonstrates to students that the kind of economic theory developed at a particular time is often a reflection of the macroeconomic conditions that the economist was observing. Keynes lived through a period where there were prolonged periods of recession and deficient demand, and his work seeks to explain this.

Kick this off by asking something like the following:

> Now, let's imagine an unfortunate scenario where you have all lost your job where you were paid £500 per week – a wage that you were happy with. Let's imagine that this is an economy where unemployment benefits are paid to those that do not have a job, and let's imagine those benefits are £350.

Make these two points very clearly on the board: previous wage: \$500; benefits worth: \$350.

> *How many of you would be willing to return to work if firms reduced the wages that they were offering to £400?*

Invariably, some students put their hand up and say that they would return to work; others do not.

> *Okay, so what do we see? We see that the existence of unemployment benefits means that some of you would not be willing to return to work at the lower wage rate. I suspect many of you would not be willing to return to work for anything less than the £500 that you were previously earning.*
>
> *This represents something that John Maynard Keynes referred to as wages being 'sticky downwards'. In other words, in reality it is very difficult to decrease the wage rate once expectations of what your labour is worth have set in.*

You can then provide further examples of intervention that may make it difficult for wages to adjust downwards. For example, a minimum wage may exist that keeps wages higher, or trade unions may negotiate to protect current wage rates.

In reality, many economies have some sort of intervention in the labour market. As a result, wages and the prices of factors of production do not adjust as quickly as the Monetarist school argues.

The key implication of this is that the economy is not going to automatically adjust back to the full employment level! Instead, Keynesian economists would argue that the economy can operate for quite a prolonged period of time below full employment level.

Use this explanation and demonstrate on the board an economy operating below full capacity. Extrapolate from this the Keynesian long-run aggregate supply, and explain that this is an alternative method of conceptualising long-run equilibrium in an economy.

Once you have drawn the curve, pick a point that is significantly below full employment level. Use this point to explain that Keynes would argue there is lots of spare capacity in that economy which can be utilised without bargaining for higher factor payments. Then identify a point where the economy is approaching full employment and highlight that at this point, the economy will grow, but the use of scarce resources will cause inflationary pressure in the economy to grow.

Then use the MWB question in Box 9.6 to check students' understanding.

Finish this topic by looking at the Great Depression and the US government's response to the crisis. This is a great way of contextualising the economic arguments that students have been studying. An example of how this can be done is shown in Box 9.7.

BOX 9.6 MWB CHECKS FOR UNDERSTANDING OF BOTH SCHOOLS SIMULTANEOUSLY

MWB checks for understanding

1. Which of the following statements is correct regarding the following diagram (Figure 9.5)?

   A. The initial equilibrium shows an economy operating below full capacity.

   B. At initial equilibrium, there will be unemployed workers.

   C. Unemployment would have been caused by initial higher price levels.

   D. The shift from SRAS1 to SRAS2 may have occurred due to lower wage costs.

   E. The shift from SRAS1 to SRAS2 may be caused by an increase in welfare payments.

Answers A, B and D are correct.

Follow this question up by asking students which economic school of thought the diagram is associated with.

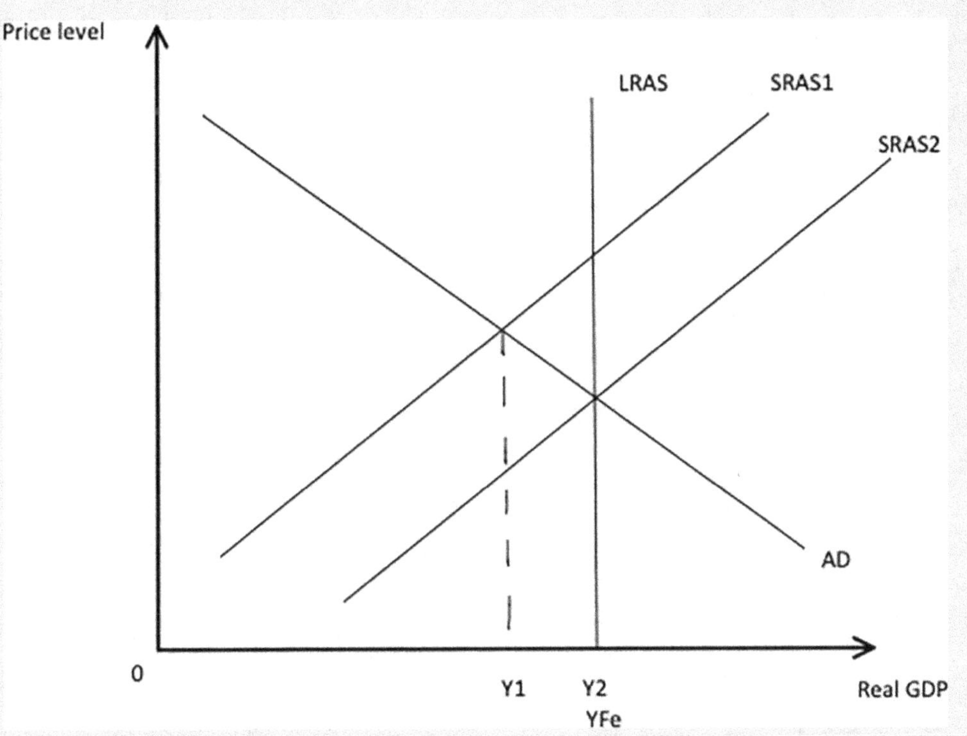

Figure 9.5 An economy operating below full employment level

1. Which of the following statements is correct regarding Figure 9.6?

   A. The economy has unemployed resources because welfare payments are too high.

   B. The distance between Y1 and YFE represents unemployed labour only.

   C. Aggregate demand can be increased without initially causing prices to rise.

   D. Firms will need to attract unemployed workers by paying higher wages.

   E. The economy could be at equilibrium Y1 for an extended period of time.

Answers C and E are correct.

Follow this question up by asking students which economic school of thought the diagram is associated with.

The use of questions where students have to interpret what each graph is showing them is a great way to check that students have a solid understanding of the differing schools of thought regarding the Keynesian and Monetarist schools. Both questions also address common misconceptions that may be true in some circumstances but are not *necessarily true*. For example, in question 1, students often assume that higher prices in the economy are causing unemployment because they reason that a fall in the general price level has returned the economy to full employment, and so the high prices must have been initially causing the unemployment. In question 2, students will often assume that spare capacity represents just unemployed labour instead of all possible resources within the economy.

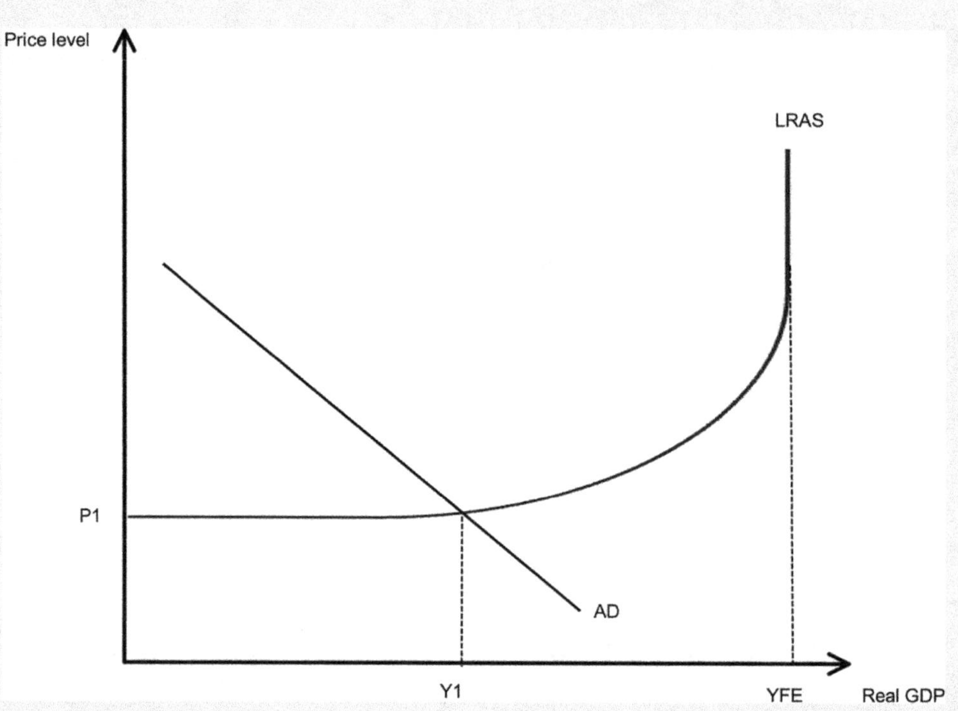

Figure 9.6 An economy operating below full employment level in a Keynesian macroeconomic diagram

Finally, ask:

3. Which of the following statements is correct regarding the Monetarist and Keynesian schools of thought?

   A. Keynesians believe that wage levels will not adjust automatically and can be sticky.

   B. Keynesians believe that the economy will naturally adjust back to the full employment level.

   C. Monetarists believe that government intervention in labour markets is a barrier to the economy adjusting back to the initial full employment level.

   D. Only Keynesians believe that the economy can operate below full employment level in the short-run.

Answers A and C are correct. D is an important option that highlights to students that it is the long run in which both schools have disagreements about adjustment to full employment level. In the short run, both schools recognise the economy can operate with unemployed resources.

BOX 9.7 CASE STUDY

Case study

During the 1920s, the stock market in the US had quickly expanded. It is estimated that approximately 3 million Americans owned stocks. Heavy investment in the stock market led to an overvaluation of stocks. In October 1929, the stock market crashed. This caused widespread panic across the economy. On October 24, known as 'Black Thursday', panicked investors sold a record 13 million stocks. This panic resulted in a large number of 'bank runs'. A bank run occurs when a large number of individuals rush to withdraw their savings from a bank. Over 9,000 banks collapsed between 1930 and 1933, causing many people to lose their savings. This loss of wealth lead to a fall in household consumption and business investment, significantly reducing aggregate demand in the US economy.

Between 1929 and 1933, it is estimated US GDP fell by 30%. In 1933, the unemployment rate in the US hit 25%. At the time, a formal unemployment benefit system did not exist. The growth in unemployment resulted in a severe decline in the standard of living in the US. Many people became homeless and started to live in shanty towns, nicknamed 'Hoovervilles' after Herbert Hoover, the US President between 1928 and 1932. This mass unemployment resulted in persistently low levels of aggregate demand within the US economy.

In response to the crisis, President Franklin Roosevelt launched the 'New Deal' between 1933 and 1935. The New Deal was a programme of government intervention designed to tackle the high rate of unemployment at the time. For example, the Works Progress Administration (WPA) employed millions of people on public service projects, such as road buildings and education programmes. The Social Security Act of 1935 provided a form of unemployment benefit for individuals that lost their jobs.

The New Deal is often seen as a Keynesian response to the Great Depression and is largely credited with restoring employment in the US economy in the 1930s. However, Monetarists would argue that the primary cause of the Great Depression was the dramatic fall in the amount of money circulating in the economy following the collapse of banks. This caused deflationary pressures, which stopped real wages, effectively adjusting to reduce the rate of unemployment in the economy.

Questions

1. Why did many people in the US lose their savings?
2. What impact did a loss of savings have?
3. Use a Keynesian LRAS curve to show the likely equilibrium position of the US economy in 1933.
4. Use a Monetarist LRAS curve to show the likely equilibrium position of the US economy in 1933. *Then show* how Monetarists would *have expected* the economy to adjust.

5. Use a Keynesian LRAS graph to show how the New Deal would have impacted macroeconomic equilibrium in the US economy.
6. Why would the New Deal have been considered a Keynesian response to the Great Depression as opposed to a Monetarist response?
7. Which economic school of thought do you believe best explains the position of the US economy during the Great Depression? Justify your answer.

The case study in Box 9.7 will require careful reading with students. It is likely that some students may need further explanation of the process of a bank run or the idea of the money supply, which is more simply referred to as 'the amount of money circulating in the economy' within the case study.

Key takeaways

- Students need to be explicitly taught the assumptions of the Monetarist and Keynesian schools of thought with regard to long-run aggregate supply. Use concrete examples to make these assumptions as clear as possible
- Teach the two schools of thought separately and check students' understanding of them separately. Once understanding is secure, use a series of questions like those shown in Box 9.6 and the case study in Box 9.7 to test their understanding of the theories simultaneously.
- Use this as an opportunity to apply the theories to the real-world economics of the Great Depression. This is a great opportunity for students to see these arguments playing out in 'real-life' economics.

Note

1 I choose to leave out that full employment will also include frictionally employed workers. At this stage of the course, adding this in here tends to cause more confusion. This does, perhaps, lead to a slight simplification of some of the arguments, but I do not find that this simplification is a barrier to understanding. Finer detail can be added in later in the course when students' understanding is more secure.

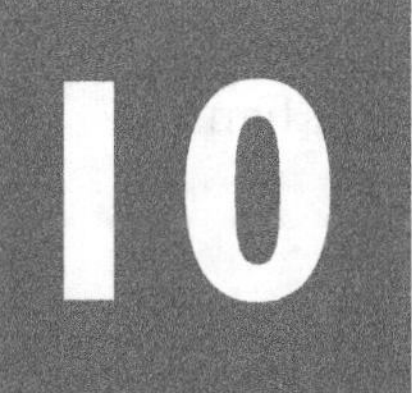

Monetary policy and quantitative easing

What's the big picture?

Monetary policy is one set of tools that policymakers use to achieve macroeconomic objectives. It refers to the actions by a central bank to manage the money supply and interest rates. While monetary policy grew in use following the Great Depression, it rose to prominence during periods of high inflation in the 1970s and the Monetarist's school's assertion that inflation was best controlled by controlling the money supply. The widespread use of quantitative easing in response to the financial crisis in 2008 and the Covid-19 pandemic put monetary policy further in the spotlight.

Monetary policy is typically overseen by the central bank. In the UK, the Bank of England has a hierarchical set of objectives. The primary objective is to maintain inflation at 2%. Its secondary objective is to support the objectives of the government and, specifically, its targets around growth and unemployment.[1]

Students need to understand that it is one of three main tools used by policymakers, alongside fiscal policy and supply-side policy. The latter two are controlled by the government. By the end of the course, students should have an in-depth understanding of government macroeconomic objectives and the ways in which the three main policy tools can interact and complement each other in order to achieve these objectives.

Why do students find this topic difficult?

Students need to understand the key aspects of monetary policy: interest rates, the money supply and control of exchange rates. In my experience, students tend to find interest rates accessible as they are familiar with the idea of receiving interest on savings, or paying 'a little extra' to the bank for any borrowed funds. Exchange rates are then typically visited in detail when students study international economics.

However, students tend to find the money supply and quantitative easing more difficult. To fully grasp quantitative easing, it is likely that students need a sound understanding of the following:

DOI: 10.4324/9781003724179-10

- The role of the central bank and its aims
- Commercial bank objectives and the relationship with the central bank
- The money supply, including narrow and broad money
- Financial securities, including bonds, bond prices and bond yields
- Inflation and its negative consequences
- Components of aggregate demand

Not only do students need to understand each of the earlier examples in isolation but they also need to understand the interrelationships between different aspects of the list earlier. Quantitative easing is, therefore, a highly technical concept and one that is likely to cause cognitive overload.

Explaining this concept

Mistakes to avoid

In an attempt to reduce cognitive load, it is tempting to simplify this topic significantly. As has been commented on in this book before, teaching an A-level necessitates that many concepts are simplified – strict adherence to academic fidelity at this stage of a students' career is likely to overwhelm. However, there is a risk of going too far. In an attempt to reduce cognitive overload, quantitative easing can become 'the central bank prints money to increase the amount of money in circulation'. Marking A-level papers, I have seen a number of instances where students conceptualise quantitative easing as this. We can avoid this, but we have to go through the topic slowly.

Explaining this concept

The following explanation is going to assume that interest rates have been taught and is going to jump straight in at quantitative easing.

We need to ensure that students have a firm understanding of the technical elements that make up quantitative easing before we introduce them to the concept itself. This means ensuring students understand the money supply and financial securities, like bonds. The explanation in this chapter as per the sequence in Figure 10.1.

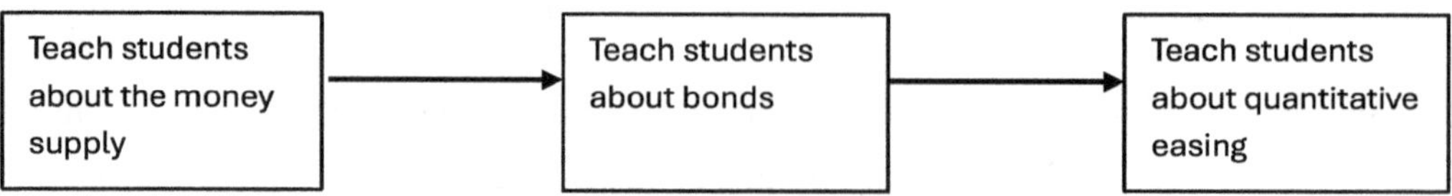

Figure 10.1 Sequence for teaching quantitative easing

In many schemes of work, an understanding of financial markets comes much later in the course. I appreciate the following sequence may, therefore, not necessarily fit with many curriculum maps. However, a specification provides a list of content that students need to be taught; it doesn't necessarily represent the best order in which to teach things. I would strongly recommend conversations around this sequencing and whether some of that content can be brought forward.

Section one – teaching students about the money supply

Students need to understand the money supply in an economy. Begin by introducing the idea that money can exist in different forms. As ever, I recommend live drawing parts of this explanation as you go along.

> *There are lots of different ways you can hold money: you could have it as physical cash, you might hold it in a current account that is connected to your debit card, you might have it in a long-term savings account like an ISA or you may own a government bond. We are going to look at government bonds in a little bit more detail later.*
>
> *Now, the key thing here is that all of these forms of money differ in how easily we can convert them as cash to use for the purchase of goods and services. We could place these forms of money on a spectrum about how easily they are converted to cash. Of course, at one end of the spectrum we have physical cash itself, which by definition is the easiest thing to convert into cash! This is shown in* Figure 10.2.
>
> *The money that we hold in a current account is also very easily convertible into cash. You can use your debit card to withdraw physical cash from an ATM, or you can use your debit card in a shop and cash will be taken from your account and credited to the account of the shop owner. As a result, money in current accounts is very closely to cash in terms of liquidity. This is shown in* Figure 10.3.

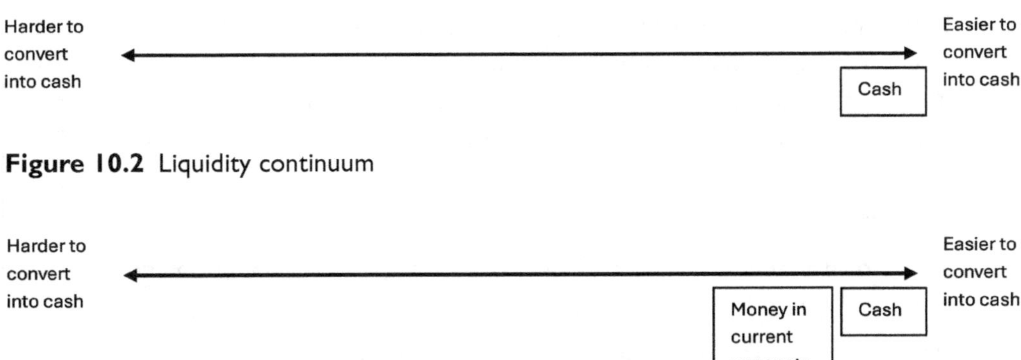

Figure 10.2 Liquidity continuum

Figure 10.3 Liquidity continuum continued

You can continue this explanation, adding in other forms of money that students may need to know for their specification. This may include savings accounts, money market funds or government bonds. You can add these to your spectrum and then use this to define the ideas of narrow money and broad money.

> *So, we can see we have many different forms of money that vary in the ease with which they can be converted into cash. We can refer to all these types of money as 'broad money', which is the total supply of money within the whole economy. In contrast, some of our forms of money that are most easily convertible to cash we refer to as 'narrow money'. We can see this on our continuum below [Figure 10.4]*

End this example by explaining the term 'liquidity' and explaining that an asset that is easy to convert into cash would be described as 'more liquid' and vice versa.

Then introduce students to the importance of measuring the money supply using a small example with some think-pair-share questions. This might look something like the scenario in Box 10.1.

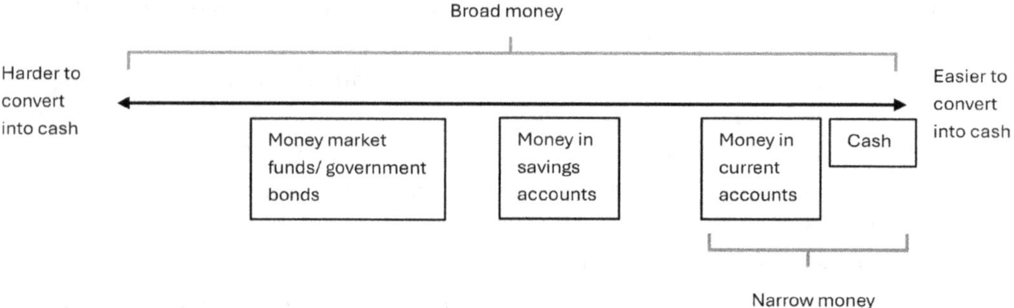

Figure 10.4 Liquidity continuum three

BOX 10.1 SCENARIO ON MONEY SUPPLY

Scenario

Imagine a country where the percentage of the total money supply in the economy that was held as narrow money was typically around 75%.

The Central Bank noticed that consumer confidence in the economy started to fall. As a result, the percentage of the total money supply that was held as narrow money reduced to 68%.

Questions

1. Why would a reduction in economic confidence result in the amount of money held as narrow money falling?
2. Why would the central bank be concerned about this?
3. What policy response may a central bank use in this situation?

The task in Box 10.1 is effective as a think-pair-share, as students should be at a stage where they can link an increase in savings to a fall in aggregate demand and recognise that a central bank would typically respond by reducing interest rates. This last point is particularly important to emphasise, as it will be revisited when students explore the reasons that quantitative easing was required as a policy during the financial crisis.

Finish the section by checking understanding with a few quick MWB questions on broad and narrow money. It is worth checking that students understand all forms of money fall under the category of 'broad money', but only the most liquid forms are 'narrow'. Check on this by giving students some forms of money and asking them to categorise them.

Section two – teaching students about bonds

Students will now be ready to move on to a specific form of financial asset: government bonds. The mechanics of government bonds are tricky to understand. I remember struggling as an undergraduate student trying to get my head around bond prices and inverse relationships with yields! As ever, we need to take students through this slowly and explicitly:

> *Let's imagine the government was looking to build a new railway line. However, they do not have enough money from tax revenue to build this railway. As a result, the government is going to need to borrow some money. How does a government actually do this? Well, they borrow it and promise to pay it back – just like any form of borrowing.*
>
> *The way that a government does this is by issuing a government bonds. Anyone can purchase one of these government bonds and essentially lend some money to the government.*
>
> *So, for example, Leila you may choose that you want to lend the government £100 and the government agree to pay you this back in 10 years' time. You would be issued with a bond certificate that might look a little bit like the one in Figure 10.5 (perhaps this is a slight over-simplification!):*
>
> *We can see that the bond is worth £100 and that the bond is going to 'mature' in October 2025 – this is essentially when the government agrees to pay Leila back.*
>
> *Now, is Leila going to lend the government £100 out of the goodness of her heart? Leila might be very nice, but she is probably going to want something in return for lending them £100. Leila is going to want a little bit of 'interest' each year as an incentive to lend the money. For example, maybe she would like a payment of £5 each year in order to part with her £100 for 10 years. When we are discussing bonds, we refer to this amount as the 'coupon' of the bond. This coupon amount is fixed for the duration of the issuance of the bond [Figure 10.6].*

Figure 10.5 Government bond certificate drawing one

Figure 10.6 Government bond certificate drawing two

Stop here and run a quick check for understanding on some of the key terms that have been introduced. You might ask some MWB questions that check the following:

- Students understand why a government issues bonds and that it represents government borrowing.

- Students understand what the 'maturity' of a bond means.
- Students understand what the 'coupon' of a bond means.

It is important to check understanding here before moving on to yields, which is the part that students find most difficult. Ensure students are confident on the foundations before we introduce the confusing bit!

It's really important we follow the next part of this explanation because this is where students sometimes get confused!

An important metric that is tracked is the proportion of the price of the bond that the coupon represents. So, in our example, the coupon is equal to £5 and the bond is priced at £100. This means that the coupon represents 5% of the price of the bond. We have calculated this by using the following formula:

$$\frac{Coupon\,amount}{Price\,of\,bond} \times 100$$

This is something that is tracked because this tells the investor their return on the bond. If they 'give up' £100 by lending to the government, the £5 is the reward they receive each year for doing so. So we convert this to a percentage and see this is the percentage reward the investor receives. We refer to this as the 'yield' on the bond.

Pause and use some very simple calculation questions to check students understand how to use this formula. You could use a question such as the one in Box 10.2.

BOX 10.2 BOND CALCULATION QUESTION

Question

Government A sells a bond for $500 with an annual coupon of $30. Government B sells a bond for $200 with an annual coupon of $8.

1. Which bond offers the highest yield?
2. Which bond would provide the greater returns to investors?
3. If the bond sold by Government B matured in five years, what would the total value of coupon payments be over the term of the bond?

After using the question in Box 10.2, you may wish to highlight to students that bonds are typically sold at par values of $100 or $1,000. However, the yield on these bonds will often be obvious and will defeat the purpose of checking students' understanding of the formula.

Then carry on with your explanation:

Right, here comes the tricky part! So far we have assumed that Leila was purchasing her bond and keeping it until maturity. However, individuals often sell their bonds again to other investors before the maturity date. This sale takes place on something called the 'secondary market'.

The key thing is that the ***price of the bond can change but the coupon amount will stay the same****. Let's have a think about that: imagine there is a huge increase in demand for government bond like the one that Leila owns on the secondary market. We can use our basic supply and demand analysis to see that this is going to increase the price of the bond in Figure 10.7.*

Leila's ***bond has increased in price from £100 to £110. However, as we have said, the coupon on the bond is going to stay at £5.*** *We can think about what this might do to the yield on the bond:*

$$\textit{Original yield} = \frac{\pounds 5}{\pounds 100} \times 100 = 5\%$$

$$\textit{New yield} = \frac{\pounds 5}{\pounds 110} \times 100 = 4.5\%$$

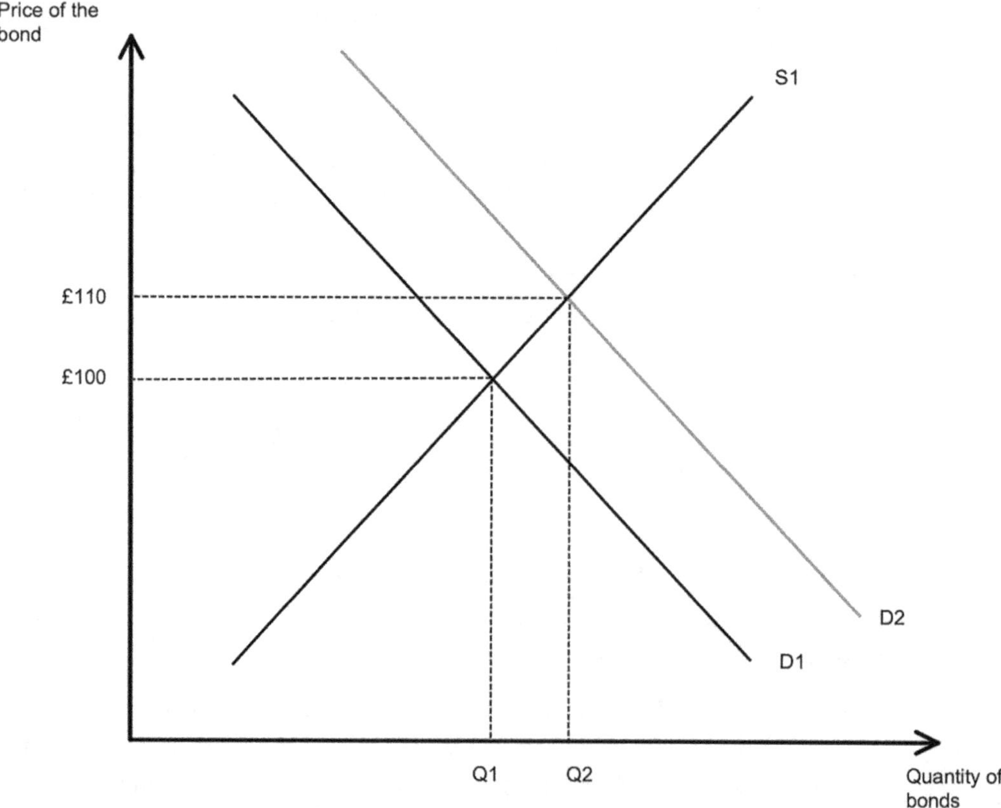

Figure 10.7 Supply and demand of government bonds

Interesting! ***We can see that the price of the bond has gone up but the coupon amount has stayed the same, which has resulted in the yield falling****. This tells us that anyone purchasing the bond now gets a slightly smaller return than Leila did when she initially brought her bond.*

Let's look at one more example. Imagine the same set of issued bonds now experience a large decrease in demand. As a result, demand for the bond shifts inwards and the price of the bond falls to £90. Ian, what do we know the coupon on the bond is still going to be?

Excellent – the coupon amount stays at £5. Estelle, how can we calculate the yield on the bond?

Perfect, we are going to divide the coupon by the price of the bond:

$$\text{New yield} = \frac{£5}{£90} \times 100 = 5.5\%$$

So we can see here that the price of the bond has gone down but because the coupon has stayed the same, the yield on the bond increases. An investor who buys the bond on the secondary market now is getting a slightly larger return than Leila did when she initially brought her bond.

These two examples demonstrate a really important relationship: the price of a bond and the yield on the bond move in opposite directions. If the price of the bond increases, the yield decreases. If the price of the bond decreases, the yield increases.

Make this relationship really clear with your live drawing. This may be as simple as drawing ↑ ***Bond price*** =↓ ***bond yield*** and vice versa on the board.

Now give students an opportunity to practice to see this relationship repeatedly. You could use something like the worksheet in Box 10.3.

Questions 3d and 3e in Box 10.3 are designed to demonstrate to students that the coupon payment will stay the same regardless of the change in price and yield of the bond. The coupon payment remains fixed at £5 and so generates an income of £25 both before and after the sale.

You want students thinking to be directed to the relationship between bond prices and yields on this task. As such, it is beneficial to give them the formula for calculating bond yields on the task. This means that students' working memory is not directed to remembering the formula, which may still not be fully secure in their minds. Instead, they are directing their efforts towards understanding the relationship.

You may feel that your students need slightly more practice of questions like one and two, which are the more simple examples. A minimum of two of these questions is required, as they demonstrate both increasing and decreasing prices of bonds and the different implications that this has for yields.

BOX 10.3 GOVERNMENT BOND TASK

Government bonds – task

Formula for calculating the yield on a bond: $\frac{\text{Coupon}}{\text{Price of bond}} \times 100$

1. A bond is initially sold for £100 with a coupon of £6. On the secondary market, the bond then sells for £108.
   a. What is the initial yield on the bond?
   b. What is the yield on the bond when it is sold on the secondary market?
   c. What do you notice about the relationship between the price and yield of the bond?
2. A bond is initially sold for £100 with a coupon of £4. On the secondary market, the bond then sells for £92.
   a. What is the initial yield on the bond?
   b. What is the yield on the bond when it is sold on the secondary market?
   c. What do you notice about the relationship the price and yield of the bond?
3. A bond is initially sold for £100 with a coupon of £5. The bond matures in ten years. After five years, the bond sells on the secondary market for £112.
   a. What is the change in the yield of the bond between issuance and its sale on the secondary market?
   b. When do investors gain a greater return on their investment – when the bond was initially issued or once it has been sold on the secondary market?
   c. Why would the price of the bond have increased?
   d. What is the total value of coupon payments made prior to the bond being sold?
   e. What is the total value of coupon payments made after the bond is sold on the secondary market until maturity?

Using your own example, explain why there is an inverse relationship between the price of a bond and its yield.

The final section of this section is to make the link between bond yields and interest rates:

> *We know from previous lessons that the central bank in a country is responsible for setting the interest rate. The central bank makes a change to their 'base rate', which then filters through the financial system. We tend to think of this as being the 'short-term interest rate'. It is the interest rate being set by the central bank based on current conditions in the economy.*

We also need to consider something called the 'long-term interest rate'.

Let's imagine that Ridhima is thinking about investing in a 10-year government bond priced at £100 with a coupon rate of 5%. Let's assume she intends to hold on to that bond until maturity. The key question for Ridhima is: is it worth me giving up £100 now to receive £5 a year for the next 10 years? This is her 'reward for saving'.

Ridhima is going to be weighing up her expectations of the long-term economic conditions of the country in which she is purchasing the bond. Is the economy going to grow? Is this government's debt levels going to increase significantly in the future? Will there be inflation in this economy in the future? Am I better off putting the money into the shares of a company?

Essentially, Ridhima is thinking about her long-term reward for saving. As such, we can think of the coupon rate on the bond as a 'long-term interest rate'. That also means that when the demand changes for the bond, the yield on the bond is going to change and our expectations of the long-term interest rate shifts.

This demonstrates to us a really important concept: the yield on a government bond can be thought of as representing a long-term interest rate. It represents the reward for saving and cost of borrowing expectations of individuals within an economy.

The earlier explanation is lengthy and needs to be accompanied with a visual aid on the board or visualiser to demonstrate the decision facing Ridhima. Notice also that this explanation is not interrupted with cold-call questions for students. I have avoided it earlier because the content demands are heavy. In scenarios where technical detail is important, it's often important to avoid breaking the narrative flow of an explanation, which can distract students away from key details. Finish this section by checking students understand the causal link shown in Figure 10.8.

This can be achieved through some simple MWB questions. I would recommend asking enough questions to the point that it feels 'over-learnt' and then reinforced with homework activities that ensures students are extremely confident in this link.

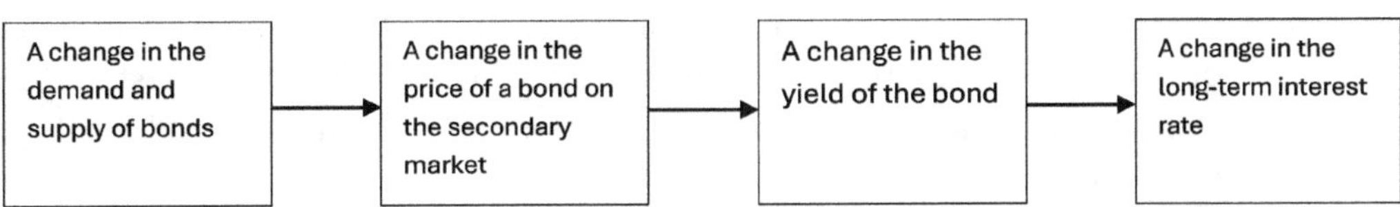

Figure 10.8 Causal link

Section three – teaching students about quantitative easing

The two sections earlier dedicate more time to the teaching of the money supply and government bonds than I would have used for much of my teaching career. I have found that the time and investment in these concepts speeds up the teaching of quantitative easing while simultaneously ensuring students have a deeper understanding of quantitative easing. The focus on these areas means that the example used to teach students about quantitative easing can be somewhat shorter.

Start this sequence by checking students' understanding of interest rates, the money supply and government bonds. Then try an explanation such as the following:

> *Imagine a scenario where economic confidence is extremely low – perhaps the economy is in a deep recession. Jonny, what we expect the central bank's base rate to be at such a point?*
>
> *Exactly, the base rate may be close to 0 – let's imagine it is 0.25%. This is to try to encourage borrowing and reduce saving, which would then increase aggregate demand.*
>
> *However, we've just said that the economy is in a deep recession and confidence is extremely low. So, despite such a low base rate of interest, consumption and investment are still extremely low. This is keeping aggregate demand in the economy low. What can you do if you are a central bank in this situation?*
>
> *Well, the central bank does have one quite unique tool available to them to try to stimulate aggregate demand a little more. Remember, the central bank of a country has the power to create money. So, a central bank could create some additional money and use that money to buy financial securities, like government bonds, from lots of financial companies, such as commercial banks.*
>
> *This is going to increase the demand for government bonds, which we now know will result in a decrease in the yields of those bonds. This reduces the long-term interest rate in our economy and, as a result, should mean that there is less money held in less liquid assets such as government bonds. Instead, more of the money supply will be held as 'narrow money' or 'liquid money'. This should help stimulate investment and consumption!*

Bring this example together to show that this action by the central bank is likely to stimulate aggregate demand in the economy at a time when short-term interest rates are not effective. Use some MWB questions to check students' understanding of this mechanism and then finish the sequence by giving students the definition of quantitative easing.

Then show students the real-world application of quantitative easing through the case study in Box 10.4. I find the case study is an effective way of consolidating

BOX 10.4 CASE STUDY ON QUANTITATIVE EASING

Case study

Prior to 2007, commercial banks and investment banks had been extremely 'bullish' about the strength of the global economy. As a result, many commercial banks had provided mortgages and loans to individuals who may not have had the credit rating to receive those loans at other periods in history. The commercial banks then sold these mortgage products on to investment banks in the form of complex financial products, known as 'collateralised debt obligations' or CDOs.

At the beginning of 2007, many economists and financial analysts started to warn that these CDOs were risky, and many were not worth the amount that investment banks had paid for them. Over the course of 2007 and 2008, some of the largest financial institutions in the world reported significant financial issues as a result of holding a significant amount of these CDOs. This led to the collapse of one of the world's largest banks, the Lehman Brothers, in September 2008. Before the collapse of the Lehman Brothers, other large banks had to be financially rescued by the governments of both the US and UK.

This 'credit crisis' led to a severe slowdown in the global economy, with many warning that the financial crisis could cause the largest recession since the Great Depression of the 1930s. In response, central banks across the globe reduced their interest rates. For example, the Bank of England reduced interest rates from 5.25% in 2007 to 0.5% by March 2009.

However, in many instances, this reduction of interest rates had little impact. In the US, UK and Eurozone aggregate demand was persistently weak, and economists still warned that the impact of the recession could be worse than that experienced in the 1930s. Consumer and business confidence was so low that even historically low interest rates were not sufficient to stimulate aggregate demand.

Central Banks needed a different mechanism to try to stimulate growth. In response, they turned to quantitative easing. Quantitative easing is a process by which the central bank uses newly created money to purchase financial securities, such as government bonds, from financial institutions in order to increase the liquidity of the financial system.

While the impacts of the financial crisis were still severe, many economists credit the use of quantitative easing with saving the global economy from the depth of impact of the Great Depression. These economists suggest that the increased liquidity within the financial system gave commercial banks more confidence to provide loans which then stimulated consumption and investment. Further, quantitative easing reduced on long-term interest rates, which also helped to stimulate aggregate demand in the economy.

However, this does not mean that the verdict on quantitative easing is clear. Many economists worry that significant increases to the money supply leads to inflationary pressure. This is because the increased supply of money reduces the value of that money. While this was not a significant issue during the financial crisis, some economists have said that excessive use of quantitative easing outside of deep recessions has led to prices being higher in the economy. For example, some have argued that the use of quantitative easing after the Covid-19 pandemic was one of the causes of the high levels of inflation witnessed during 2022 and 2023.

Questions

1. What was the *intended* impact of the Bank of England's reduction in interest rates from 5.25% to 0.5%?
2. Why did this reduction in interest rates *not* have the impact intended?
3. What kind of unemployment were economies likely to be experiencing at this time?
4. Why did quantitative easing stimulate aggregate demand in several economies?
5. Draw a Keynesian AD/LRAS diagram to show the following:
   a. The likely macroeconomic position of economies before quantitative easing
   b. The likely macroeconomic position of economies after quantitative easing
6. With reference to your diagrams, explain why the inflationary pressures of quantitative easing during the financial crisis were not as severe.
7. Why would quantitative easing lead to inflationary pressure outside of deep recessionary periods?

students' understanding of the concept and introducing the possible negative impacts of quantitative easing. The case study is one that I tend to go through slowly with students and often pause after the second paragraph to make sure students have a sufficient (although too much depth isn't required!) of CDOs. This is a nice opportunity to bring this topic to life by showing pictures of investment bankers at Lehman Brothers clearing their desks or pictures of Barack Obama and Timothy Geithner looking rather serious.

The set of questions in Box 10.4 are useful for helping students to draw links between different areas of content that they would have studied. For example, they can make links between quantitative easing, inflationary pressure and the shape of the Keynesian long-run aggregate supply curve.

Notes on elements left out

The explanations provided earlier do not make reference to the impact of quantitative easing on the wealth effect or the value of a country's currency. For many specifications, these are important aspects of teaching the topic. These should not be ignored, but they add significant complexity to the topic, and as such, I would teach them as part of a separate follow-up lesson.

Key takeaways

The key takeaways of this chapter are as follows:

- The concept of quantitative easing relies on the understanding of other technical concepts, such as the money supply and government bonds. Invest the time in teaching these concepts first and in detail; a sound understanding of these is likely to significantly reduce the cognitive load when teaching quantitative easing.
- This topic requires significant chunking of explanations, interspersed with regular checks for understanding. Plan these carefully, and don't move on until you are confident students have a secure understanding of each 'chunk'.
- Let the financial crisis do the heavy lifting for you with regards to quantitative easing. It's a greater example of real-world economics that really helps to consolidate the concept.

Note

1 The US Federal Reserve also has a dual mandate, but it is not hierarchical. The US Federal Reserve's dual mandate places equal weighting on maintaining price stability and low unemployment. Students in the UK do not need to know this, but it can make for interesting discussion.

11 Inflation and price stability

What's the big idea?

Inflation represents a decrease in the purchasing power of money. Steady, creeping inflation often signals that an economy is growing sustainably over time as a result of increases in demand. However, unpredictable or high levels of inflation will erode real incomes and push up the cost of living for citizens within an economy. Inflation can also erode the value of individual's wealth and punish lenders over borrowers.

Despite the negative effects of increasing prices, it's important students recognise that falling prices may also be a bad thing. Persistent deflation can lead to a deflationary spiral and a fall in asset values, which also makes everyone worse off.

Ultimately, students need to recognise that whether inflation is 'good' or 'bad' is going to depend on the cause and magnitude of changes in the price level.

Inflation is a key concept that underpins a strong understanding across a range of topics. For example, students need to recognise the impact of inflation when differentiating between real and nominal figures. It is, therefore, important not to treat inflation as an isolated topic. Instead, teachers need to explicitly model how to adjust for inflation when analysing data sets, ensuring students build the habit of questioning whether the figures they are looking at represent a genuine increase in volume or merely a change in the price level.

Why do students find this topic difficult?

Inflation seems simple enough to understand initially. Students grasp the idea that inflation represents an increase in the general price level with relative ease. However, the effects of inflation can often seem invisible. It is difficult to 'see' a slowly creeping increasing in price levels that may erode real incomes and wealth. Inflation is difficult because of the following:

- Students need to consider its impact on 'real' values, which can feel abstract if not grounded in concrete examples.

DOI: 10.4324/9781003724179-11

- The concept of weights when measuring inflation is also understood at a superficial level, rather than an understanding of its importance within a measure of the cost of living.
- Students find it difficult to discern between inflation, disinflation and deflation. This is because many students fail to understand the difference between an absolute decrease and a decreasing rate.

Explaining this concept

Mistakes to avoid

The amount of content required to teach can sometimes lead to inflation being rushed as a topic. Avoid this. As outlined in the 'Big picture' section, an understanding of inflation is so important to understanding broad macroeconomic trends.

It is also easy to assume that concepts like 'real incomes' are easy for students to conceptualise. Remember that students aren't earning an income yet and don't need to do a weekly grocery shop. As such, they don't always experience the impacts of inflation on their purchasing power in the same way that we do as adults.

Finally, don't make the same mistake that I did and rush over the teaching of weights because it seems like a small point on the specification list. This is an important component when considering inflation as a measure of changes in household's costs of living. Make sure you give it the appropriate time.

Explaining this concept

Inflation is one of the larger topics in many specifications. A complete sequence for teaching all the content listed in specification documents is outside the scope of this book. Instead, this section will focus on addressing the misunderstandings or misconceptions identified earlier:

1. The impact of inflation on purchasing power and 'real values'
2. The concepts of weights when measuring inflation
3. Inflation, disinflation and deflation

Please note that this may not, therefore, demonstrate a completely linear sequence. For example, you may wish reorder this sequence and introduce students to disinflation and deflation before point 1 earlier. Similarly, you may decide to teach students about the limitations of inflation measuring in between points 2 and 3.

Section one – the impact of inflation on real values

An understanding of 'real' and 'nominal' values is fundamental to the understanding of inflation. Begin your explanation of explaining what inflation is. I usually begin by showing an extreme example, such as the change in the price of a Mars bar over the past 30 years. I then provide an example of a change in the price of a good over the past year to demonstrate that inflation doesn't have to be a long-term phenomenon.

I often find this doesn't take too long, and most students grasp the idea fairly quickly. We then need to think about the impact on individuals' purchasing power. This is where we need to spend a little more time. Start with the explanation in Box 11.1.

The explanation in Box 11.1 gives students an example of how inflation reduces purchasing power *when income doesn't* change. Students tend to find this fairly easy to understand. However, we then need to run through this idea with changing nominal incomes. The following explanation shows this:

> *Now, let's go back to scenario 2, where the price of Will's basket had gone up by 20% and so now costs £120. Let's imagine that this time Will's income has increased from £100 to £105. This is great for Will – his income has gone up!*
>
> *But has his income **really** increased? Not in terms of what it can purchase him! Even though Will has had an increase in his income, he still can't afford the same basket of goods that he did last year.*

Students should now be familiar with the idea of inflation reducing the purchasing power of incomes. They now need to see how this is calculated in percentage terms:

> *Now we tend to see changes in wages and price levels represented as percentages. We are going to introduce a formula for calculating this.*
>
> *In the last example, we saw that Will's income had increased by 5% from £100 to £105. At the same time, prices had increased by 20%. We therefore want to work out what has happened to Will's purchasing power.*
>
> *We are going to use index numbers to help us calculate this. Remember, an index number is a value that measures the change in a variable compared to a base period, which we always set to 100. So, if Will's income has increased by 5% then we represent this as 105. Price levels have gone up by 20% so we represent this as 120. This is showing us the **change** in these variables in comparison to a base year. Now, to compare the changes in these variables we are going to do the following sum:*
>
> $$\frac{105}{120} \times 100 = 87.5$$
>
> *This tells us that after the changes in income and price levels, Will's income now only represents 87.5% of the basket of goods he wants to buy. Will's purchasing power has fallen by 12.5%.*

BOX 11.1 INFLATION EXPLANATION

Step one

Figure 11.1 Inflation

Will earns £100 a month. Now, let's imagine Will spends all of that money on a basket of goods and services. The basket of goods will contain lots of things: maybe some bread, pasta, milk, his transport to and from work.

Step two

Figure 11.2 Inflation when nominal incomes do not increase at the same rate

Let's fast-forward a year. Will hasn't had a pay rise and so is still earning £100 a month. However, there has been some inflation in the economy. On average, prices have gone up by 20%. As a result, that basket of goods that used to cost Will £100 now costs him £120.

This is going to cause Will a bit of a problem! His income no longer affords him the same basket of goods that he bought last year. Will is going to have to buy a little bit less – maybe he is going to have to buy less pasta or start finding alternative transport methods to get to work. This demonstrates to us a real important impact of inflation: it reduces the quantity of products that can be purchased in comparison to the year before. This therefore impacts individual's standard of living.

Then present the students with multiple examples in the form of MWB questions. These need to expose students to a variety of changes:

- A question where the increase in nominal income is less than the increase in inflation (e.g. income rises by 4% and prices by 6%)
- A question where the increase in nominal income is greater than the increase in inflation (e.g. income rises by 4% and prices by 2%)
- A question where the increase in nominal income and inflation is the same
- A question where nominal income is increasing but inflation is decreasing
- A question where nominal income is decreasing and inflation is decreasing by a greater amount

Students need a variety of these questions to show them the various relationships between nominal and real values. I would finish the sequence off with a MWB question like the one shown in Box 11.2.

BOX 11.2 MWB CHECK FOR UNDERSTANDING

MWB question

An individual's nominal income increases by more than the inflation rate. Which of the following statements is correct? There may be more than one correct answer.

A. The change in the individual's real income is negative.

B. The change in the individual's real income is positive.

C. The inflation rate must be negative.

D. The individual's purchasing power has increased.

E. The individual's purchasing power has decreased.

F. The individual's real purchasing power has increased by less than their nominal purchasing power.

Answers B, D and F are correct.

Answer A and B checks whether a student understands that real incomes increase when a nominal change in income is greater than the price change.

Answer C checks that a student does not confuse an increase in real incomes with a negative inflation rate.

Answers D and E check whether a student understands the relationship between real income changes and purchasing power.

Finally, answer F differentiates to check whether a student understands that although real purchasing power has increased, a positive inflation rate means that this real change will always be less than the nominal change.

Section two – weights and the cost of living

An understanding of weights in inflation measurement is important to understand changes in household's cost of living. Students find this difficult and can often struggle to see why it is important to use a weighting when calculating the inflation rate of a basket of goods. The example shown in Box 11.3 is an extreme and unrealistic example. However, in my experience, students need to see this extreme example to understand the point being made and to show the difference between a simple average and a weighted average. Once this example is done, Box 11.4 provides a more realistic example that will help students think about this more accurately. However, begin your explanation with my Box 11.3.

My first question is this, which change in price do we think Jack cares most about?

Get students to think-pair-share this question. After 30 seconds of conversation, most pairs will have come to a decision that Jack will care more about the change in the price of pasta because he is buying this more frequently and spending more money on this product.

> *Now remember one reason we measure inflation is to track the change in the cost of living. We therefore need to think about what the inflation rate is for Jack. Let's take a simple average: the price of pasta has gone up by 50% and the price of ironing boards by 2%. To take a simple average we would divide the total by 2, which would give us 26%.*
>
> *Does this feel right? Does it feel right that Jack is experiencing a 26% increase in his cost of living?*

Notice the specific wording in this question: Is Jack *experiencing* a 26% increase in his *cost of living?* We are trying to highlight here to students that one of the most important impacts of inflation is the experience of households when they are purchasing goods and services that they need. Again, I would ask students to think-pair-share this question. Hopefully, most recognise that 26% seems a little bit low.

> *To more accurately represent the change in Jack's cost of living, we need to take a weighted average of the price changes. Now, I am going to do this approximately and we'll then look at a more precise version in a moment. In Year 2, Jack has spent a total of £98.40 – £78 on pasta and £20.40 on an ironing board. I am therefore going to say that Jack has spent 80% of his total spending on pasta, and 20% on ironing boards.*
>
> *To calculate a weighted average, I am going to multiply each price change by the proportion of total spending:*

$$50\% \times 0.8 = 40\%$$

$$2\% \times 0.2 = 0.4\%$$

BOX 11.3 WEIGHTING IN THE BASKET OF GOODS

PASTA
PRICE = £1
QUANTITY = 52
TOTAL EXPENDITURE : £52
IRONING BOARD
PRICE = £20
QUANTITY = 1
TOTAL EXPENDITURE : £20

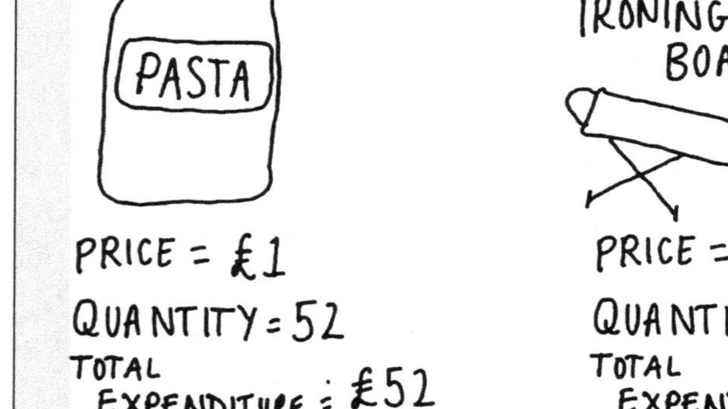

Figure 11.3 Inflation weighting

I'm in charge of an economy that Jack lives in. In the first year, Jack only bought two things: pasta and an ironing board. Jack bought 52 packs of pasta in the year at £1 per pack. So Jack's overall spend on pasta is £52.

The other product Jack bought was one fairly cheap, table-top ironing board at a price of £20.

ONE YEAR LATER...
PASTA
PRICE = £1.50
QUANTITY = 52
TOTAL EXPENDITURE : £78
IRONING BOARD
PRICE = £20.40
QUANTITY = 1
TOTAL EXPENDITURE : £20.40

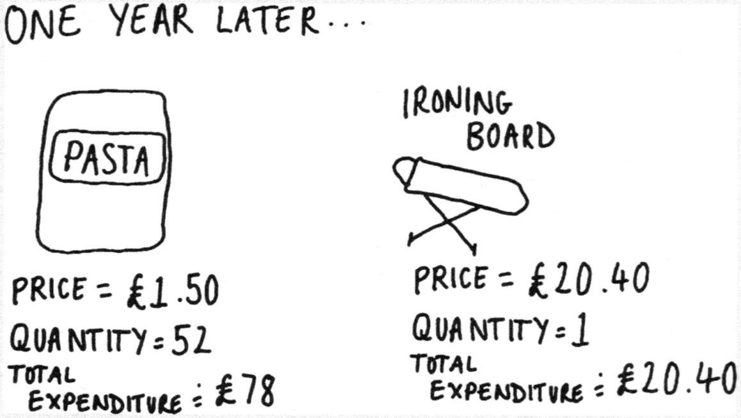

Figure 11.4 Inflation weighting

Now we fast-forward a year and Jack still purchases one pack of pasta a week. We are going to make a bit of an assumption for now that Jack can't substitute this pasta out and purchase another product, like rice.

Unfortunately his ironing board broke and so he needs to buy a new one. Jack is interested in measuring the change in price of these items over time and how much more he is going to have to pay for the pasta and ironing board this year.

The price of pasta has gone up by 50% to £1.50 a pack. This means Jack now spends £78 each year on pasta.

The price of ironing boards has only gone up by 2% to £20.40.

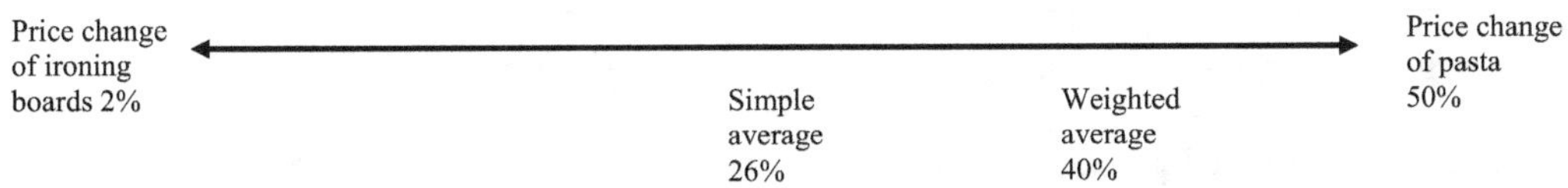

Figure 11.5 Continuum for showing the difference between simple and weighted averages

I am then going to add these answers together to give me my total weighted average, which is equal to 40.4%.

What do we notice about this weighted average compared to our simple average? It is much much closer to the price change of pasta, which is what Jack is buying far more frequently. This is therefore a much better representation of change in cost of living that Jack is experiencing.

Help students visualise this with a continuum, like the one shown in Figure 11.1. The continuum is a really excellent visual to help students see how the weighted average moves the reported inflation rate closer to the price change of pasta (Figure 11.5).

Give the students another example, possibly one in which there is a product which is not purchased regularly with a high inflation rate and a product that is bought very regularly with a low inflation rate. Again, emphasise the difference in the simple average and the weighted average and why the weighted average shows a much more accurate reflection of the change in the cost of living for an individual.

Highlight that so far, you have explained the process with a very simple two-good basket. Explain to students that inflation is measured this way using a basket of goods that contains hundreds of different products that are categorised to represent the key areas of household spending. Once this has been explained and you have used a few MWB comprehension questions, give students a task like the one shown in Box 11.4.

The task in Box 11.4 is a simple case study, but it is important to show them a 'more real-world' example of inflation measuring. Up until this point, we have been using fairly unrealistic examples that are designed to introduce a concept. The task in Box 11.4 is then designed to consolidate and deepen understanding. It brings out a large number of questions that can be used to test students' understanding of weights and to help them make links between their previous learning on nominal and real rates. The questions are designed to ensure students can differentiate between a simple (3.6%) and weighted average (2.9%) and recognise why there is the difference.

Question 8 is designed to test students' ability to manipulate the data. Inflation may increase further because a product with a fairly significant price change (leisure) is going to make up a more significant proportion of household spending. However, students would need to know the size of the decrease in household

BOX 11.4 TASK ON THE BASKET OF GOODS

Task – Basket of goods weighting

Economists in a country have been measuring changes in the price level to assess changes in citizens' cost of living. An overview of some of their findings is shown in Table 11.1a

Table 11.1 Inflation weighting

Product category	Proportion of household expenditure	Price change of category
Food and beverages	18%	4.8%
Clothing and footwear	12%	4.2%
Housing	26%	0.8%
Transport	22%	1.2%
Leisure	16%	4.4%
Other	6%	6.2%

The economists have also been monitoring the change in household income over the past year. On average, nominal incomes across the country have risen by 2.6%.

Economists are expected the proportion of household income spent on housing costs to fall next year because of a decrease in the price of gas and electricity bills. It is expected that this reduction in bills along with other economic factors will lead to an increase in household confidence over the course of the next year. Based on survey data and historical trends, economists are confident that this is likely to lead to an increase in the proportion of household income spent on leisure.

Questions

1. Which category of products/services do households in this economy devote most of their expenditure towards?
2. Which category of products/services has experienced the largest change in price over the past year?
3. Using the information provided in the table, calculate a *simple average* inflation rate for this economy.
4. Using the information provided in the table, calculate a *weighted average* inflation rate for this economy.
5. Why is there a difference between the weighted average inflation rate and the un-weighted average?
6. Which product category caused the most significant change in the price level of this economy?

7. Based on the information provided, what has been the overall change in purchasing power within the economy?
8. Read the last paragraph regarding economists' predictions for the upcoming year. Excluding housing, assume all price changes stay the same but the weighting of household expenditure changes according to the case study:
    a. How would you expect the inflation rate to change in the following year? Explain your answer.
    b. Assume nominal incomes increase by 4.5%. How would these changes impact the purchasing power of individuals within this economy?
    c. Do you think the answers to question A and B are certain? What more information would you need to answer this question more confidently?

spending on housing and the corresponding increase in leisure spending. This question is designed for students to recognise uncertainty in economic predictions.

Section three – inflation, disinflation and deflation

Students get confused when distinguishing by an increasing rate of inflation, a decreasing rate of inflation and a negative rate of inflation. The use of explicit examples helps students to master this distinction quite quickly. As with previous content, exposure to multiple examples is vital to secure understanding.

Start by distinguishing between inflation and disinflation as per the two examples in Box 11.5. Intersperse your explanations with cold-call questions to check students are following.

Practice this distinction a few times with some follow-up MWB questions. Avoid the temptation to move on to deflation as soon as you have finished the first example. Make sure that students have 'over-learnt' and practised the distinction between scenarios where there is and is not disinflation occurring. Notice also that the examples are slightly differentiated – disinflation occurs in Year two in the first example and in Year three in the second example. These are simple changes that ensure students are paying attention to the examples, rather than expecting a pattern.

Once this has been embedded, repeat similar examples with deflation introduced. One example is shown in Box 11.6.

As with disinflation, it is strongly recommended that students are provided with another example of deflation and then some MWB checks for understanding. Once some simple checks for understanding have been completed, use some of the questions in Box 11.7 to expose students to other questions on inflation, disinflation and deflation. Box 11.7 differentiates between an 'okay' example and a better example of a question to ask to check students' understanding.

BOX 11.5 INFLATION AND DISINFLATION EXPLANATION

	Step one – Year one	***Step two – Year two***	***Step three – Year three***
Example one	*The average price level increases from £100 to £110.* *This is a 10% increase in prices.* *This is* ***inflation.***	*The following year, average prices increase from £110 to £115. This is a 5% increase in prices.* *Are prices increasing?* *Yes – so we have* ***inflation.*** *What do we notice about the size of the increase? It is 5% this year compared to 10% the year before, so the rate of increase has slowed down. This is* ***disinflation****.*	*The following year, average prices increase from £115 to £124. This is an 8% increase in prices.* *Are prices increasing?* *Yes – so we have* ***inflation.*** *What do we notice about the size of the increase? It is 8% this year compared to 5% the year before, so the rate of increase has sped up. This is* ***not disinflation.***
Example two	*The average price level increases from £60 to £65. This is an 8% increase in prices.* *This is* ***inflation.***	*The following year, average prices increase from £65 to £72. This is an 11% increase in prices.* *This is* ***inflation.*** *The rate of increase has gone from 8% to 11%, so it is increasing. This is not* ***disinflation.***	*The following year, average prices increase from £72 to £74. This is a 3% increase in prices.* *Prices are increasing – this is* ***inflation.*** *However, the rate of change has slowed from 11% to 3%. This is* ***disinflation****.*

BOX 11.6 INFLATION, DISINFLATION AND DEFLATION

	Step one – Year one	***Step two – Year two***	***Step three – Year three***
Example one	*The average price level increases from £80 to £86.* *This is a 8% increase in prices.* *This is* ***inflation.***	*The following year, average prices increase from £86 to £88. This is a 2% increase in prices.* *We have* ***inflation and disinflation.***	*The following year, average prices decrease from £88 to £85. This is an 3% decrease in prices.* *Are prices increasing?* *No – the average price level has fallen. This is referred to as* ***deflation****.*

BOX 11.7 MODERATE VERSUS BETTER EXAMPLE OF FORMATIVE ASSESSMENT QUESTION

Assessment questions – moderate versus good question

Moderate example

1. The following table gives the price index of a country over four years. All values are compared to the base year (2021).

Year	Price index
2021	100
2022	98
2023	104
2024	105
2025	102

Which of the following statements is correct?

A. There was deflation in 2023.

B. There was deflation in 2022.

C. There was disinflation in 2023.

D. Inflation shows the increase in the general price level.

This is a moderate example because it does not truly reveal that students can distinguish between inflation, disinflation and deflation. The only correct answer is B, which is the most obvious example of deflation in the table because it is the only example below 100. The question does not require students to get into some of the more technical detail of index figures and how they represent the various forms of inflation.

A better example

1. The following table gives the price index of a country over four years. All values are compared to the base year (2021).

Year	Price index
2021	100
2022	98
2023	104
2024	105
2025	102

Which of the following statements is correct?

A. Prices in 2025 were higher in comparison to 2021 but lower than 2024.

B. Disinflation occurred between 2021 and 2022.

C. Prices in 2023 were higher than in 2022 but were probably still lower than 2021.

D. The only time deflation occurred was between 2021 and 2022.

E. Disinflation occurred between 2023 and 2024.

The correct answers are A and E.

As we have seen previously, including the possibility of multiple answers in a question ensures that students need to check all possible responses.

This question is also stronger than the previous example because answers reveal a deeper understanding of index numbers and types of inflation. For example, at a surface level, students will not recognise 2025 as a year of deflation and, therefore, may be inclined to answer D. This is because they see anything above 100 as inflation and do not check to understand the percentage change between each year. Prices in 2025 are nearly 3% lower than in 2024, although they are still higher than 2021. It would be important to follow up this question with some cold-call questions to ensure students understand *why* answer D is incorrect.

Answer B ensures students recognise the difference between disinflation and deflation, which was missing from the previous set of answers.

Some other good examples of questions that can be used to check students' understanding of types of inflation are shown in Box 11.8.

Bringing it all together

The case study in Box 11.9 should be used at the end of the overall teaching sequence. It should help students bring together their understanding of nominal and real rates, the measurement of inflation and types of inflation. It is a good case study to use, as it brings in other concepts that are important to the understanding of economics as a subject, such as the importance of underlying metrics as well as headline figures and the idea that economic forecasts are regularly being updated. This implicitly is building students' understanding of what it may mean to 'think like an economist'.

BOX 11.8 MWB CHECKS FOR UNDERSTANDING

Good examples of diagnostic questions

1. Table 11.2 later shows the year-on-year change in price levels within an economy and the average changes in nominal incomes.

Table 11.2 Changes in price and incomes

Year	Change in prices	Change in nominal incomes
2016	4.2%	4.4%
2017	2.1%	1.9%
2018	0.9%	1.3%
2019	−0.7%	0%

Which of the following statements is correct?

A. Disinflation occurred in both 2017 and 2018.

B. Deflation occurred in 2017, 2018 and 2019.

C. Prices were higher in 2018 than in 2016.

D. Real incomes increased in every year.

E. The greatest increase in real incomes occurred in 2018.

Answers A and C are correct.

Answer C is a great option that students often get confused about. Students see that the rate of inflation is decreasing and so have the misconception that prices must be decreasing. However, prices in 2018 are 0.9% higher than 2017, where prices were 2.1% higher than 2016. This *must* mean that price levels in 2018 are higher than 2016. This is a really great question to check that students *really* understand what disinflation is showing.

Answer E is incorrect because the greatest increase in real incomes actually occurs in 2019. This is because nominal incomes stay constant but price levels decrease by 0.7%. This is a good way of checking students' understanding of real and nominal values.

Figure 11.6 shows the inflation rate in an economy over five years.

Which of the following statements is correct?

A. Price levels were lowest in 2023.

B. The economy experienced disinflation in 2021 only.

C. The economy experienced inflation in four out of the five years.

D. Price levels in 2022 were lower than 2021.

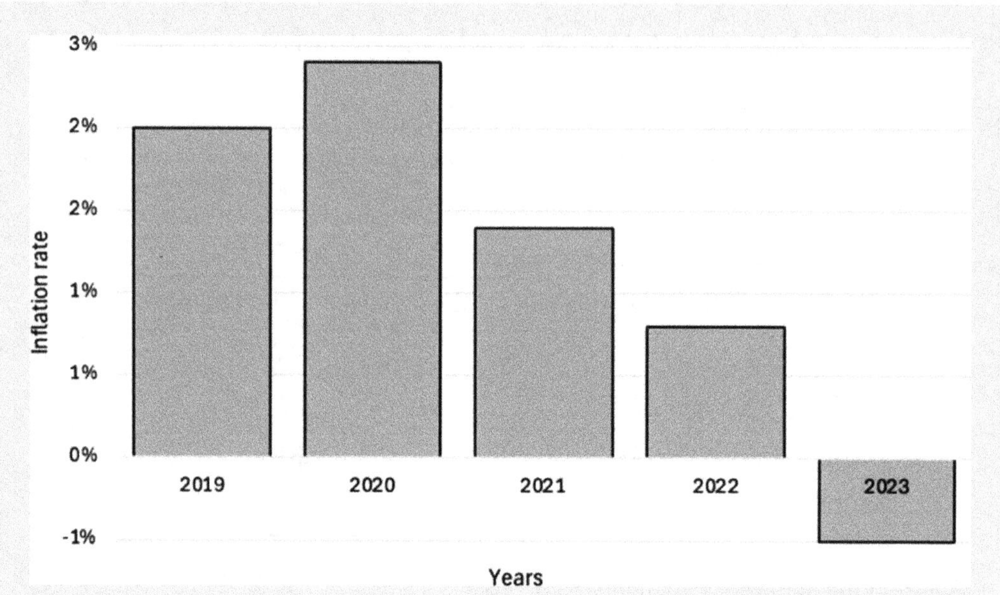

Figure 11.6 Inflation data

The only correct answer here is C. As long as students know that you regularly include more than one correct answer in many questions, they are still likely to check through and disregard every other option. This is because they know there is a possibility that you may include more than one correct answer.

Answer A again ensures students can distinguish between price indexes and inflation rates. Prices are decreasing in 2023, but the general price level is likely to be higher than most years because the economy has been regularly experiencing increasing price levels prior to 2023.

Answer D ensures that students distinguish between a decreasing rate of inflation (disinflation) and falling prices (deflation).

BOX 11.9 CASE STUDY ON INFLATION

Case study

The change in price levels and nominal incomes for an economy over the course of four years can be seen in Table 11.3.

The country's central bank has an inflation target of 2%. The central bank had been worried about the persistently high levels of inflation in 2022 and 2023, although were glad to see price changes closer to the target rate in 2024 and 2025.

Table 11.3 Changes in price and incomes

Year	Price change	Change in nominal incomes
2022	3.2%	1.6%
2023	2.8%	1.9%
2024	1.8%	1.5%
2025	1.7%	1.9%

However, while inflation may have fallen, the price inflation of some items has remained stubbornly high. Housing and associated costs, such as electricity bills, have been increasing by over 3% in each of the years analysed. These make up the largest category within the basket of goods, accounting for nearly 30% of all household spending within the economy. The headline rate has been dragged down by very small price increases in other categories, such as leisure and entertainment. The price change in the clothing and footwear category has been negative in both 2024 and 2025.

Some economists had previously been concerned about future deflationary pressures in the economy. In 2024, these economists worried that years of falling real incomes was depressing aggregate demand and that this may lead to decreasing price levels in the future. These concerns have been slightly reduced by the increase in real incomes in 2025.

Figure 11.7 shows forecasts made by economists for future price changes in the economy. The blue line represents inflation forecasts made in 2024, whereas the orange line represents updated forecasts made in 2025.

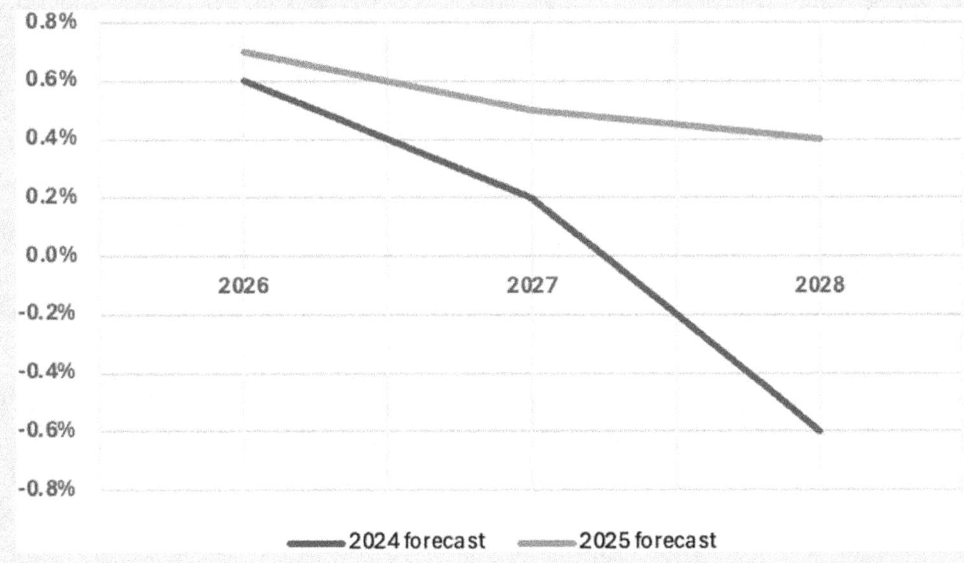

Figure 11.7 Inflation graph

Questions

1. What was the change in real incomes in the following?
   a. 2022
   b. 2025
2. With reference to changes in real incomes, explain why economists would have been concerned that aggregate demand may fall in subsequent years.
3. With reference to information contained within the case study, explain how inflation is measured using the concept of weights.
4. Why would economists be concerned that price inflation in areas such as housing has stayed 'stubbornly high'?
5. With reference to inflation, disinflation and deflation: explain the types of inflation that economists in 2024 forecast would occur in the economy over the next three years.
6. Using information provided in the case study, explain why there is a difference between inflation forecasts made in 2024 and 2025.

Key takeaways

- Show students several examples of inflationary impacts on real incomes. Show examples where inflation causes real incomes to fall significantly and other examples where inflation depresses real incomes but does not necessarily cause them to become negative.
- Spend time going through the weighting process in the basket of goods measurement. Use visual aids like a continuum to help students distinguish between a simple and weighted average.
- Do not rush the teaching of inflation, disinflation and deflation. Introduce the ideas one at a time, and use multiple examples to help students differentiate between the types.
- Ensure students see a large range of questions that test their understanding of inflation. Students need to build flexible knowledge that is familiar with seeing inflation discussed in a variety of different concepts.

The Phillips curve and the natural rate of unemployment

What's the big idea?

The short-run Phillips curve suggests that there is a trade-off between macroeconomic objectives of low unemployment and low and stable inflation. However, students need to understand that it is argued that this trade-off disappears in the long run and that the economy will adjust back to the natural rate of unemployment. This is used as an argument against demand-side interventions to reduce the unemployment rate below the natural rate of unemployment.

Students should see these arguments in the context of debates between Monetarist and Keynesian schools of economic thought, helping students to deepen their understanding of these debates. This topic represents an opportunity to link back to prior learning on the shape of the long-run aggregate supply curve and the disagreements between the two schools of thought here.[1]

Why do students find this topic difficult?

As with long-run aggregate supply, students can find it difficult to do the following:

1. Understand there is a conflict between how different schools of thought may interpret the same situation.
2. Understand that economic conditions will be different in the short-run and long-run.

Students' understanding of the long-run Phillips curve is also complicated by the idea of rational expectations. At present, exam boards do not require students to understand the nuance between anchored expectations or adaptive expectations. This is for good reason. These concepts will increase the cognitive load in a topic that is already tricky for students to understand. However, this can mean that explanations of inflation expectations are reduced to a surface level, and paradoxically, this can make it harder for students to understand the theory.

DOI: 10.4324/9781003724179-12

Explaining this concept

Mistakes to avoid

I have previously introduced this topic with the short-run Phillips curve alongside the AD/LRAS diagram depicting macroeconomic equilibrium. However, I believe this leads to heavy cognitive overload early on in the topic. In my experience, many students already find the Monetarist LRAS the trickier of the two long-run positions to understand, and so using this diagram while trying to introduce new content makes it difficult for students to focus their attention on the new content. Instead, the following sequence will introduce the short-run Phillips curve on its own without making an explicit link to how this situation can be depicted on an AD/LRAS diagram. Once students then have a strong understanding of the short-run Phillips curve, then you can help them make this link.

Explaining this concept

It is assumed that by this point in the curriculum sequence that students have an understanding of the following:

- Government macroeconomic objectives of growth, inflation and unemployment
- The types of unemployment (frictional, structural and cyclical) and, therefore, the natural rate of unemployment
- The concepts of demand-pull and cost-push inflation

The short-run Phillips curve

Students typically find the short-run Phillips curve easier to understand. Start by explaining that you are going to be exploring a possible conflict between the macroeconomic objectives of inflation and unemployment. This is likely to build on conflicts you have examined between economic growth and inflation and environmental sustainability

Then construct the diagram with students. The original Phillips curve was constructed with wage growth on the y-axis, but subsequent models substitute this for the inflation rate. At A-level, I keep this simple by using the inflation rate. This is the common labelling of the graph now and is usually the one that exam boards expect students to use. Your explanation of the short-run Phillips curve may look something like the one included in Box 12.1.

Then connect these points with a curved short-run Phillips curve. Explain to student that the line is not straight because there is not a constant trade-off. For example, as the number of unemployed individuals gets smaller and smaller, the

BOX 12.1 INTRODUCTION TO THE PHILLIPS CURVE

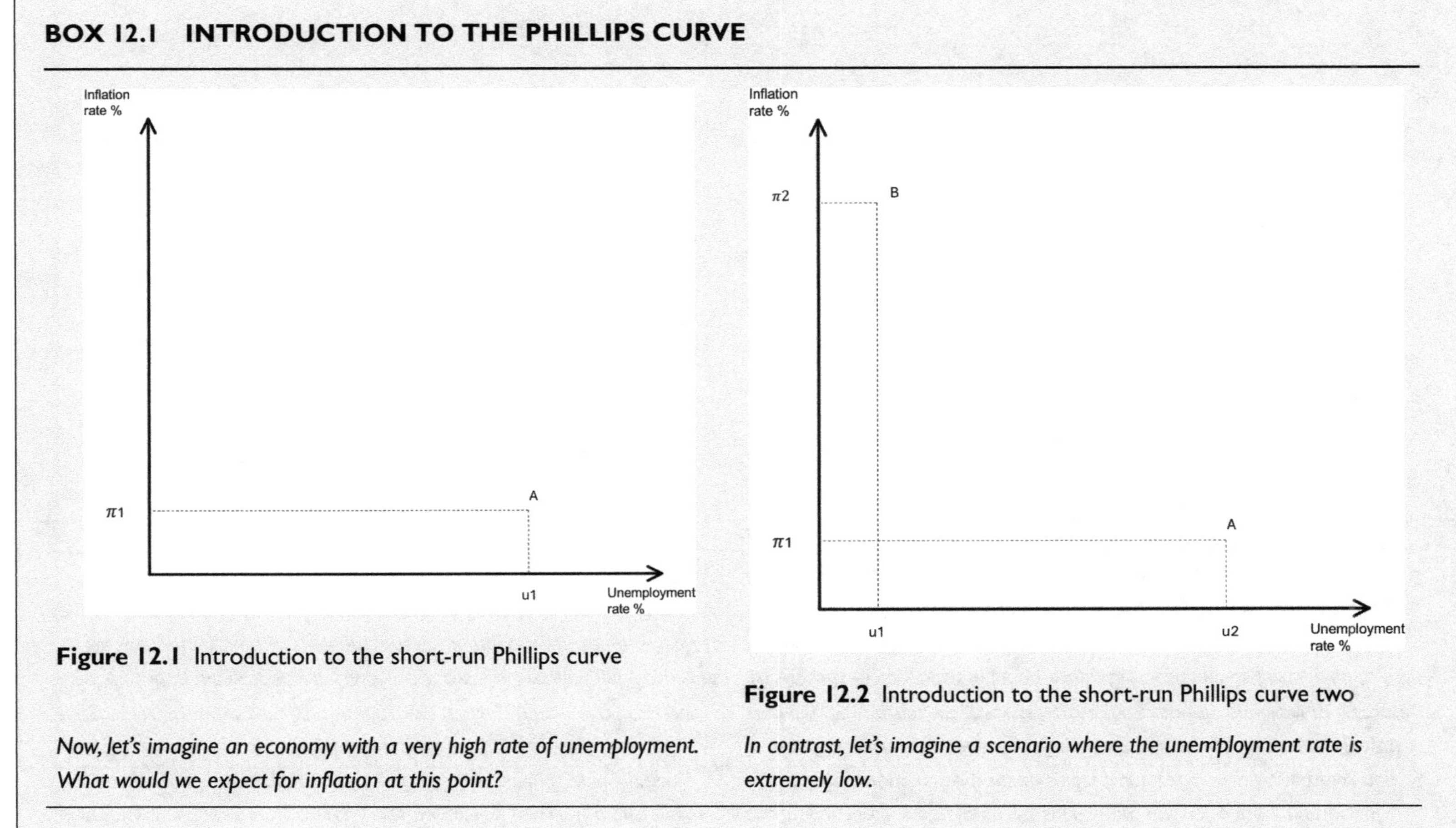

Figure 12.1 Introduction to the short-run Phillips curve

Now, let's imagine an economy with a very high rate of unemployment. What would we expect for inflation at this point?

Figure 12.2 Introduction to the short-run Phillips curve two

In contrast, let's imagine a scenario where the unemployment rate is extremely low.

A large number of unemployed workers is likely to mean that those unemployed workers have limited wage bargaining power. If a firm needs to hire new workers, they have a large number of unemployed workers available to employ, so each individual does not have much power to bargain for higher wages. As a result, there is likely to be limited cost-push inflation within the economy because wage costs will remain fairly constant. *As such, when there is high amount of unemployment there is likely to be low levels of inflation. We can see this as Point A on* Figure 12.1.	*At this point, unemployed labour is a scarce resource as most of the labour force is employed. As such, there are not a large number of unemployed workers for firms to select from if they need to employ new labour. This increases the wage bargaining position of these unemployed workers. As a result, wage levels across the economy are likely to increase. This results in cost-push inflation within the economy as firms need to pay higher wages to attract new workers.* *As such, when there is a low amount of unemployment there is likely to be high levels of inflation. We can see this as Point B on* Figure 12.2.

wage bargaining power of those individuals increases at a larger rate, and so the 'cost' in terms of wage inflation increases more and more.

Then introduce students to the trade-off that the short-run Phillips curve suggests occurs between employment and inflation targets:

Let's suppose the unemployment rate is relatively high in a country and is above the government's target. As such, the government wants to reduce unemployment. They do this by using some expansionary fiscal policy, such as increasing government spending.

Given that labour is a derived demand, this should lead to an increase in the demand for labour. As a result, the unemployment rate falls – we can see this by the movement from U1 to U2 in Figure 12.3. However, we can see that this results in the inflation rate increasing from $\pi 1 to \pi 2$.

We can see that the government's policy to reduce unemployment has resulted in an increase in the inflation rate.

This relationship could work the other way round: suppose the inflation rate was initially at $\pi 2$ and the government wanted to reduce this. Maybe they could use some sort of contractionary policy to reduce aggregate demand, which would reduce the inflation rate from $\pi 2$ to $\pi 1$. However, the

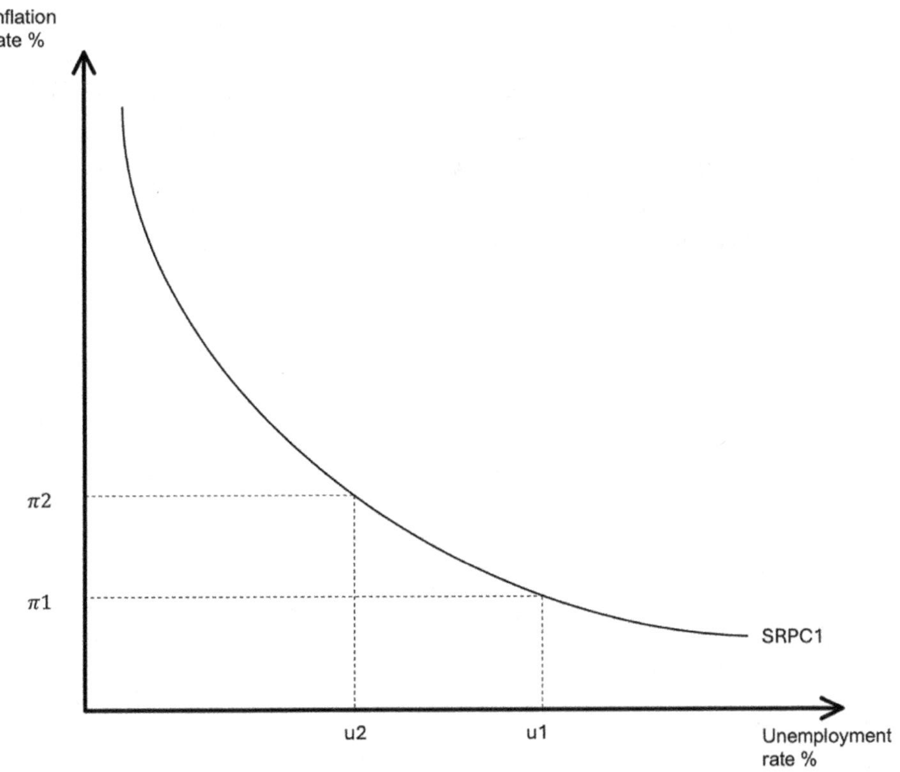

Figure 12.3 Short-run Phillips curve

unemployment rate would increase from U2 to U1 – the government's action to reduce inflation has resulted in higher unemployment.

This demonstrates the key implication of the short-run Phillips curve: it is difficult for the government to achieve both its aims of low unemployment and low, stable inflation at the same time.

Then check students' understanding of the short-run Phillips curve with some MWB checks. This may include the following:

- Checking students' ability to reproduce the graph, labelling axes correctly.
- Checking students' ability to demonstrate the trade-off of objectives demonstrated by the graph. This would involve giving students initial starting rates of unemployment and inflation and then giving a government policy that would result in these changing.
- Checking students understand why the trade-off exists – e.g. why lower rates of unemployment are likely to be linked with higher rates of inflation

The long-run Phillips curve

Now is the time to introduce the curve side-by-side with a Monetarist AD/LRAS diagram. This is a good foreground to move on to the long-run Phillips curve.

We are going to start by imaging an economy that is in equilibrium at the full employment level. We can show this on our Monetarist AD/LRAS curve as per the diagram in Figure 12.4. We can show the corresponding position on the short-run Phillps curve. Notice that the rate of unemployment at this full employment level is equal to the natural rate of unemployment.

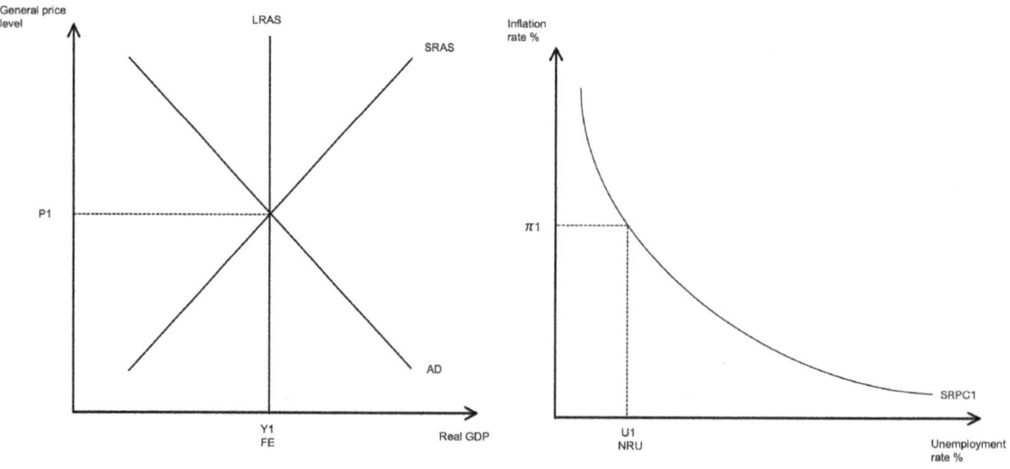

Figure 12.4 Short-run Phillips curve and macro equilibrium

Let's imagine there is some sort of fiscal stimulus in the economy – perhaps an increase in government spending. What impact is that going to have on our AD/LRAS diagram . . . Fiona?

Exactly . . . we are going to get an outward shift of aggregate demand. We can see the impact of that in Figure 12.5.

We can see the impact that this has had and the link between our two diagrams. National income has increased above the full employment level, which is also represented by our drop in unemployment below the natural rate. At the same time, price levels in the economy have increased from P1 to P2, which is also shown by the increase in inflation to $\pi 2$ on our Phillips curve.

Pause here and check students' understanding with some quick whiteboard checks. For example, give them a starting equilibrium and ask them to show the impacts of different fiscal policies on macro equilibrium and the short-run Phillips curve.

Once you are confident students understand this, introduce them to the idea of inflation expectations. With a strong cohort, I have previously introduced the idea of anchored and adaptive expectations. However, I do not think this is advisable for the vast majority of classes. As such, I tend to explain inflation expectations in the following way:

So we have an economy where unemployment is initially equal to U1, which is also the economy's natural rate of unemployment. Let's say that is 4%. At that rate of unemployment, inflation is equal to $\pi 1$. Let's say that is 2%. *As we saw, expansionary fiscal policy then increased aggregate demand, which reduced unemployment – let's say to 3.5%. This increases the price level, leading to an inflation rate of 4%.*

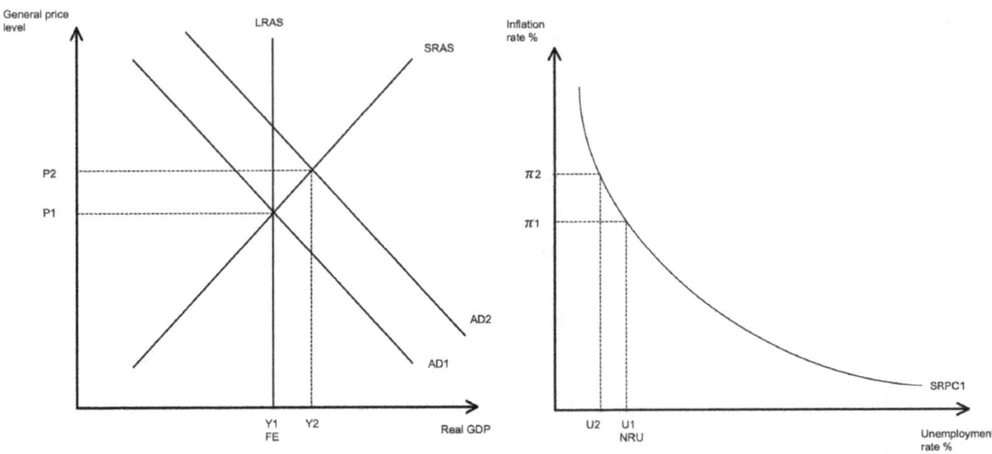

Figure 12.5 Short-run Phillips curve and macro equilibrium two

Annotate your previously drawn diagram with these figures to make the narrative clear for students.

> *Let's imagine that the government doesn't enact any sort of policy to try to reduce this inflation rate and the economy stays in this equilibrium for an extended period of time, with inflation at 4%. How are individuals going to start reacting? If this inflation has been present for an extended period of time, then individuals are going to expect that it may persist for longer and will want higher wages to compensate for this. So suddenly workers across the economy may start demanding wage increases that are equal to at least 4%. This pushes up firms' costs by 4%, which may lead to an inflationary spiral as firms pass on these higher costs to consumers.*
>
> *This is a really important part of this theory: the expectation that the current rate of inflation will persist into the future leads individuals to demand wages to match the inflation rate. As a result, this pushes up cost-push inflation. This higher rate of inflation has become 'embedded' within the economy.*
>
> *Now, firm's facing these costs may decide that they don't want to keep paying a 4% increase in wages each year. So how do they respond? They respond by letting go of workers. So now we have a situation where 4% inflation is embedded, and firms want to make workers unemployed. This means inflation stays at a rate of 4% but unemployment is going to start to increase. Now this is interesting – the unemployment rate is going to adjust back to 4% but the inflation rate is embedded at the higher rate! What do we notice? The economy has adjusted back to its natural rate of unemployment in the long-term. We can see this at Point A in Figure 12.6.*

Avoid the split-attention effect by annotating directly on the graph and getting students to do the same. Then carry on the explanation:

> *Notice that Point A is not on our original short-run Phillips curve. We are therefore operating on a new short-run Phillips curve – SRPC2 as shown in Figure 12.7.*

Run through one more example where the government tries to reduce unemployment again by using expansionary fiscal policy. This will lead to a shift onto a third short-run Phillips curve and will show the economy always adjusting back to the natural rate of unemployment but at higher inflation rates. You can then use this to derive the shape of the long-run Phillips curve and demonstrate that the trade-off between unemployment and inflation breaks down in the long run. Keep emphasising the importance of inflation expectations in this theory: if individuals and firms expect inflation to stay at the elevated level, unemployment will increase back to the natural rate and inflation will persist.

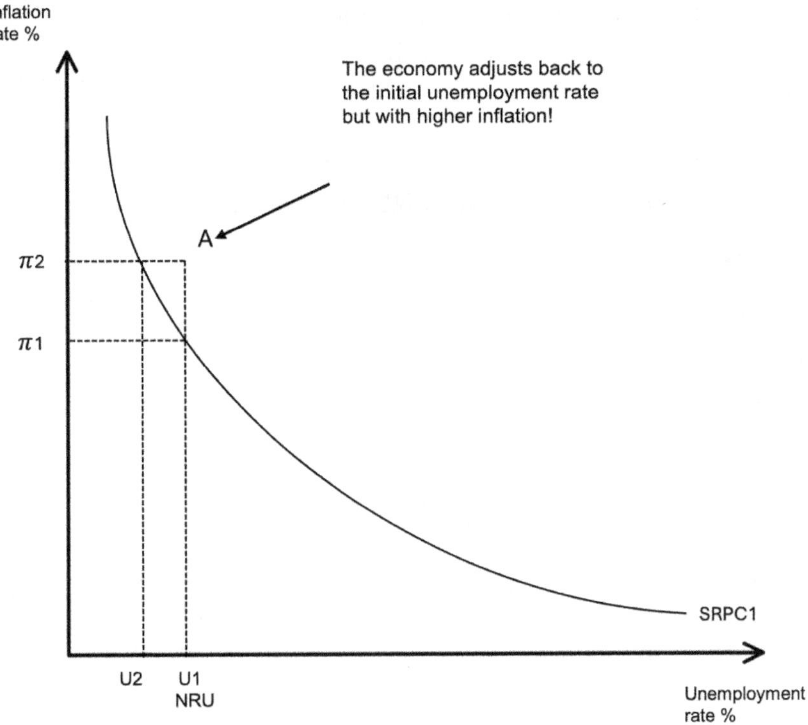

Figure 12.6 Derivation of the long-run Phillips curve

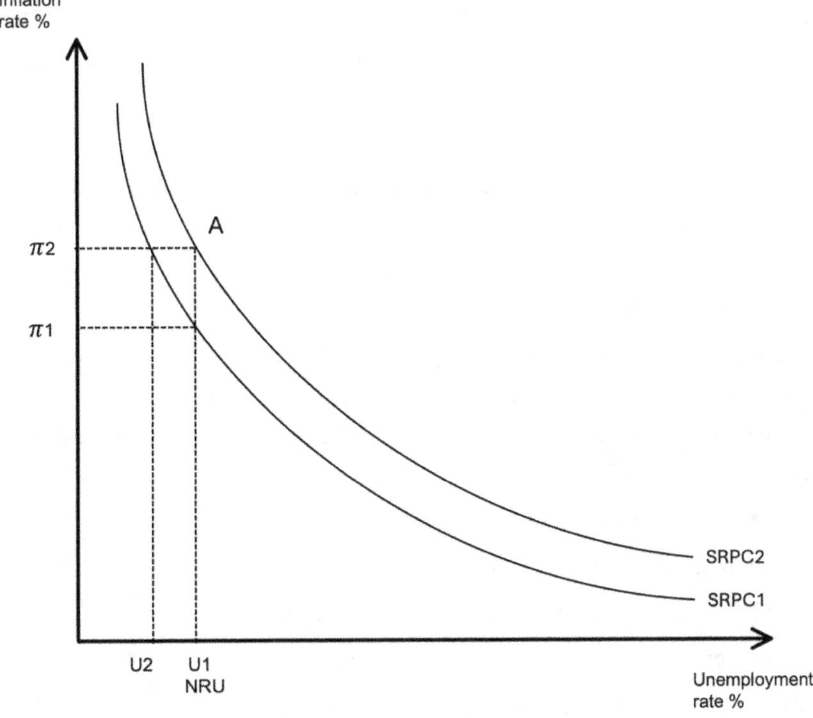

Figure 12.7 Derivation of the long-run Phillips curve two

Check students' understanding with a series of MWB questions that check students' understanding of the long-run Phillips curve. I would use a question like the ones in Box 12.2.

BOX 12.2 MWB CHECK FOR UNDERSTANDING

MWB question

Look at the following graph.

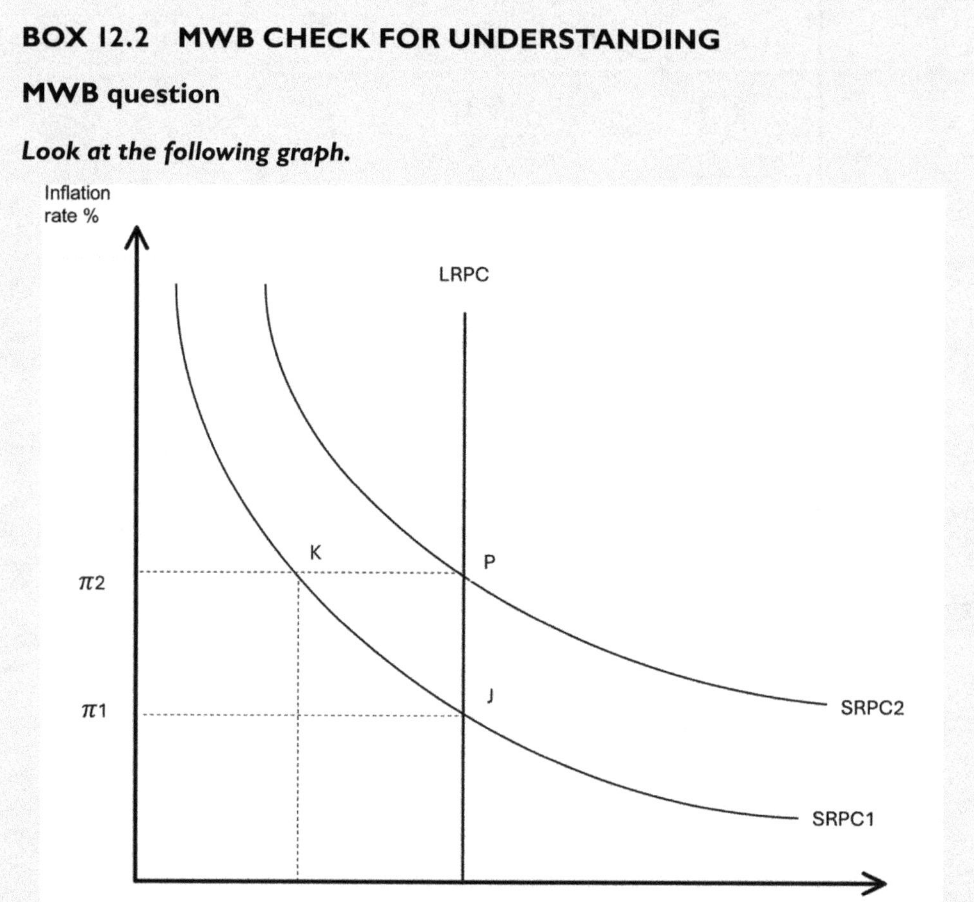

Figure 12.8 Phillips curve check for understanding

1. The economy is initially operating at point J. The government uses expansionary demand-side policy to reduce the rate of unemployment. Which of the following statements is correct regarding the impacts of this policy according to the expectations-augmented Phillips curve?

   A. In the long-term, the economy will operate at point K.

   B. In the long-term, the economy will return to point J.

   C. In the long-term, the economy will operate at point P.

   D. U1 represents the natural rate of unemployment.

   E. U2 represents the natural rate of unemployment.

2. The economy is initially operating at point J. The government uses expansionary demand-side policy to reduce the rate of unemployment. Which answer represents the change in short-run and long-run equilibrium positions?

   A. J to K to J

   B. J to P to J

   C. J to K to P

   D. J to P to K

The correct answers for question 1 are C and D. The correct answer for question 2 is D.

These questions should test that students understand the relationship between the short-run and long-run Phillips curve and the mechanism by which the economy will return back to the natural rate of unemployment.

I often re-model this process one more time for students. Model this explicitly on the board with the two diagrams side-by-side, ensuring you show each key stage together:

Step one: *The economy is initially in equilibrium at point 1. This demonstrates the economy at full employment level at the natural rate of unemployment. This is shown in* Figure 12.9.

Step two: *The government decides to try to reduce the rate of unemployment using expansionary demand-side policy. We can see on the AD/LRAS graph that this would lead to an outward shift of aggregate demand, pushing the economy to operate above full employment level. As a result, prices increase to P2.*

This is then reflected on the Phillips curve – the unemployment rate falls to u2 but inflation increases from $\pi 1$ *to* $\pi 2$.

Step three: *Higher wage demands embed within the economy, forcing up firms' costs of production. As a result, short-run aggregate supply shifts inwards and the economy returns to full employment level. This return back to full employment level means workers have become unemployed.*

This can be seen on the Phillips curve – the movement back to full employment level increase the unemployment rate but higher inflation is now embedded within the economy. As such, the economy is operating on a new short-run Phillips curve and has returned to the natural rate of unemployment.

Finish off the explanation by bringing students back to the big picture:

The implication of the long-run Phillips curve is that the use of expansionary demand-side policy to try to reduce the natural rate of unemployment will eventually only lead to an adjustment back to the natural rate but with higher inflation embedded in the economy. This is a Monetarist position and links back to their theory that, as long as there is no government intervention in the

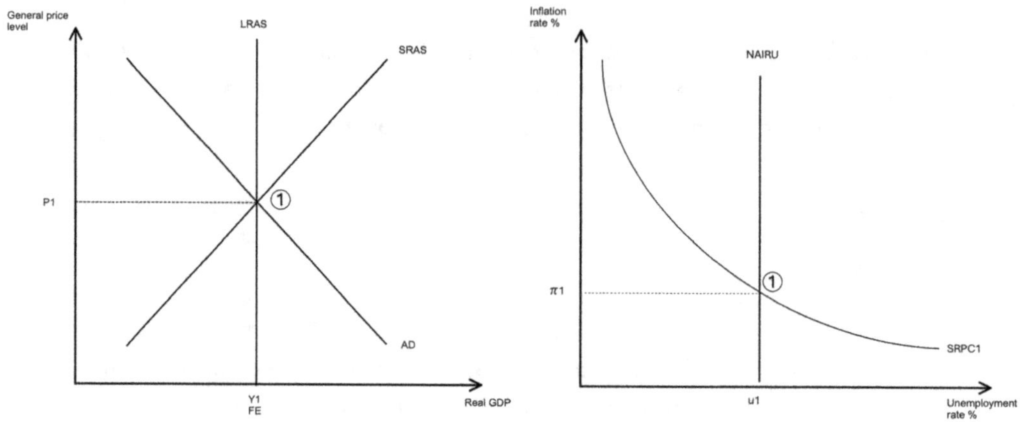

Figure 12.9 Macro equilibrium and the long-run Phillips curve step one

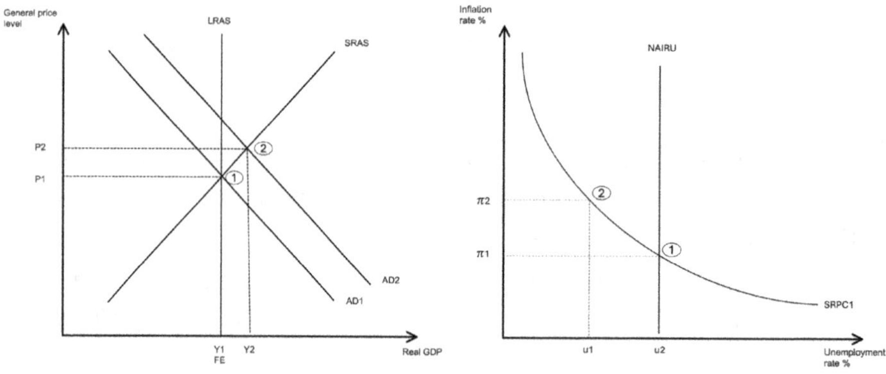

Figure 12.10 Macro equilibrium and the long-run Phillips curve step two

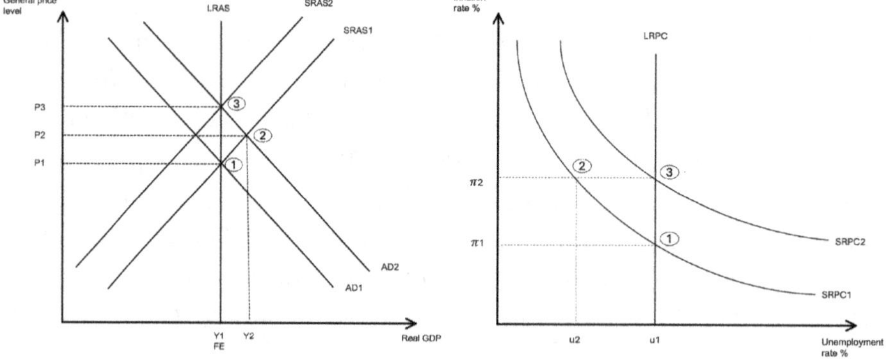

Figure 12.11 Macro equilibrium and the long-run Phillips curve step three

labour markets, the economy will adjust back to the initial long-run equilibrium position of the economy.

Once this is complete, I would provide a comprehension like the one shown in Box 12.3.

BOX 12.3 PHILLIPS CURVE COMPREHENSION TASK

Comprehension task

An economy currently has an unemployment rate of 4.4%. It is estimated that the natural rate of unemployment for the economy is 4%.

The government of the economy would like to reduce the level of unemployment. They plan a fiscal stimulus to stimulate aggregate demand in the economy. The government reduces the basic rate of income tax by one percentage point and increases government spending by 1.5%. This initial injection into the economy stimulates aggregate demand and reduces unemployment to 4%. However, multiplier effects result in further increases in aggregate demand. As a result, the unemployment rate falls to 3.6%.

Before the fiscal stimulus was fully implemented, major trade unions and leading economic commentators forecast that the policy would lead to inflation rising above the Central Bank's 2% target. As a consequence, many large firms and key employee groups began negotiating contracts that incorporated a 3% expected price increase for the following year.

At this point, the government also considers implementing policies to increase the flexibility of the labour market. For example, the government providing funding for local councils to increase their provision of job information provided to local residents. The intention of this policy would to increase the efficiency of job matching, as local residents would have greater information about the jobs available and skills required to fulfil the role. The government is also implementing legislation to reduce the power of trade unions, which it believes will increase the flexibility of the labour force.

Questions

1. Use a Monetarist macroeconomic equilibrium diagram to show the *initial* equilibrium position of the economy.
2. Why would a reduction in the basic rate of income tax stimulate aggregate demand?
3. Why may an increase in government spending cause multiplier effects?
4. Go back to the graph you drew for question 1. Show the impact of multiplier effects on the macroeconomic equilibrium position of the economy.
5. Use a short-run Phillips curve to demonstrate the impact of the multiplier effects on the economy.
6. With the use of information from the text, explain why higher inflation expectations are likely to become embedded within the economy.
7. Use a long-run Phillips curve to show the long-term impacts of the government stimulus in the economy.
8. Show the possible impact of government policies to increase the flexibility of the labour market on the following:
   a. A Monetarist macroeconomic equilibrium diagram
   b. A long-run Phillips curve

The comprehension task is effective at bringing together students' knowledge from a range of macroeconomic topics, including the multiplier, Monetarist macroeconomic equilibrium and the Phillips curve. This should help in the building of complex schema and facilitate a deeper understanding of the links between economic concepts.

Finishing the sequence by using some of the questions in Box 12.4 to check students' understanding of the Phillips curve.

BOX 12.4 CHECKING FOR UNDERSTANDING

Question one

Table 12.1 gives some information regarding two country's unemployment and inflation rates.

Table 12.1 Unemployment and inflation in Country X and Y

	Country X unemployment (%)	Country X inflation (%)	Country Y unemployment (%)	Country Y inflation (%)
2015	3.6	2.4	5.2	0.7
2016	3.8	2.1	4.8	1.1
2017	3.9	1.9	4.1	1.7
2018	4.2	2.2	3.9	1.9

Which of the following statements is correct?

A. Both Country X and Country Y demonstrate a typical short-run Phillips curve relationship.

B. Country X follows a typical short-run Phillips curve from 2015–2017.

C. Country X is likely to have a lower natural rate of unemployment than Country Y.

D. The Phillips curve theory would suggest wage inflation in Country Y is increasing as unemployment falls.

E. Policies to stimulate aggregate demand in Country Y will lead to an increase in the unemployment rate.

Answers B and D are correct. The table does not provide any information regarding the estimated natural rate of unemployment in either country, and so conclusions regarding C and E cannot be made. A is incorrect as 2018 does not demonstrate a typical Phillips curve relationship in Country X.

Question two

Country X currently has an unemployment rate of 3.9%, which is estimated to be its approximate natural rate of unemployment. The government implements a programme of expansionary fiscal policy. Which of the following are likely impacts of this stimulus according to the long-run Phillips curve?

A. The economy's natural rate of unemployment will reduce below 3.9%.

B. Expectations of future increases in the price level will decrease.

C. If the government persists with the stimulus, both inflation and unemployment will accelerate.

D. Long-term unemployment will remain at 3.9% but inflation will accelerate.

E. The economy's natural rate of unemployment will reduce but at the cost of higher inflation.

Answer D is the only correct answer.

Question three

An economy is initially in an equilibrium position corresponding with point 1 shown in the following graph.

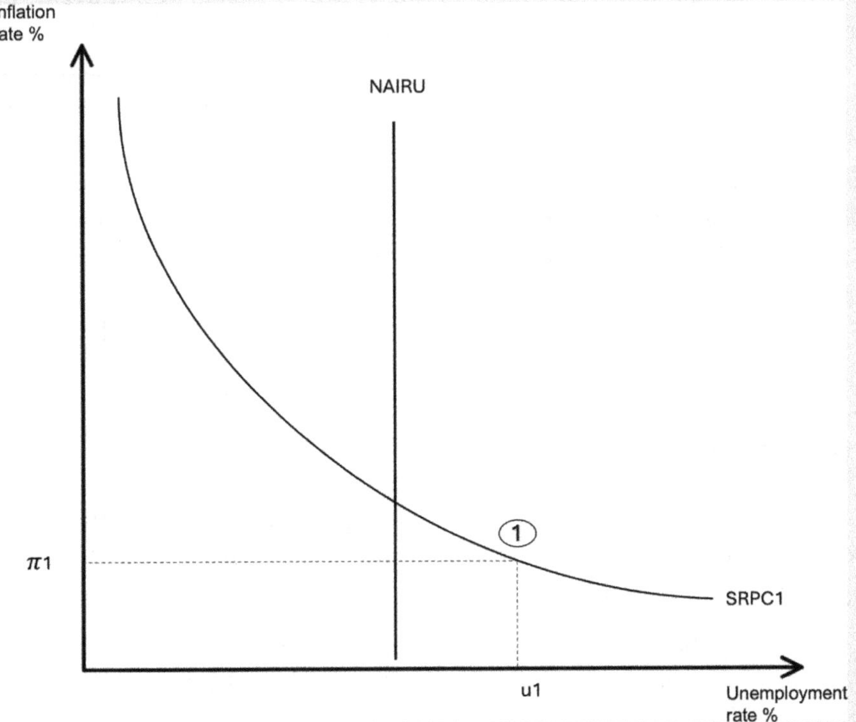

Figure 12.12 Checking for understanding the long-run Phillips curve

Which of following statements is correct regarding this diagram?

A. Expansionary demand-side policy will not reduce the unemployment rate below U1.

B. Expansionary demand-side policy can be used to reduce the unemployment rate without increasing inflation.

C. Policies to increase the flexibility of the labour force should decrease the natural rate of unemployment but would be inflationary in the long-term.

D. The economy is initially operating below full employment level.

Answer D is the only correct answer here. Answer A is important to ensure students do not confuse the equilibrium unemployment rate in an economy at a given time with the natural rate of unemployment. Answer C is a good distractor answer because the first part of the answer is correct: increasing the flexibility of the labour force should decrease the natural rate of unemployment. However, it is unlikely to be inflationary as the short-run Phillips curve would also shift down and to the left, resulting in the economy operating at a lower inflation rate with a lower natural rate of unemployment.

The explanations and questions in Box 12.4 focus on the derivation of the long-run Phillips curve as the result of demand-side shocks. Students also need to recognise that supply-side shocks can be used to explain the long-run Phillips curve, and indeed, the oil crises of the 1970s were one of the original reasons that the phenomenon was observed. I introduce the topic using demand-side analysis first because I find it is easier for students to understand. However, in the next lesson, I would recommend exploring the concept as a result of supply-side shocks. Using the oil crises of the 1970s broadens students' understanding of economic history. It is also a good way of deepening their understanding of central bank inflation targeting and the key role that this has in anchoring inflation expectations.

Key takeaways

- Introduce students to these curves in a sequential manner, going step-by-step through each process. Live draw the process and annotate directly onto the graphs to avoid the split attention effect.
- Show the links between the AD/LRAS model and Phillips curve *after* you have introduced the short-run Phillips curve. Don't try to do this straight away.
- Introduce the topic using demand-side shocks first and then show the same phenomenon occurring as a result of supply-side shocks.

Note

1 Disagreements between the schools regarding the Phillips curve are now more nuanced. The 'New Keynesians', for example, would not necessarily reject the findings of the long-run Phillps curve. Students do not need to understand the intricacies of these debates at A-level.

13 Absolute and comparative advantage

What's the big picture?

Absolute and comparative advantage help to explain the growth of international trade, forming the basis for globalisation. These theories underpin the growth in trade between nations, which has increased the access to goods and services for citizens across the globe over the past 200 years. It helps to explain why globalisation has led to greater choice and lower prices for consumers and why it has led to structural unemployment in certain industries in high-income countries. Students must not lose sight of this big picture. This is a topic that requires understanding of comparisons between opportunity cost ratios, which can lead to students becoming bogged down in the detail and losing sight of the big picture. An understanding of the big picture provides the basis for students to go on to understand arguments around globalisation and protectionism.

Why do students find this topic difficult?

This topic requires students to understand opportunity cost ratios. Students are likely to have first encountered opportunity cost ratios when they learned about production possibility curves, often in the beginning weeks of an economics course. At this stage, they probably had to calculate the opportunity cost of producing one product in terms of another (e.g. Good A and Good B). However, to understand comparative advantage, students need to be able to compare opportunity cost ratios between two different countries. This is often represented by matrix grids, which can contain lots of numbers. This can quickly become overwhelming for students. As such, we need to take students through explicit examples nice and slowly and not rush through the content.

This topic becomes complicated further when students are introduced to the idea of a trading price based on the opportunity cost ratios calculated. Trading prices are tricky for students to understand because of the following:

1. An 'acceptable' trading price is one that is acceptable for both Country A and Country B. Students, therefore, have to be able to express the trading price in terms of both countries.

DOI: 10.4324/9781003724179-13

2. Point 1 is a complication students find with standard exchange rates. Trading prices are complicated further by the fact that we are not dealing with currency, which students are familiar. Instead, we are dealing with a price expressed in terms of the value of two items. This makes the concept seem abstract and confusing.

Explaining this concept

Mistakes to avoid

It's easy to jump straight into opportunity cost calculations without setting the scene. Students can often then get lost in the technical detail and don't realise why they are studying these opportunity cost ratios in the first place! Don't rush this topic or lose sight of the big picture!

Once the scene has been set, go through an example nice and slowly. Avoid jumping straight in with the production possibilities of two countries and their respective opportunity cost ratios. This is a lot of information to be encountering at once and is a sure-fire way to overload working memory.

Explaining this concept

Absolute advantage

Start by introducing students to the big picture:

> *In the 1700s and 1800s, the vast majority of goods and services consumed in a country were produced within that country. Some estimates suggested 95% of all goods and services would have been produced domestically. Fast forward to the 21st century, and the value of international trade is now over half of the world's economic output. Over the course of the next few lessons we are going to try to think about how that developed, the impacts of this development and how it may explain the current political and economic climate of today.*
>
> *We can think of this in terms of the timeline shown in Figure 13.1.*

The timeline in Figure 13.1 represents an oversimplification of the development of international trade. However, its purpose is to help students see the big picture

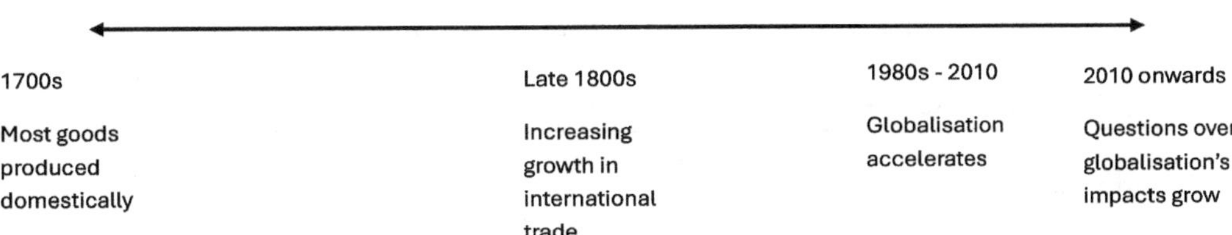

Figure 13.1 Timeline of international trade

to understand why absolute and comparative advantage are important. I think it does this well. It also helps to provide a narrative for topics on international trade and globalisation. Of course, you can tell students can be told that the narrative displayed in Figure 13.1 can be studied in much greater detail, and perhaps you may wish to enrich students' understanding here with a homework task on this.

Once this narrative is set, begin by thinking about absolute advantage:

How did the pattern of trade start to develop initially in the 1700s? Let's consider a simple model based on two countries: Country A and Country B. At the moment, Country A and Country B are not trading with each other.

Let's assume that both Country A and B have 100 'resources'. These resources are made up of land, labour, capital and enterprise.

We are going to assume that Country A and Country B only produce two goods: apples and wheat. This is clearly an unrealistic assumption, but it is going to help us develop our theory. We will then consider later how much of a limiting factor these assumptions are.

Country A can produce a maximum of 1,000 apples or 500kg of wheat. Let's assume that they split their resources equally between both, so that they can produce 500 apples and 250kg of wheat at the same time. Country A's production choice is shown in **Table 13.1.**

Let's then consider Country B. Country B can produce more wheat than Country A: they can produce 1,000kg wheat. However, they then produce fewer apples, with production of 500 apples. Again, let's assume that they split their resources between both, so that they can produce 500kg of wheat and 250 apples. Country B's production choice is shown in **Table 13.2.**

The total production of goods is shown in **Table 13.3.**

We may have noticed something interesting here. The total production is actually lower than the maximum that each country could produce of each good. So what if they decided to specialise in the products that they can produce the most of? This would mean that Country A would produce 1,000

Table 13.1 Country A production

	Country A
Apples	500
Wheat	250 kg

Table 13.2 Country A and B production

	Country A	Country B
Apples	500	250
Wheat	250 kg	500 kg

Table 13.3 Total production of Country A and B

	Country A	Country B	Total production
Apples	500	250	750
Wheat	250 kg	500 kg	750 kg

Table 13.4 Gains from specialisation

	Total production before specialisation	Total production after specialisation	Net gain
Apples	750	1,000 (produced by Country A)	+ 250 apples
Wheat	750 kg	1000 kg (produced by Country B)	+ 250 kg wheat

apples and Country B would produce 1000kg wheat. We would end up in the situation shown in **Table 13.4.**

So by specialising in the goods with which each country can produce more, we end up in a situation where total production increases. Country A and B could then trade some apples for wheat in order for each country to have access to both products. For example, Country A could trade 250 apples for 250kg wheat. This would leave both countries better off than if they didn't trade.

This demonstrates the theory of absolute advantage. A country is said to have an absolute advantage when they are able to produce more of a product than another country with the same level of resources.

This helps us to understand why countries initially began trading: both countries could benefit if they both specialised in the goods with which they had an absolute advantage and then traded.

The tables discussed here should be drawn live with students. For example, with Table 13.4, the net gain calculation should be modelled live to students. This ensures they understand the process by which this was calculated and are not overloaded by a confusing table with lots of information displayed at once.

At this stage, check students' understanding with MWB checks for understanding. An example of such a question is provided in Box 13.1.

BOX 13.1 MWB CHECK FOR UNDERSTANDING

MWB check for understanding

Country A and B do not currently engage in international trade. Both countries produce two goods, with their resources split equally between these goods. The maximum production of each country is shown in Table 13.5.

Table 13.5 Country A and B production possibilities

	Country A	Country B
Coffee	400 kg	550 kg
Rice	650 kg	600 kg

Assume both countries decide to specialise in the production of goods with which they have an absolute advantage and then trade at a mutually favourable exchange rate. Which of the following statements is correct?

A. Total production of rice will increase from 1,250 kg to 1,300 kg.

B. Total production of coffee will decrease from 950 kg to 800 kg.

C. Country A will produce rice.

D. Country A will be better off in terms of rice, but Country B will be worse off.

E. Total production of coffee will increase but rice will decrease.

Answers A and C are correct. This question tests whether students can identify which product each country has the absolute advantage in and then checks their understanding of specialisation in these products.

Comparative advantage

Now pose this question for students:

If trade is based on absolute advantage, what happens if a country has the absolute advantage in the production of both goods? Should they still trade?

We might also ask, what if two countries have very similar capability in producing goods? For example, Germany and the USA may have very similar capabilities in the production of cars and machinery. Should they still trade? We need to consider a slightly different model to answer these questions.

Let's look at an example. **Table 13.6** *shows the maximum productive potential of rice and coffee for both Country A and B.*

Which country has the absolute advantage in the production of rice . . . Alex?

Table 13.6 Country A and B production

	Country A	Country B
Rice	800 kg	600 kg
Coffee	1,000 kg	300 kg

Yes, Country A has the absolute advantage because they could produce 800kg of rice compared to Country B's 600kg if they both put 100% of their resources into the production of rice. Now, which country has the absolute advantage in the production of coffee . . . Iain?

Yes, Country A also has the absolute advantage in the production of coffee. So Country has the absolute advantage in the production of both products. What does this mean in terms of trade?

Well, in this scenario we need to consider how efficiently each country produces each good. To do this, we need to consider their opportunity cost each country experiences when they choose to specialise in the production of a particular product.

Now we recapped in our 'starter questions' today that the formula for calculating opportunity cost per unit is: $\frac{Loss}{Gain}$

So, let's consider this for Country A producing rice. If Country A specialises and produces only rice, then they gain 800kg of rice and 'give up' the possibility of producing 1000kg of coffee. So our formula would be:

$$\frac{1000kg\,coffee}{800kg\,rice} = 1.25kg$$

This number tells us that for every kilogram of rice that Country A produces, they 'give up' 1.25kg of coffee.

Now let's consider that for Country B:

$$\frac{300kg\,coffee}{600kg\,rice} = 0.5kg$$

Interesting! ***Country B only 'gives up' 0.5kg of coffee for every kilogram of rice that they produce****. So, Country B's opportunity cost of producing rice is lower than that of Country A, even though Country A can produce more absolutely.*

Let's keep track of this on the board [Box 13.2].

BOX 13.2 DISPLAY ON BOARD

Board

If Country A produces 1 kg RICE, then they give up 1.25 kg COFFEE.
If Country B produces 1 kg RICE, then they give up 0.5 kg COFFEE.

I find it is advantageous to have this visual on the board before we put the numbers into the table. The table overwhelms with students, whereas writing the narrative on the board as we do the calculations as a class provides greater clarity. It means

Table 13.7 Opportunity cost ratios

	Country A	**Country B**
Produces 1kg rice	Give up **1.25 kg** coffee	Give up **0.5 kg** coffee
Produces 1kg coffee	Give up **0.8 kg** rice	Give up **2 kg** rice

that the students' focus is going into what the calculation is telling them, rather than trying to figure out what the table means.

Now ask the students:

On your whiteboards I want you to do the same calculation for me for the production of coffee.

Once students have calculated this, add the answers to the board in the same way that it was written previously.

Okay, so we've calculated our opportunity cost ratios for each country and each product. We are now going to place this into a table. I am going to label the rows and the contents quite specifically to make sure we are really clear what this is telling us. This is shown in Table 13.7.

So we can see that each country has a product with which their opportunity cost is lower than the other country. We refer to this as a ***comparative advantage:*** *this is the ability to produce a good with a lower opportunity cost than a rival.*

Pause there and make sure that students have plenty of practice in calculating the opportunity cost ratios and identifying the products that each country should produce. Give them several matrix tables and repetition of calculating the opportunity cost ratios. In the final few questions, get students to identify which country has the absolute advantage, as well as the comparative advantage. This helps students to see instances in which a country has both absolute and comparative advantage and scenarios in which they only have one of the two.

Trading price and the law of comparative advantage

The final part of this sequence is to ensure students understand that trade is beneficial if appropriate trading prices are set. I use 'trading prices' instead of 'exchange rates', as is listed in some textbooks. The use of 'exchange rates' here can cause confusion for students when thinking about typical exchange rates that they are familiar with.

Students need to be shown several examples and non-examples to understand this.

Now, the idea that countries will trade based on their comparative advantage is dependent on the exchange rate that each country decides to trade at. Let's go through this slowly, step-by-step:

Before trading, *we said that if Country A produces rice then they have to 'give up' 1.25kg coffee. So we could rephrase that by saying that each unit of rice is going to cost Country A 1.25kg coffee.*

Now, let's assume that Country A decides to specialise in producing coffee, which means they don't produce any rice. They are now going to have to purchase their rice from Country B. What kind of trading price would Country A be happy with?

Let's say the trading price is 1kg rice = 1kg coffee. Country A are going to be happy with this! To get 1kg rice, they only have to give up 1kg coffee – this is less than the 1.25kg they would have to give up if they didn't specialise.

What if the trading price was 1kg rice = 1.1kg coffee? Well Country A would still be happy because this is less than 1.25kg coffee they were given up before.

What if the trading price was 1kg rice = 1.3kg coffee? At this point, Country A would not be happy – they are giving up more coffee than if they produced on their own.

So we can see that Country A is happy as long as the trading price is below 1kg rice = 1.25kg coffee.

It is really important that you annotate on the board to show students the key elements of this explanation. For example, you may simply write up the various exchanges with a tick or a cross based on whether Country A would be happy to trade at that exchange rate. If you don't do this, the narrative will be very difficult for students to follow. I find that demonstrating this initially to students on the board is better than showing them an initial worked example, which is likely to be text heavy and appear daunting.

We now need to consider this in terms of Country B. When Country B produce rice, they give up 0.5kg coffee. We could think of this as Country B's 'cost' of producing rice. So, what exchange rate will they be happy with?

Let's go the initial trading price, set at 1kg rice = 1kg coffee. Well, Country B will have given up 0.5kg coffee when they produced the 1kg rice. Now they are getting 1kg back in return. Country B will be happy with this – they are gaining 0.5kg coffee for every unit of rice that they trade!

Would Country B accept a trading price of 1kg = 0.8kg coffee? Well, this is still above the 0.5kg cost of producing, so yes, they would.

Would Country B accept a trading price of 1kg = 0.4kg coffee? Producing 1kg of rice has cost them 0.5kg coffee, and they are now only receiving 0.4kg coffee back in return. As a result, Country B would not be happy with this trade.

So we can see that a trading price of 1kg rice = 0.5kg coffee is the minimum price that Country B will accept.

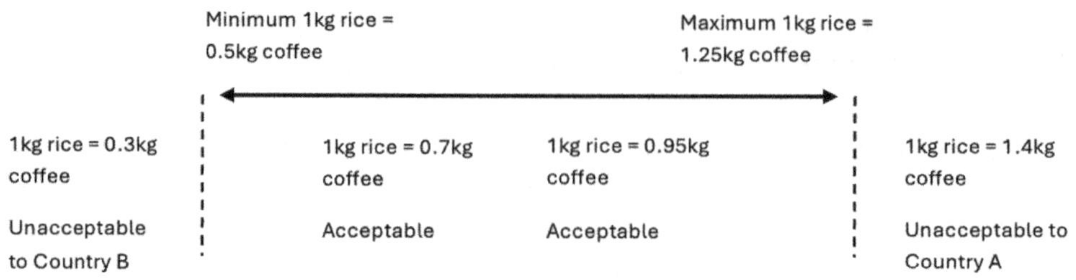

Figure 13.2 Continuum of acceptable trading prices

This is interesting: 1kg rice = 1.25kg coffee is the maximum price Country A will accept, and 1kg rice = 0.5kg coffee is the minimum price that Country B will accept. We can think of this as the range of trading prices that both countries will be willing to accept.

Show this to students using a continuum like the one shown in Figure 13.2.

The continuum in 13.2, if added to incrementally, is an extremely powerful tool for helping students to visualise acceptable trading prices for both countries.

Bring this all together by explaining to students that this demonstrates a really important concept in international trade:

Comparative advantage is a really important concept in international trade, because the law of comparative advantage tells us that ***both*** *countries can benefit from specialising in the good with which they have a comparative advantage and then trading.*

So, Country A will benefit from producing coffee and purchasing rice from Country B if the trading price is set appropriately. This occurs even though they have the absolute advantage in the production of both products.

Now give students questions to check their understanding of this content. Begin with two worked examples as shown in Box 13.3 and 13.4. Similar to the worked examples provided in *Chapter 3: Price Elasticity of Demand*, these worked examples include a more straightforward example and a difficult question. The majority of questions that students encounter will, therefore, fall between these two extreme ranges.

BOX 13.3 WORKED EXAMPLE ONE

Worked example one

Question: Table 13.8 shows the maximum trading possibilities of two countries, both producing rubber and tin.

Table 13.8 Country A and B production

	Country A	Country B
Rubber	400 kg	600 kg
Tin	250 kg	300 kg

Which country has the comparative advantage in the production of tin?

Answer:

Step one: calculate opportunity cost ratios for each country.

You have been asked to calculate comparative advantage in the production of tin, which means we need to find the opportunity cost of producing tin for each country.

The formula for opportunity cost is as follows:

$$\frac{Loss}{Gain}$$

If each country produces tin, then they are 'giving up' production of rubber. The calculation for each country is therefore the following:

Country A: $\frac{400}{250} = 1.6kg\ rubber$

Country B: $\frac{600}{300} = 2kg\ rubber$

Step two: compare the opportunity cost ratios.

Country A has the lower opportunity cost because they only give up 1.6 kg rubber every time they produce a 1 kg tin, compared to 2 kg for Country B.

Country A, therefore, has the comparative advantage in the production of tin.

BOX 13.4 WORKED EXAMPLE TWO

Worked example two

Question: Table 13.9 shows the maximum trading possibilities of two countries, both producing rubber and tin.

Table 13.9 Country A and B production

	Country A	Country B
Rubber	620 kg	800 kg
Tin	310 kg	500 kg

1. Which country has the comparative advantage in the production of each good?
2. What would be the acceptable trading price range for each country in order to benefit from trade? Give your answer in the form 1 kg rubber = tin.

Answer:

Step one: calculate opportunity cost ratios for each country for both products.

You have been asked to calculate comparative advantage in the production of tin, which means we need to find the opportunity cost of producing tin for each country.

The formula for opportunity cost is as follows:

$$\frac{Loss}{Gain}$$

The opportunity cost ratios for each country and product are shown in Table 13.10.

Table 13.10 Country A and B production

	Country A	**Country B**
Producing 1 kg rubber	0.5 kg tin	0.625 kg tin
Producing 1 kg tin	2 kg rubber	1.6 kg rubber

Step two: identify which countries have the comparative advantage in the production of each product.

Country A has the comparative advantage in the production of rubber, as their opportunity cost ratio of 1 kg rubber = 0.5 kg tin is lower than Country B's. Country B has the comparative advantage in the production of tin, as their opportunity cost ratio of 1 kg tin = 1.6 kg rubber is lower than Country A's.

Step three: identify the acceptable trading price range in terms of rubber.

Highlight the product that the trading price needs to be given in terms of; e.g. rubber.

Read across this row to find the two opportunity cost ratios of producing rubber. Country A's is 0.5 kg tin and Country B's is 0.625 kg tin. The trading price must sit between these two values.

Therefore, 1 kg rubber = 0.5 kg – 0.625 kg tin

Finish off this sequence by bringing this together in a consolidation task that reinforces the importance of the big picture of this topic: that international trade has increased as a result of the law of comparative advantage. This task is shown in Box 13.5.

BOX 13.5 CASE STUDY ON ABSOLUTE AND COMPARATIVE ADVANTAGE

Case study

Country A and Country B are the only two countries in the world. They have never previously traded internationally. They both produce wheat and cheese. The maximum amounts of each product that Country A and Country B can produce are shown in the following Table 13.11:

Table 13.11 Country A and B production

	Country A	Country B
Wheat	800 kg	500 kg
Cheese	200 kg	200 kg

As the result of an increase in technology and transport systems, it has become easier for Country A and Country B to trade with each other. The governments of Country A and Country B are considering whether to trade with each other and whether they will benefit from this.

Questions

1. Before trade, assume that each country allocates 50% of their resources to the production of each good. What would total world production be of wheat and cheese under these terms?
2. Who has the absolute advantage in the production of both goods?
3. Who has the comparative advantage in the production of each good?
4. If both countries choose to specialise in the good with which they have a comparative advantage and then trade, what would total world production of each good become?
5. What would the acceptable trading price range be for each country? Express your answers in terms of 1 kg wheat.
6. How does this example demonstrate the law of comparative advantage?
7. Why do the countries trade cheese even though they can both produce the same absolute amount?

Answers

Country A has the absolute advantage in the production of wheat. Neither country has the absolute advantage in the production of cheese, as they can both produce the same amount.

Total world production prior to trade would be 650 kg wheat and 200 kg cheese. The opportunity cost ratios of each country and product can be seen in Table 13.2.

Table 13.12 Opportunity cost answers

	Country A	**Country B**
Producing 1 kg wheat	Give up 0.25 kg cheese	Give up 0.4 kg cheese
Producing 1 kg cheese	Give up 4 kg wheat	Give up 2.5 kg wheat

Country A, therefore, has the comparative advantage in producing wheat, and Country B has the comparative advantage in the production of cheese. Based on this, total world production after specialisation and trade would be 800 kg wheat and 200 kg cheese. We can see that total world production of wheat would increase, whereas cheese would stay the same. The key is to demonstrate that the law of comparative advantage states that overall production will increase, not necessarily that production of each good will increase. Despite this, both countries can still benefit from producing the goods with which they have a comparative advantage as total world production will increase.

The acceptable trading price range would be 1 kg wheat = 0.25 kg − 0.4 kg cheese.

Key takeaways

- Start and finish by setting the big picture for students. The topic quickly becomes quite technical, and so it is important that students understand why this is an important topic and its macro implications.
- Provide concrete examples and add information incrementally. For example, do not start by introducing students to two countries and their opportunity cost ratios in the production of two goods. Instead, go slowly: introduce students to Country A first, and consider its production possibilities before introducing Country B.
- Use visuals to help students comprehend the idea of a trading price. An acceptable trading price will sit between the opportunity cost ratios of both countries.

14 Terms of trade

What's the big picture?

A country's terms of trade is a measure of the ratio of export prices and import prices. A favourable terms of trade means that a country's export prices have increased relative to their import prices. This means that a country has to sell fewer exports in order to afford the same level of imports. In contrast, an unfavourable terms of trade means that a country needs to sell a greater number of exports in order to afford the same number of imports. An unfavourable terms of trade represents a reduced purchasing power for a country and can mean that a country may have difficulty in generating the foreign currency required to pay for foreign debts. The terms of trade, therefore, have an important impact on a country's standard of living: if a country needs to sell an increasingly larger number of exports to afford their imports, it is likely that standards of living in a country will start to deteriorate.

This is a topic that is also important when considering economic development. According to the Prebisch-Singer hypothesis, if a low-income country is reliant on the export of primary products that are income inelastic, then over time the country's terms of trade will deteriorate, and the country may find it difficult to import the capital goods required for development. This then has significant implications on development strategies within those nations.

Why do students find this concept difficult?

I think this is one of the most difficult to teach and one that students find one of the hardest to understand. I don't think this is unique to my classroom. I marked assessment papers for an exam board in 2025 which featured a relatively simple terms of trade calculation, but it was one of the worst answered questions across the paper. Students consistently gained 0 marks on a question that should have been a simple 2 marks.

I think this is difficult because of the following:

- The terms of trade have a complex relationship with the current of the balance of payments. Increasing export prices may be positive for the current account

DOI: 10.4324/9781003724179-14

due to the price effect but negative due to the volume effect. The relationship with the balance of payments is, therefore, dependent on the price elasticity of demand for exports and imports, which adds further complexity to the topic.

- Linked to the prior point, the language uses in terms of 'favourable' or 'unfavourable' movements in the terms of trade seems to be inconsistent with other concepts within international trade. For example, students often see a depreciation of the exchange rate as a 'good' change because it reduces the relative price of exports and, therefore, typically increases aggregate demand. Yet this would be described as an 'unfavourable' terms of trade movement. Similarly, domestic inflation can be (somewhat simply) seen by students as negative, and yet this would be 'favourable' with regards to the terms of trade.
- Students often find index numbers difficult to understand.
- Finally, it can feel relegated to a small bullet point on the specification list, invariably only featuring in exam papers as short-mark calculation questions. As a result, it can be tempting for teachers to place focus on learning the formula above deep conceptual understanding.

The points earlier provide a perfect mix for a lack of conceptual understanding: limited curriculum time is given to a topic that poses lots of challenge in terms of students' cognition.

This is not intended as a criticism of economics departments across the country! It is perfectly natural that less curriculum time is allocated to topics which are not considered 'core knowledge' for A-level specifications. I also suspect that with the time allocated to terms of trade, most teachers will spend most time on the Prebisch-Singer hypothesis. I hope to show later that by investing a little more time in the concept and the formula, the time required to teach the Prebisch-Singer hypothesis can be significantly reduced.

Explaining this concept

Mistakes to avoid

As with elasticity topics, I have seen so many lessons that follow the following structure:

1. Provide a definition of the concept.
2. Provide the formula that is used to calculate the concept.
3. Practice the formula repeatedly.
4. Explore further what the formula tells students and why it is important.

I think this is the process that leads to students trying to memorise formulae, and I believe it is one of the reasons lots of students found the calculation question in the 2025 exams difficult. Many students knew the formula had *something* to do with exports and imports, but the variation in answers was huge. Some answers given were simply $\frac{\text{Exports}}{\text{Imports}}$; others were $\frac{\text{Export prices}}{\text{Import prices}}$. To me this signalled that many students were trying to remember the formula, rather than understanding what it meant.

Explaining this concept

Teach this topic in the following sequence:

1. Recap how trade occurs.
2. Introduce the idea of the terms of trade and its importance.
3. Introduce the formula for the terms of trade.
4. Examine the factors that cause a change in the terms of trade.
5. The Prebisch-Singer hypothesis (if required by specification).

This chapter will focus predominantly on points 1–3 from the list earlier.

Explaining this concept – revisiting prior knowledge

Start your lesson by recapping index number calculations. For example, you could have a starter activity that requires students to compare some price level data that you have looked at when studying inflation. Make sure that students remember that a value of 100 is used to represent the base year and that other values represent the size of a variable in comparison to this base year. For example, a price index of 112 shows that prices are 12% higher than the chosen base year. It is important to start your lesson in this way to mitigate against the final bullet point from the 'Why do students find this concept difficult?' section.

Then revisit the mechanism of currency exchange in international trade. This may or may not have been something you covered when introducing exchange rates. However, I would argue that students' understanding of this is even more important for a conceptual understanding of the terms of trade. Regardless of whether it was taught or not, spend some time before teaching terms of trade to ensure that students are clear. The process you need to revisit is shown in Figure 14.1.

You need to ensure that students understand that an increase in export generally represents an increase in earnings of foreign cash, whereas an increase in imports generally represent an increase in spending of foreign cash.

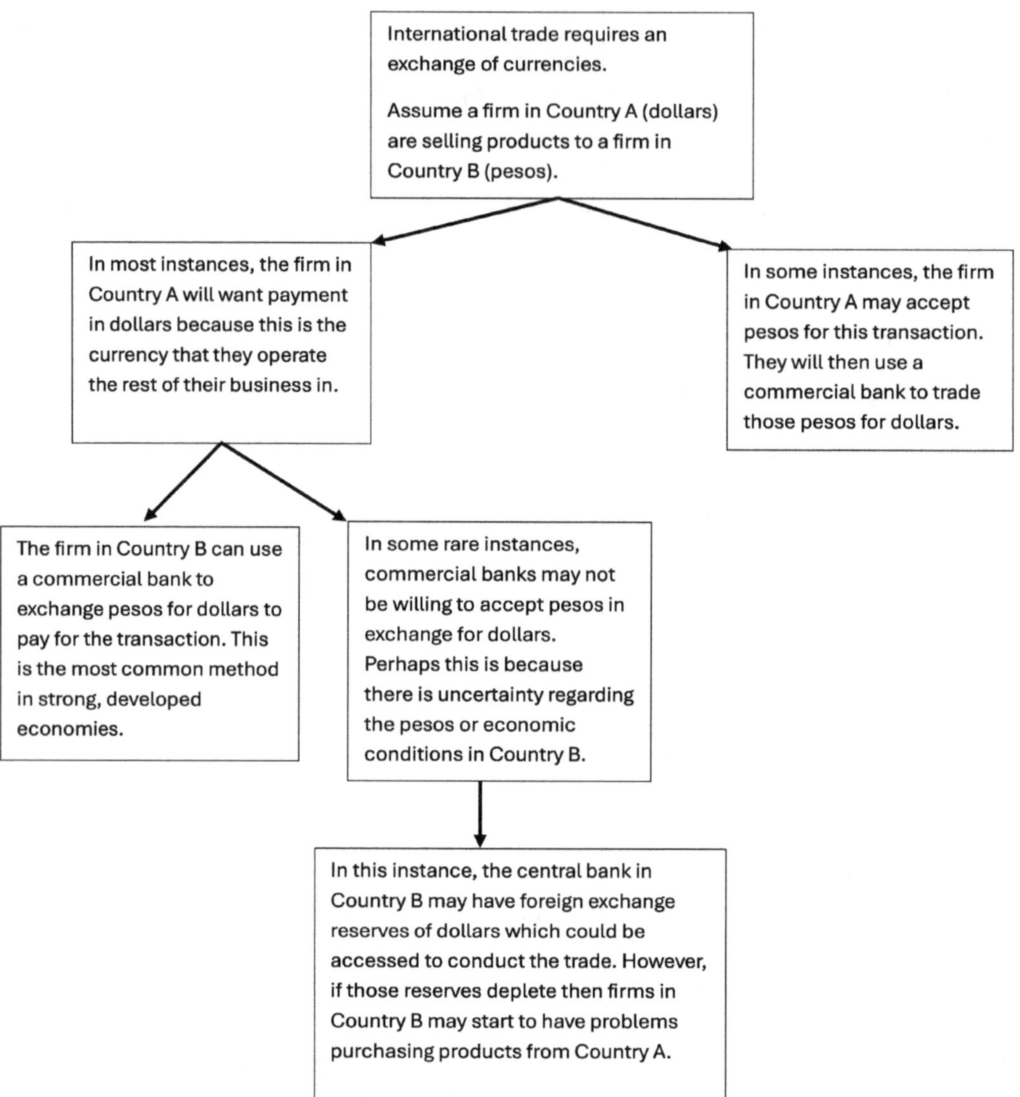

Figure 14.1 Foreign exchange reserves and international trade

Explaining the terms of trade

Start by being explicit that this is something that students find difficult. Explain that it may seem counterintuitive when thinking about other concepts like the current account on the balance of payments and exchange rates.

> *We are going to look at a concept that students often find difficult. Part of the reason for this is because it seems to contradict some of the other things we have learnt this year with regards to exchange rates and international trade. We will deal with those seeming contradictions a little bit later, so try to put them to the back of your mind for now! It's also why it is really important that*

we recapped the importance of foreign exchange reserves at the start of this lesson. Try to hold that in your heads.

Let's imagine a really simple trade transaction. Firms in Country A grow and sell coffee. Firms in Country A buy rice from Country B.

Country A uses euros and Country B uses dollars. We are going to keep it nice and simple and assume that the exchange rate is currently €1: $1.

There are already a couple of assumptions that we are making here. Pause there and recap these points so that all students are clear. I'd also have a simple overview of this drawn on the board to make sure it is nice and clear for students.

Notice we give an exchange that represents parity. This simplifies things somewhat and is unrealistic. However, we want students' working memory to be focused on conceptual understanding of the terms of trade and don't want to muddy things by requiring them to calculate the exchange rate at the same time. We can introduce complexity a little later and correct this simplification.

Continue your explanation:

Let's imagine that Country A's sells its coffee for €5 and sells 100 units of coffee. It is therefore generating €500 of export revenue.

Let's also imagine that it buys rice for $5 and buys 100 units. It is therefore spending $500 on imports.

In this scenario, Country A is okay: firms can exchange the €500 it receives from exports and use these to buy rice. Country A is generating enough export revenue to purchase all its imports.

Have this represented visually on the board. A simple table like Table 14.1 will be helpful:

Reiterate and emphasise the point that at these prices and quantities, the export revenue generated by Country A is enough to afford their imports of rice.

Now, let's imagine there are good weather conditions in Country A that reduce the costs of producing coffee. As a result, the price that firms in Country A sells their coffee for falls to €4. At the same time, the price of rice that they import stays the same. How does this impact our calculations? Well, firms in Country A are now going to need to sell more coffee than they did before in

Table 14.1 Terms of trade explanation step one

	Price	Quantity	Value
Exports coffee	€5	100	€500
Imports rice	$5	100	$500
Net value			0

Table 14.2 Terms of trade explanation step two

	Price	Quantity	Value
Exports coffee	€4	125	€500
Imports rice	$5	100	$500
Net value			0

Table 14.3 Terms of trade explanation step three

	Price	Quantity	Value
Exports	€4	115	€460
Imports	$5	100	$500
Net value			–$40

order to be able to purchase the same amount of imports. We can see this in Table 14.2.

Firms in Country A are going to have to increase their quantity sold by 25% if they want to want to ensure that their export revenue can afford the same level of imports. We can say that this means Country A's exports are having to ***'work harder'*** *– each export is generating less revenue and so firms in Country A needs to sell more in order to retain parity.*

Emphasise the phrase 'work harder' in this explanation. I think it shifts focus onto the idea that a decreasing price of exports is not *always* a good thing because we are going to need to sell more of them to generate the same revenue.

A key assumption here is that firms in Country A do manage to increase their quantity exported by 25%. What if exports only increase by 15% in response to the decrease in price?

Country A has a bit of a problem! Their export revenue is only €460. Assuming Country A exchanges this to dollars to purchase their rice, they are going to be $40 short! Country A is not going to have enough currency to purchase the imports that they need. We can see this in Table 14.3.

As you will have gotten used to in this explanations, we haven't given a name to this concept yet (we haven't used the phrase terms of trade). We want students to focus on conceptual understanding before we label the concept.

Check students' understanding with some MWB checks for understanding, such as the questions in Box 14.1.

BOX 14.1 CHECK FOR UNDERSTANDING ONE

MWB check for understanding

Country A's currency is euros. They purchase imports in dollars. Country A has the average price and quantities of exports and imports shown in Table 14.4.

Table 14.4 Country A exports and imports information

	Price	Quantity	Value
Exports	€8	90	€720
Imports	$9	80	$720
Net value			0

1. The average price of Country A's exports decrease to $6. Which of the following statements is correct?
   A. If Country A exports 110 units, they will be able to purchase the same level of imports as previously.
   B. Country A will need to export 120 units or more to be able to purchase the same level of imports as previously.
   C. If Country A exports the same number of units, they will only be able to afford 60 units of imports.
   D. Assuming Country A still sells 90 units, they will still be able to purchase the same number of imports.

Answers B and C are correct.

2. The average price of imports to Country A decreases to $8. Which of the following statements is correct?
   A. Assuming the same level of imports, Country A's expenditure on imports will decrease to $640.
   B. Country A could reduce the quantity of exports to 70 and still afford the same level of imports.
   C. Assuming all quantities stay the same, Country A would have a surplus of $80 export revenue.
   D. Assuming export quantities stay the same, Country A could now import 100 units and retain parity in terms of export revenue and import expenditure.

A and C are correct. For answer B, Country A would need to sell 80 units to afford the same level of imports. For answer D, Country A would be able to import 90 units if the quantity of exports remained the same.

The second question is important, as it shows students an example where it is import prices that are changing, rather than export prices.

Then explain to students a further reason that the terms of trade are important.

Let's go back to the situation that we have on the board here – because of the fall in price of each export and because Country A has been unable to increase export volumes significantly, their export revenue is $40 lower than its import expenditure. Where does Country A get the money from to afford these imports?

Well, they have two options. They could either borrow this money, or they could use foreign exchange reserves that are held at the central bank. Both of these solutions can create problems if the situation persists: if Country A needs to continue borrowing then eventually they will run out of potential creditors, and if they need to keep using foreign exchange reserves then eventually the Central Bank is going to run out of reserves.

It may take a while for this to be a problem if Country A is a rich, developed nation. However, if they are a developing country this could quickly turn into an issue. If they are consistently short in terms of export revenues then the will eventually struggle to import the rice that they need to feed their population.

The first line is important to emphasise in this explanation. The terms of trade are linked to a change in export prices relative to import prices. However, the consequences and impact of terms of trade *are* linked to the value of trade. The first line of this explanation tries to clearly reference that the cause is the change in prices and that the impact is the knock-on effect that this has in terms of export value.

Finish your explanation by highlighting on the board that if export quantities do not increase sufficiently, then a key impact of a declining terms of trade is that either:

1. The country will need to borrow money to afford their imports; or
2. The country will need to use some of their foreign exchange reserves to afford their imports.

Before you move on to the formula, check students' understanding with a variety of scenarios on MWBs:

1. An unfavourable terms of trade movement and a less-than-proportionate increase in the demand for a country's exports

2. An unfavourable terms of trade movement and a more-than-proportionate increase in the demand for a country's exports
3. A favourable terms of trade movement and a less-than-proportionate increase in the demand for a country's exports
4. A favourable terms of trade movement and a more-than-proportionate increase in the demand for a country's exports

In each scenario, you want to also check that students recognise the possible impacts on either a country's borrowing requirement or their foreign exchange reserves. We still haven't necessarily labelled these figures as the terms of trade or used the phrases 'favourable' or 'unfavourable', and so you are going to want to avoid using those terms in your examples. A question might look something like the one in Box 14.2.

Explaining this concept – the formula

Start by re-emphasising the key point here:

So we've looked at an example where a country's export prices decrease, and we've seen how this means that the country's exports need to 'work

BOX 14.2 CHECK FOR UNDERSTANDING TWO

MWB check for understanding

1. Information about Country A's export and import in Year one and Year two can be seen in Tables 14.5 and 14.6. We are assuming an exchange rate of €1:$1.

Table 14.5 Year one

Year one	Price	Quantity
Exports	€5	100
Imports	$10	50

Table 14.6 Year two

Year two	Price	Quantity
Exports	€4	120
Imports	$10	50

Question: Explain the impact that this change in the terms of trade will have on either Country A's borrowing requirement or their level of foreign exchange reserves.

harder' to generate enough revenue to afford the same level of imports. Similarly, we have seen how an increase in the price of imports means that a country will need to be able to sell more exports in order to afford the same level of imports as before. ***The key thing here is that we are looking at changing export and import prices, and the impacts that these have****.*

We refer to this as a country's 'terms of trade'. A 'favourable' terms of trade means that a country's export prices have increased relative to import prices, because this means that those exports have to work 'less hard' to purchase the same level of imports. In contrast, an 'unfavourable' terms of trade means that export prices have decreased relative to imports and that these exports are now going to have to work harder! This may seem inconsistent with the idea that a country may like decreasing export prices because it can sell more exports. However, with terms of trade, we are only considering 'how hard' those exports are going to have to work!

It's important to explicitly reference where students often see a contradiction. Signpost this to students so that it isn't a question that they are silently considering! Then explain that you are going to introduce a formula that uses index numbers to describe the relative changes between export and import prices. Start by a decrease in export prices, as this aligns with the example you have been using for most of the lesson and so requires the least cognitive work for students.

So, let's imagine country A export prices have recently decreased by 10%. The price that they pay for imports has stayed the same. Clearly, we are in a situation where their exports are going to have to work harder! We can demonstrate this by showing the ratio of these changes. Export prices have decreased by 10% and so would have an index value of 90, whereas import prices have stayed the same and so would have an index value of 100.

We are going to plug that into the following formula:

$$\textit{Terms of trade} = \frac{\textit{Price index of exports}}{\textit{Price index of imports}} \times 100$$

$$\frac{90}{100} \times 100 = 90$$

An index value of 90 is less than a 'par value' of 100. This tells us that export prices are decreasing relative to import prices. Essentially, if the quantity of export sales remained the same then country A would only be able to afford 90% of the imports that they previously purchased.

Through a mixture of teacher-led examples and MWB questions, students need to see the following:

1. An example where export prices increase
2. Examples where import prices increase/decrease but export prices stay constant
3. Examples where import prices and export prices both increase but by different magnitudes
4. Examples where import prices and export prices both decrease but by different magnitudes
5. Examples where import prices and export prices move in opposite directions

For each scenario given, students need to be quizzed on what their answer tells them. It is only through repeated practice of these different scenarios that students will become familiar with the calculation and what the answer provided gives them.

Then once you are confident that students are comfortable with the formula and have completed sufficient independent practice, consolidate their understanding with the case study in Box 14.3.

BOX 14.3 CASE STUDY ON THE TERMS OF TRADE

Case study

Country A is a developing nation. Its currency is generally seen as weak by the majority of its trading partners. Its major exports are agricultural products, such as tea, coffee and textiles. They tend to import the majority of capital required for manufacturing and construction.

In 2025, the country experienced an extremely good harvest. As a result, the costs of production for tea and coffee fell substantially. This resulted in a decrease in the prices charged for these products. Given the weighting of these products in Country A's overall exports, this led to a 3% fall in the total average price of Country A's exports in comparison to 2024.

At the same time, the price of imports increased. Other nations cited increasing labour costs and global trade tensions as reasons for increasing costs. This led to an increase in import prices to country A of 1%.

Economists currently predict that Country A's export prices are likely to recover slightly in 2026. They should recover to be 1% lower than they were in 2024. However, import prices in 2026 are expected to continue rising and are likely to be 3% higher than they were in 2024.

The central bank of Country A has a limited amount of foreign exchange reserves.

Questions

1. Use a supply-and-demand diagram to show why Country A's export prices decreased in 2025.

2. Using the information provided, calculate the following:
   a. Country A's terms of trade in 2025
   b. Country A's terms of trade in 2026
   c. The percentage change in the country's terms of trade between 2025 and 2026
3. In your own words, explain how the change in Country A's 2025 terms of trade will impact their ability to purchase imports.
4. Based on your answer to question 2, use an AD/LRAS diagram to show the potential impact of the change in Country A's ability to import capital.
5. Explain the likely impact of the change in Country A's terms of trade on the level of their foreign exchange reserves.
6. Based on information contained within the case study, explain a likely reason why Country A has a limited amount of foreign exchange reserves.

The case study in Box 14.3 is useful because it reinforces the formula used to calculate the terms of trade, while also highlighting to students the 'big picture' of terms of trade. It also provides a foundation for understanding the Prebisch-Singer hypothesis without confusing students with technical terms too early.

Finish by checking students' understanding with some of the questions included in Box 14.4.

BOX 14.4 CHECKS FOR UNDERSTANDING THREE

MWB questions

1. A country has a terms of trade of 102. Which of the following statements can be inferred?

   A. The country will be running a current account surplus.

   B. The country will be running a current account deficit.

   C. The volume of exports will decrease.

   D. The volume of imports will decrease.

   E. The country can afford more imports with the same level of exports.

Answer E is the only correct answer here. All other answers address common misconceptions that students have on the terms of trade. This is because students wrongly infer that a change in the terms of trade can signal something about the current account. For example, students assume that increasing export prices must signal a decrease in the quantity of exports and, therefore, widening current account deficit. It is important to tackle this misconception and explain that without the information on changing quantities, terms of trade numbers do signal anything about changes in current account balances.

2. Country A is a developing nation that imports capital that they use for infrastructure development. The country has a terms of trade of 106. Which of the following statements can be inferred?

   A. The price of capital that Country A imports is decreasing.

   B. The price of Country A's exports is increasing.

   C. Country A will be able to afford more imported capital, even if export volumes stay the same.

   D. Country A should be able to afford more imported capital for the use of infrastructure development.

Answer C and D are the only correct answers. Students correctly identifying these answers will demonstrate that they understand the importance of the terms of trade for developing nations. Answer A and B are common misconceptions: a favourable terms of trade shows that export prices are increasing relative to import prices. However, this doesn't *necessarily* mean that export prices are increasing. For example, export prices could be staying constant, and import prices could be decreasing. Similarly, for Answer A, export prices could be increasing and import prices could be staying constant (not to mention that the price of capital will only be one market impacting the average price of imports for Country A).

Key takeaways

- Foreground your explanation by telling students that there may appear to a contradiction between this topic and their understanding of export prices. This is likely to make students feel more comfortable with the cognitive dissonance that they are likely to experience and so they are less likely to become distracted by it.
- Introduce the concept and develop students' understanding before introducing the formula. Students need to understand what the formula is helping them understand, and so they need to understand the terms of trade conceptually before they experience it.
- Provide students with simple concrete examples first to help them understand the concept. Don't overcomplicate these examples with difficult exchange rate calculations or more complex multiplication sums.

Index

Note: Page numbers in *italics* indicate a figure and page numbers in **bold** indicate a table on the corresponding page.

For Product Safety Concerns and Information please contact our EU representative GPSR@taylorandfrancis.com
Taylor & Francis Verlag GmbH, Kaufingerstraße 24, 80331 München, Germany

www.ingramcontent.com/pod-product-compliance
Lightning Source LLC
LaVergne TN
LVHW081259100826
845148LV00005B/923

* 9 7 8 1 0 4 1 2 0 3 0 9 4 *